Published by the Syndics of the Cambridge University Press
Bentley House, 200 Euston Road, London N.W.1
American Branch: 32 East 57th Street, New York, N.Y.10022

© Cambridge University Press 1970

Library of Congress Catalogue Card Number: 66–73798

Standard Book Number: 521 07587 4

Printed in Great Britain
at the University Printing House, Cambridge
(Brooke Crutchley, University Printer)

THE SCHOOL MATHEMATICS PROJECT

TEACHER'S GUIDE
FOR BOOK 5
(METRIC)

CAMBRIDGE
AT THE UNIVERSITY PRESS
1970

THE
SCHOOL MATHEMATICS
PROJECT

When the S.M.P. was founded in 1961, its objective was to devise radically new mathematics courses, with accompanying G.C.E. syllabuses and examinations, which would reflect, more adequately than did the traditional syllabuses, the up-to-date nature and usages of mathematics.

The first stage of this objective is now more or less complete. *Books 1–5* form the main series of pupil's texts, starting at the age of 11+ and leading to the O-level examination in 'S.M.P. Mathematics', while *Books 3T, 4* and *5* give a three-year course to the same O-level examination. (*Books T* and *T4*, together with their Supplement, represent the first attempt at this three-year course, but they may be regarded as obsolete.) *Advanced Mathematics Books 1–4* cover the syllabus for the A-level examination in 'S.M.P. Mathematics' and in preparation are five (or more) shorter texts covering the material of various sections of the A-level examination in 'S.M.P Further Mathematics'. There are two books for 'S.M.P. Additional Mathematics' at O-level. Every book is accompanied by a Teacher's Guide.

For the convenience of schools, the S.M.P. has an arrangement whereby its examinations are made available by every G.C.E. Examining Board, and it is most grateful to the Secretaries of the eight Boards for their cooperation in this. At the same time, most Boards now offer their own syllabuses in 'modern mathematics' for which the S.M.P. texts are suitable.

By 1966, it had become clear from experience in comprehensive schools that the mathematical content of the S.M.P. texts was suitable for a much wider range of pupil than had been originally anticipated, but that the presentation needed adaptation. Thus it was decided to produce a new series, *Books A–H*, which could serve as a secondary school course starting at the age of 11+. These books are specially suitable for pupils aiming at a C.S.E. examination; however, the framework of the C.S.E. examinations is such that it is inappropriate for the S.M.P. to offer its own examination as it does for the G.C.E.

The completion of all these books does not mean that the S.M.P. has no more to offer to the cause of curriculum development. The team of S.M.P. writers, now numbering some thirty school and university mathematicians, is continually testing and revising old work, and preparing for new. At the same time, the effectiveness of the S.M.P.'s work depends, as it always has done, on obtaining reactions from active teachers—and also from pupils—in the classroom. Readers of the texts can therefore send their comments to the S.M.P. in the knowledge that they will be warmly welcomed.

Finally, the year-by-year activity of the S.M.P. is recorded in the annual Director's Reports which readers are encouraged to obtain on request to the S.M.P. Office at Westfield College, University of London, London, N.W.3.

This Teacher's Guide is based on the original contributions of

R. H. BAKER	A. B. BOLT	JOYCE HARRIS
D. A. HOBBS	D. J. HOLDING	A. HURRELL
J. D. PRYCE	D. R. SKINNER	A. R. TAMMADGE
A. THOMAS	J. M. TRURAN	J. V. TYSON

and has been edited by P. G. BOWIE.

ACKNOWLEDGEMENTS

We are much indebted to the Cambridge University Press for their cooperation and help at all times in the preparation of this book.

The Project owes a great deal to its Secretaries, Miss J. Sinfield and Mrs J. Whittaker; also to Mrs E. L. Humphreys for her assistance and typing in connection with this book.

CONTENTS

1

AREAS AND GRAPHS

This chapter is concerned with different ways of estimating areas of irregular plane shapes. In particular it looks at the area under a graph and the different meanings which can be attached to it. The work can be seen as a background to post O-level integral calculus but it has practical value at the level for which it is written.

1. AREAS OF IRREGULAR FIGURES

Here the emphasis is not on getting an exact area (in practice this is impossible) but on appreciating the degree of inaccuracy in the numbers obtained.

(*a*) 84 small squares. 21 m².
Cost £63.

In practice, because of the necessity to match the patterns and avoid too many joins, a fitted carpet would cost more than this. A better estimate would probably be obtained from the cost of the area of the smallest rectangle which includes the room. £72 in this example.

(*b*) There is no need to find an exact area. As the current price of land is £2·50 a square metre it should be possible to buy a plot of approximately 480 m² for £1200. By drawing in an ordinate (see Figure 3 in the text) and finding the area of a trapezium and a triangle it is quickly seen that the area is about 400 m² so the asking price for the plot is rather high.

(*c*) $AB = 20$; $BC = 20$; $CE = 15$; $CD = 7.5$.

$$\text{Area } ABCE = 350 \text{ m}^2.$$

$$\text{Area } ECD = 56.25 \text{ m}^2.$$

$$\text{Area } ABDE = 406.25 \text{ m}^2$$

which is less than the area of the plot.

(d) Taking B as the origin of coordinates, the points B, A, P(3, 20), Q(20, 16), R(27½, 5) and D form a polygon enclosing the plot whose area is 435 m².

Comparing areas by weighing is best done with a reasonably heavy material such as hardboard and then a good pair of kitchen scales is sufficiently accurate.

(e) Figure A shows one way of approximating to the area.

$$\triangle ACH + \text{trapezium } HBEG + \triangle GDF$$

is a region inside the garden. The garden lies inside

$$\triangle ACH + \text{trapezium } HCDG + \triangle GDF.$$

This method gives

$$1100 \text{ m}^2 < \text{area of garden} < 1220 \text{ m}^2.$$

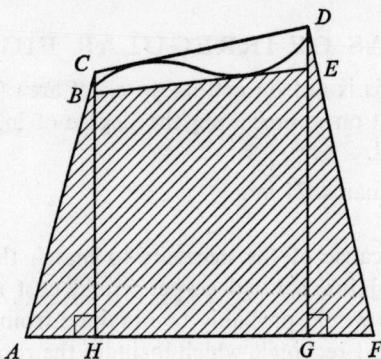

Fig. A

Accuracy can be increased by using more polygons to obtain a better approximation to the region.

(f) Length 80 m; area 1000 m².

(g) Area of the triangles and trapezium is 36800 m². 73 houses can be built on the site.

Exercise A (p. 4)

A practical technique for counting squares is to cover the diagram in the book with tracing paper and shade (or number) each square as it is counted.

1. Approximately 48 small squares which is equivalent to 12 m². 720 grams of seed required.

2. (*a*) Approximately 30 small squares which is equivalent to an area of 300000 m².

(*b*) Volume change for 5 cm rise is

$$300000 \times 100 \times 100 \times 5 = 15000000000 \text{ litres}$$
$$= 1 \cdot 5 \times 10^{10} \text{ litres}.$$

Is the plan of the reservoir constant for different water levels?

3. This question and the next have been introduced to ensure that the area of a trapezium is known and can be computed from a formula. The dotted lines in the figure are to suggest possible ways of finding the area other than counting squares.
(*a*) 22 square units; (*b*) 11 square units; (*c*) 18 square units; (*d*) 8 square units.

4. Depending on how the area is deduced from the diagram the formula will take different forms and a discussion around the equivalence of these is important.

$$A = \tfrac{1}{2}(a+b)\,d = \frac{d}{2}(a+b) = \left(\frac{a+b}{2}\right) d = \tfrac{1}{2}ad + \tfrac{1}{2}bd.$$

5. One small square represents 100 m². Number of small squares approximately 362. Total area, 36200 m² approximately. Cost approximately £2900. With ordinates at 500 m intervals the area of the resulting trapeziums is 36250 m² with a cost of £2900.

6. Square counting gives (*a*) 3200 m², (*b*) 9100 m². The percentage increase in the area of sand is 184 % approximately.

7. Area of vertical cross-section: approximately 112 squares, each representing 16 m² giving 1800 m².

Volume of 100 m length of dam is 180000 m³.

Weight of concrete 324000 tonnes.

8. Best answered by comparing the regions between the original road surface and the proposed surface and matching squares and parts of squares. In this way it will be found that the regions differ by a cross-sectional area of approximately 11 small squares representing an actual area of 110 m². Volume of earth needed is 1320 m³ approximately.

3

2. AREA UNDER A GRAPH

The point of this section is to show how the area under a graph can be used to represent quantities other than area in a meaningful way.

(a) 4 km/h.

(b) The boy was slowing down.

(c) 12.30 p.m. to 1.30 p.m.

(d) 8 km.

(e) 2 km.

(f) $5\frac{1}{2}$ large squares which represents 11 km.

(g) 17 km.

(h) Area of shaded square represents

$$\frac{2 \text{ km}}{4} = \tfrac{1}{2} \text{ km}.$$

(i) Area approximately 112 small squares. A good approximation to this area can be obtained by drawing a line, such as that from (0, 6) to (2, 8), which cuts the graph in such a way that there is as much area above it as below it and finding the area under it.

Distance travelled by car is 14 km approximately.

(j) 7 km/l.

(k) The car travelled 1·25 km further on the second litre.

Exercise B (p. 8)

1. (a) 15 l; (b) 90 doz; (c) 56 N; (d) 48 passengers; (e) 40 cm³; (f) 5000 cm³.

2. (a) 1 hod of coal.
   (b) 23 large squares.
   (c) $3\frac{2}{7}$ hods.

3. (a) Shaded square represents 20 thousand litres.

   Area under graph is 15 large squares approximately.

   Volume of water used is 300 thousand litres approximately.

   (b) More water used between 3 p.m. and 6 p.m.

   (c) Water entering the reservoir in the period under consideration is 336 thousand litres which exceeds the volume used. Hence the water level will be higher at 6 a.m.

4. (*a*) 500 m.

$AB \approx 4150$ m; $BC \approx 4250$ m.

(*b*) Average speed from *A* to *B* $\approx$ 830 m/min.

Average speed from *B* to *C* $\approx$ 1200 m/min.

(*c*) Goods train covers 8400 m in $10\frac{1}{2}$ min at an average speed of approximately 800 m/min.

5. (*a*) See Figure B.

(*b*) 10 m/s², the acceleration due to gravity.

(*c*) See Figure C.

6. See Figure D and Figure E.

Notice that to obtain a reasonable graph for the volume of water in the bath it is necessary to start the volume scale well above zero.

Loss of water per day $\approx$ 10000 litres.

FALLING BODY

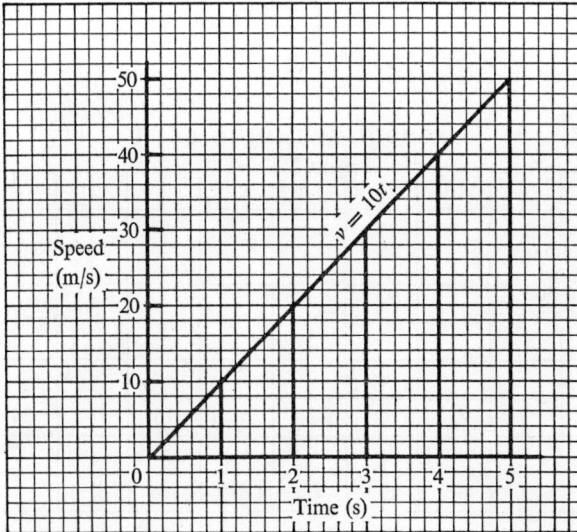

Fig. B

FALLING BODY (*cont.*)

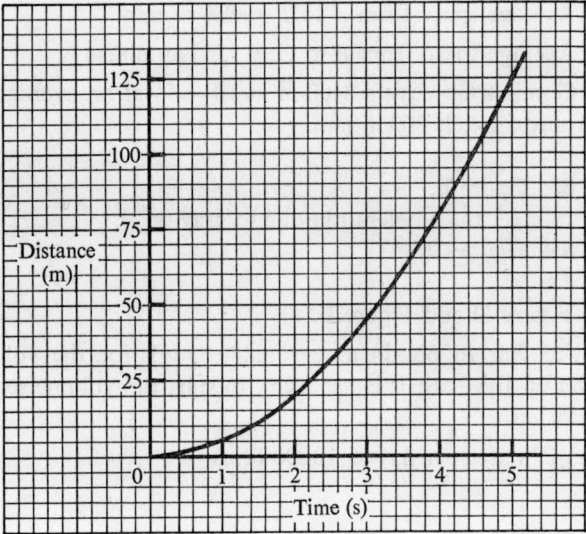

Fig. C

SCHOOL SWIMMING BATH

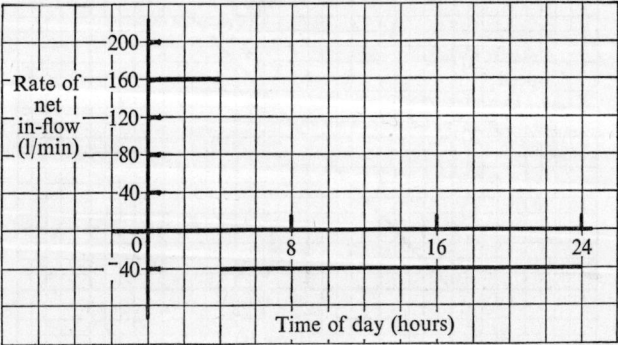

Fig. D

6

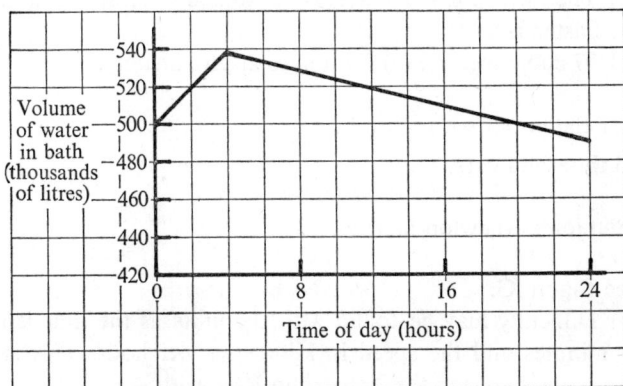

Fig. E

3. THE TRAPEZIUM RULE

Trapeziums have already been used in approximating to shapes. The main point of the Trapezium Rule is that when a set of trapeziums all have their parallel sides the same distance apart the calculation is particularly easy.

(a) 272·5 square units.

(b) 227 square units.

A better estimate could be obtained by using more trapeziums. It is not possible to say whether the estimate is large or small.

(c) $A = 126$ in each case.

(d) Area of the third trapezium is $47\frac{1}{2}$ square units.

It is not expected that all the questions in the following exercise will be attempted by any one pupil.

Exercise C (p. 12)

1. (a) 128 square units; (b) 124 square units.
A better approximation can be obtained by increasing the number of ordinates—it is common to double the number.

2. 2220 m/s.

7

3. (*a*) The measurements are approximately those of a statue on Easter Island;
   (*b*) 37 cubic metres; (*c*) 70 tonnes approximately.

4. For the graph see Figure F.
   13 thousand cars.

5. 8860 joules (newton metres).

6. See Figure G.
   (*b*) Difficulty may be found with the units as the time is given in minutes and the speed in kilometres per hour. This is best overcome by using the Trapezium Rule with $d = \frac{1}{60}$.

   Distance travelled in 8 minutes is 2·27 kilometres approximately.
   (*c*) From the graph it can be seen that the acceleration (which corresponds to the gradient) is greatest from the 4th to the 6th minute and is equal to 7 km/h/min.

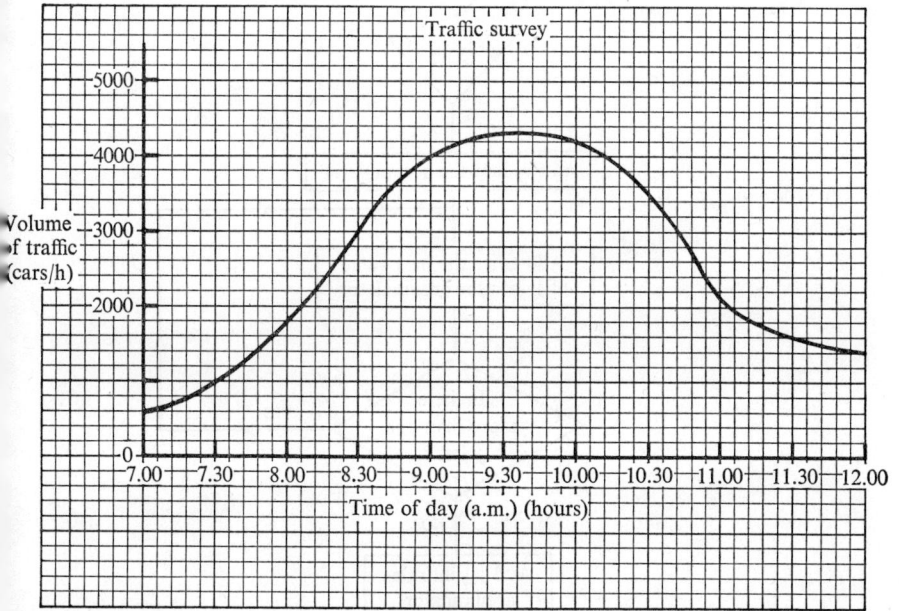

Fig. F

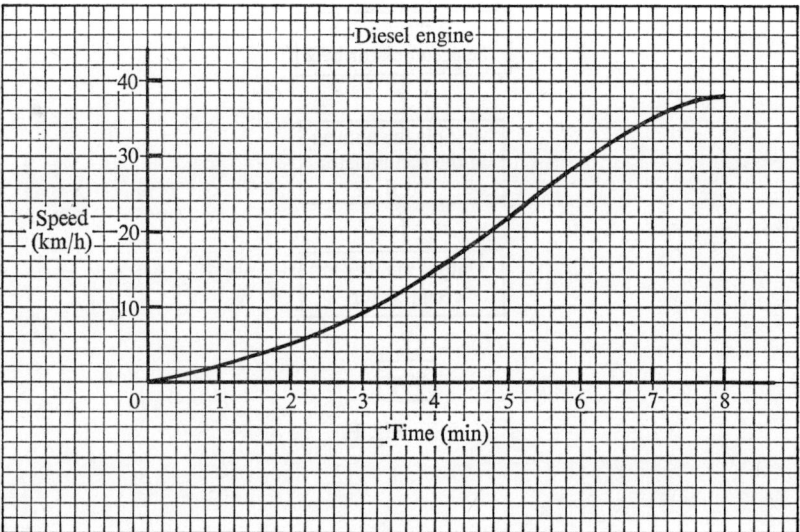

Fig. G

7.

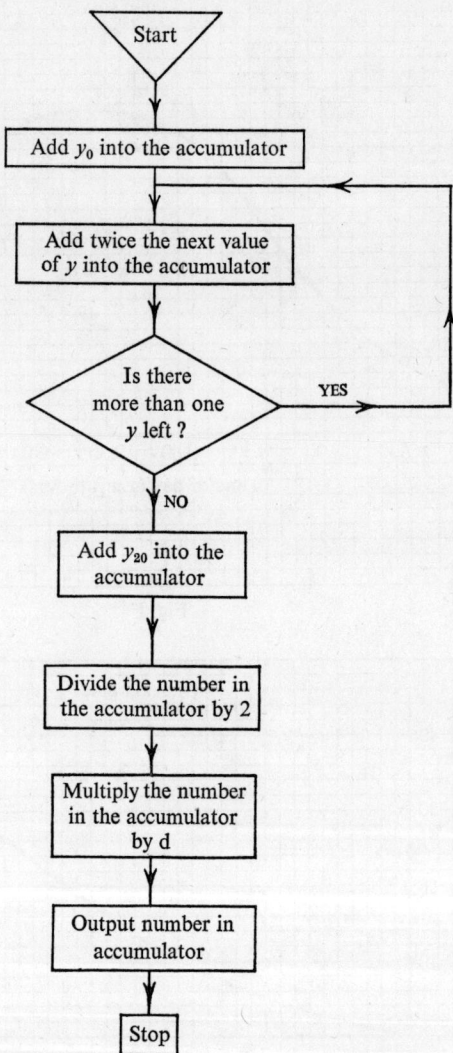

Fig. H

10

2

VECTORS AND TRIGONOMETRY

In this course, vectors were first mentioned in *Book* 2, Chapter 7: displacements were discussed there, and also ordered sets of numbers with a similar additive property. Position vectors were introduced in *Book* 3, Chapter 3 and used in *Book* 4, Chapter 12. The present chapter attempts to unify and revise these ideas and, incidentally, provides some revision of trigonometry.

A note about the development of vectors may be appropriate here. The idea of a vector came originally from physics. Some quantities which have magnitude and direction, such as, for example, displacements, velocities and forces, have a common method of combination —the triangle (or parallelogram) rule. Such quantities were called 'vector quantities'.

[*Note*. As the *Nuffield Physics Teacher's Guide III* points out, it is not sufficient to say that a vector is something with magnitude and direction—the law of combination must also be stated A thermometer reads 50 °C, and points in a direction 030°. Is this a vector?]

A vector quantity can be represented by a directed line segment, and hence by using a coordinate framework an ordered set of numbers can be given to describe a vector quantity. It follows that combination of these ordered sets is by addition of corresponding elements. This method of combination is called 'addition of vectors'.

Mathematicians have abstracted this idea so that a vector has become an ordered set of numbers with certain properties, not necessarily representing a physical quantity. The list of properties is lengthy, but the most important are that addition takes place component-wise, and multiplication by a scalar is defined. For more details see *A Survey of Modern Algebra*, by Birkhoff and MacLane.

The following articles are also recommended (if only to show the numerous pitfalls):

Mathematical Gazette, February 1964, page 34.
Mathematical Gazette, December 1966, page 397.
Mathematical Gazette, May 1966, page 101.

Mathematical Gazette, February 1968, page 42.
Mathematics Teaching, Summer 1968, page 72.

We do not want to go to a deep level of abstraction in this course, and we content ourselves with pointing out in Section 1 that the same pattern occurs in a non-physical example (taken from *Book* 2, Chapter 7) as in the physical case of displacements.

1. VECTORS—A REMINDER

(a)	B.B.C. 1	8	(b) Distance east	8
	I.T.V.	7	Distance north	7

2. DISPLACEMENT VECTORS

This section deals with the combination of two displacements by the addition of the vectors representing them. Displacements have been combined previously in *Book* 2, Chapter 7, by scale drawing and by component-wise addition in simple cases (for example, chess), and in *Book* 2, Chapter 12, more complicated cases were dealt with by trigonometry, although the method was not formalized. This work has also been introduced in *Book* 3T, Chapter 5.

The method of this section has been used in preference to the cosine and sine formulae because it needs no new knowledge, and is more general. It is also the method used in some navigational computers to find, for example, an aircraft's ground velocity knowing its velocity relative to the air, and knowing the wind velocity.

All answers are given to 3 significant figures.

(b) Distance east = 70 sin 30° = 35·0 km.

Distance north = 70 cos 30° = 60·6 km.

Exercise A (p. 19)

1.   (a) 5·00, bearing 036·9°;   (b) 9·90, bearing 045·0°;
    (c) 84·8, bearing 045·0°;   (d) 35·0, bearing 059·0°.

2.   (a) (i) $\begin{pmatrix} 10 \\ 11 \end{pmatrix}$,   (ii) $\begin{pmatrix} 90 \\ 78 \end{pmatrix}$;

    (b) (i) 14·9, 042·3°,   (ii) 119, 049·1°.

3. (a) $\begin{pmatrix} 18 \cdot 1 \\ 8 \cdot 46 \end{pmatrix}$;   (b) $\begin{pmatrix} -17 \cdot 4 \\ 20 \cdot 7 \end{pmatrix}$;

(c) $\begin{pmatrix} -28 \cdot 6 \\ -16 \cdot 5 \end{pmatrix}$;   (d) $\begin{pmatrix} 17 \cdot 5 \\ -30 \cdot 3 \end{pmatrix}$.

4. (a) $\begin{pmatrix} 18 \cdot 8 \\ 6 \cdot 84 \end{pmatrix}$;   (b) $\begin{pmatrix} 3 \cdot 89 \\ 14 \cdot 5 \end{pmatrix}$;   (c) $\begin{pmatrix} 22 \cdot 7 \\ 21 \cdot 3 \end{pmatrix}$;

(d) 31·1 m,   43·2°.

5. 339 km, 244°.   6. 166 km, 043·3°.

7. 4·84 km, 062·0°.   2·96 min.   8. 24·8 km.

3. VELOCITY VECTORS

Since a velocity is a displacement in unit time, velocities can be combined in the same way as displacements. The same technique is used here as in Section 2.

A simple device for illustrating the combination of velocities was described in *Mathematics Teaching*, Autumn 1963.

Exercise B contains a few questions on forces for those pupils who have met the idea in physics. We do not feel that we can give a full treatment here (an experiment is required), to show that forces can be combined in the same way as displacements.

(c) 330 km/h; 075·9°.   (d) 322 km/h; 082·9°.

Exercise B (p. 23)

1. (a) See Figure A.

(b) (i) $\begin{pmatrix} 10 \cdot 0 \\ 17 \cdot 3 \end{pmatrix}$;   (ii) $\begin{pmatrix} 30 \cdot 3 \\ -21 \cdot 2 \end{pmatrix}$;

(iii) $\begin{pmatrix} -35 \cdot 2 \\ -26 \cdot 5 \end{pmatrix}$;   (iv) $\begin{pmatrix} -10 \cdot 0 \\ 11 \cdot 1 \end{pmatrix}$.

2. (a) 50·0,   036·9°;   (b) 50·0,   143°;
   (c) 49·9,   213°;   (d) 61·9,   326°.

3. (a) $\begin{pmatrix} 480 \\ 0 \end{pmatrix}$;   (b) $\begin{pmatrix} 0 \\ 80 \end{pmatrix}$;   (c) $\begin{pmatrix} 480 \\ 80 \end{pmatrix}$;

(d) 487 km/h,   080·5°.

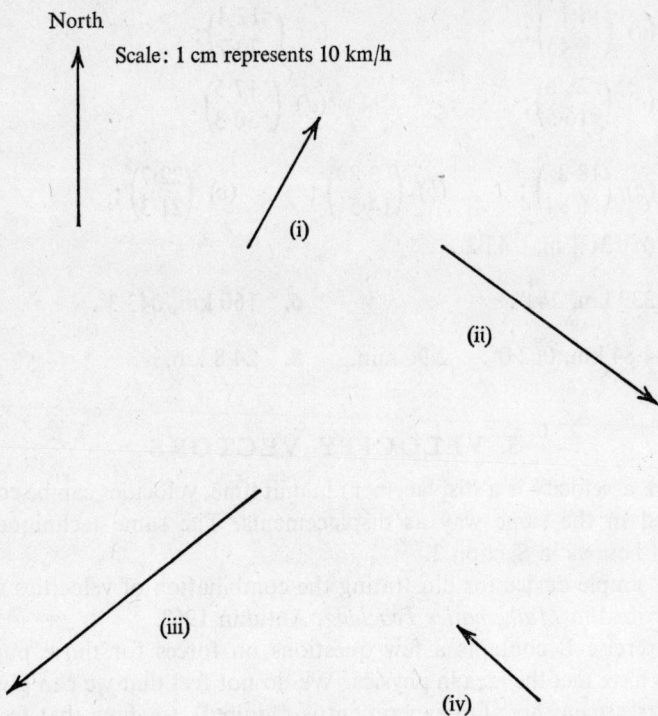

North

Scale: 1 cm represents 10 km/h

(i)

(ii)

(iii)

(iv)

Fig. A

4. At an angle of 18·4° to the attempted direction.

5. 33·3 m.

6. $\begin{pmatrix} 189 \\ 341 \end{pmatrix}$ or 390 km/h at 029·0°.

7. (a) $\begin{pmatrix} 14·1 \\ 14·1 \end{pmatrix}$; (b) $\begin{pmatrix} 3·66 \\ 1·63 \end{pmatrix}$.

   $\begin{pmatrix} 10·4 \\ 12·5 \end{pmatrix}$ or 16·2 knots at 039·8°.

8. Suppose that in the absence of wind the aircraft would be travelling at 300 km/h due east, and that the wind is from the south.

Then the resultant velocities are

$$\begin{pmatrix} 300 \\ 15 \end{pmatrix} \quad \text{or} \quad 300 \text{ km/h} \quad \text{at} \quad 087 \cdot 1°;$$

$$\begin{pmatrix} 300 \\ 30 \end{pmatrix} \quad \text{or} \quad 302 \text{ km/h} \quad \text{at} \quad 084 \cdot 3°;$$

$$\begin{pmatrix} 300 \\ 45 \end{pmatrix} \quad \text{or} \quad 303 \text{ km/h} \quad \text{at} \quad 081 \cdot 5°.$$

9. $\begin{pmatrix} 15 \\ 0 \end{pmatrix}$; $\begin{pmatrix} 0 \\ 30 \end{pmatrix}$; $\begin{pmatrix} 1 \cdot 50 \\ 2 \cdot 60 \end{pmatrix}$.

$$\begin{pmatrix} 16 \cdot 5 \\ 32 \cdot 6 \end{pmatrix} \quad \text{or} \quad 36 \cdot 5 \text{ km/h} \quad \text{at} \quad 026 \cdot 9°.$$

10. Suppose the velocity of the aircraft in still air is V km/h on a bearing of $a°$, and that the wind velocity is W km/h on a bearing of $b°$.

A possible program is:

$$\text{Input} \quad V \quad \text{to} \quad S_1$$
$$\text{Input} \quad a \quad \text{to} \quad S_2$$
$$\text{Input} \quad W \quad \text{to} \quad S_3$$
$$\text{Input} \quad b \quad \text{to} \quad S_4$$

Replace S_5 by sin S_2
Replace S_6 by cos S_2
Replace S_7 by sin S_4
Replace S_8 by cos S_4
Replace S_5 by $S_1 \times S_5$
Replace S_6 by $S_1 \times S_6$
Replace S_7 by $S_3 \times S_7$
Replace S_8 by $S_3 \times S_8$
Replace S_5 by $S_5 + S_7$
Replace S_6 by $S_6 + S_8$
Replace S_7 by $S_5 \times S_5$
Replace S_8 by $S_6 \times S_6$
Replace S_7 by $S_7 + S_8$
Replace S_7 by $\sqrt{S_7}$
Replace S_5 by $S_5 \div S_6$
Replace S_5 by inverse tangent of S_5
Output the numbers in S_7 and S_5

15

11. 8.87×10^6 N at an angle of $2.5°$ with the direction of the ship.

12. 284 N on a bearing of 067°.

13. 17·0 N vertically downward.

4. VECTORS UNDER ROTATION

In *Book* 3, Chapter 3 and *Book* 3T, Chapter 13, matrices for some simple transformations, for example, rotation about the origin through 90° were considered. We now extend this to rotation about the origin through any angle.

(*a*) $\begin{pmatrix} 2 \\ 1 \end{pmatrix}$ is mapped onto $\begin{pmatrix} 4 \\ 7 \end{pmatrix}$.

(*b*) (i) The image of $\begin{pmatrix} 0 \\ 1 \end{pmatrix}$ is $\begin{pmatrix} b \\ d \end{pmatrix}$; (ii) $\begin{pmatrix} 5 & 6 \\ 4 & 5 \end{pmatrix}$.

4.2. Rotation matrices

$$OJ' = \begin{pmatrix} -0.500 \\ 0.866 \end{pmatrix}. \quad \begin{pmatrix} 0.866 & -0.500 \\ 0.500 & 0.866 \end{pmatrix}.$$

Exercise C (p. 26)

1. $(\tfrac{-4}{5}, \tfrac{3}{5})$. $\quad\quad\quad\quad \begin{pmatrix} \tfrac{3}{5} & \tfrac{-4}{5} \\ \tfrac{4}{5} & \tfrac{3}{5} \end{pmatrix}$.

2. (*a*) $\begin{pmatrix} 0.707 & -0.707 \\ 0.707 & 0.707 \end{pmatrix}$. $\quad\quad$ (*b*) $\begin{pmatrix} -0.707 \\ 3.54 \end{pmatrix}$.

3. $\begin{pmatrix} 0.866 & -0.500 \\ 0.500 & 0.866 \end{pmatrix} \begin{pmatrix} -3 \\ 4 \end{pmatrix} = \begin{pmatrix} -4.60 \\ 1.96 \end{pmatrix}$.

4. See Figure B. Rotation about O through $+90°$, followed by a translation $\begin{pmatrix} 4 \\ 2 \end{pmatrix}$.

(1, 3).

5. See Figure C. Rotation about O through $-90°$, followed by a translation

$$\begin{pmatrix} 2 \\ -2 \end{pmatrix}, \quad (0, -2).$$

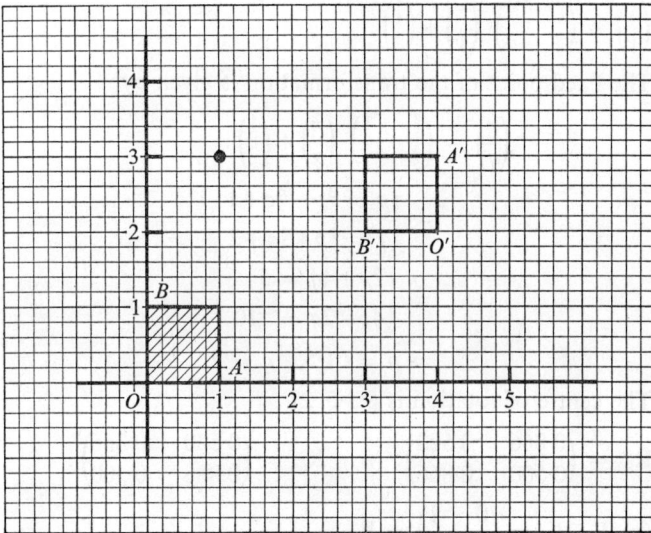

Fig. B

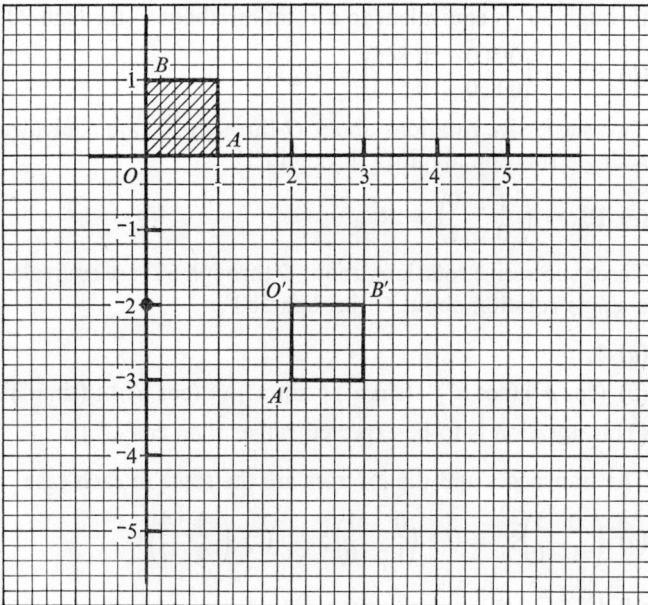

Fig. C

17

6. $\begin{pmatrix} x \\ y \end{pmatrix} \rightarrow \begin{pmatrix} \frac{3}{5} & \frac{-4}{5} \\ \frac{4}{5} & \frac{3}{5} \end{pmatrix} \begin{pmatrix} x \\ y \end{pmatrix} + \begin{pmatrix} 1 \\ 2 \end{pmatrix}.$

The fixed point of the transformation is given by

$$\begin{pmatrix} p \\ q \end{pmatrix} = \begin{pmatrix} \frac{3}{5} & \frac{-4}{5} \\ \frac{4}{5} & \frac{3}{5} \end{pmatrix} \begin{pmatrix} p \\ q \end{pmatrix} + \begin{pmatrix} 1 \\ 2 \end{pmatrix}.$$

$$\Rightarrow \begin{cases} p = \frac{3}{5}p - \frac{4}{5}q + 1 \\ q = \frac{4}{5}p + \frac{3}{5}q + 2 \end{cases}$$

$$\Rightarrow \begin{cases} 2p + 4q = 5 \\ 4p - 2q = {}^-10 \end{cases}$$

$$\Rightarrow p = {}^-1{\cdot}5, \quad q = 2.$$

The centre of rotation is $({}^-1{\cdot}5, 2)$.

7. $\mathbf{R}_{30} = \begin{pmatrix} 0{\cdot}866 & {}^-0{\cdot}500 \\ 0{\cdot}500 & 0{\cdot}866 \end{pmatrix};$ $\mathbf{R}_{60} = \begin{pmatrix} 0{\cdot}500 & {}^-0{\cdot}866 \\ 0{\cdot}866 & 0{\cdot}500 \end{pmatrix}.$

(a) $\mathbf{R}_{30}\mathbf{R}_{60} = \begin{pmatrix} 0 & {}^-1 \\ 1 & 0 \end{pmatrix} = \mathbf{R}_{90}.$

A rotation about O through 60° followed by a rotation about O through 30° is equivalent to a rotation about O through 90°.

(b) $\mathbf{R}_{30}^2 = \begin{pmatrix} 0{\cdot}500 & {}^-0{\cdot}866 \\ 0{\cdot}860 & 0{\cdot}500 \end{pmatrix} = \mathbf{R}_{60}.$

Two successive rotations about O through 30° are equivalent to a single rotation about O through 60°.

(c) $\mathbf{R}_{60}^3 = \begin{pmatrix} {}^-1 & 0 \\ 0 & {}^-1 \end{pmatrix} = \mathbf{R}_{180}.$

Three successive rotations about O through 60° are equivalent to a single rotation about O through 180°.

8. (a) 1.

(b) $(\cos \alpha°)(\cos \alpha°) - (\sin \alpha°)({}^-\sin \alpha°) = (\cos \alpha°)^2 + (\sin \alpha°)^2.$

(This notation is to be expected rather than $\cos^2 \alpha°$.)

9. The transposes and the inverses are the same in each case

(a) $\begin{pmatrix} 0 & 1 \\ {}^-1 & 0 \end{pmatrix};$ (b) $\begin{pmatrix} 0 & {}^-1 \\ 1 & 0 \end{pmatrix};$ (c) $\begin{pmatrix} \frac{3}{5} & \frac{4}{5} \\ \frac{-4}{5} & \frac{3}{5} \end{pmatrix};$

(d) $\begin{pmatrix} \cos \alpha° & \sin \alpha° \\ {}^-\sin \alpha° & \cos \alpha° \end{pmatrix}.$

10. Matrices with the property that their transpose equals their inverse are said to be orthogonal. If A' is the transpose of A, then

$$A' = A^{-1} \Rightarrow AA' = I.$$

Taking determinants, it follows that $(\det A)^2 = 1$, since

$$\det A' = \det A.$$

Thus orthogonal matrices preserve area ($\det A = \pm 1$). The converse of this is not true; the matrix of a shear for instance is not orthogonal. It can be shown that a transformation with an orthogonal matrix preserves angles, in particular right-angles (hence the name orthogonal). All isometries can be represented by orthogonal matrices. For more details see *A Survey of Modern Algebra*, by Birkhoff and MacLane.

3

THE SPHERE

1. CIRCLES IN THREE DIMENSIONS

A brief reminder of the meaning of the technical terms 'cut' and 'touch' will be required. A suitable model for Figure 1 consists of a cardboard rectangle with a slit cut in it together with a cardboard circular disc. It is worth discussing why it is necessary to push the disc through the slit for (a) but not for (b) since this emphasizes the idea that for intersection it is necessary to enter and depart from the half-space defined by the plane. In case (a), $p \cap c = \{A, B\}$; (b), $p \cap c = \{T\}$; (c), $p \cap c = \varnothing$. The situation in Figure A should

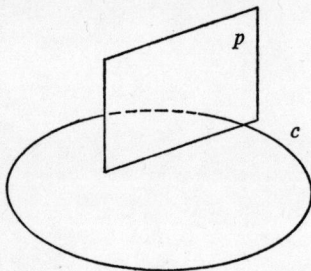

Fig. A

also be discussed. It will be necessary to stress that the cardboard rectangle represents only part of an infinite plane, which obviously cannot be represented completely, and that if it is imagined to be extended another intersection is inevitable in case (a) but not in case (b), when no possible extension can cause another intersection. Some time may have to be spent on this. The concept is not as easy as it may at first appear.

In Figure 1(a), there is an infinity of planes through A, B, all containing the line AB. In Figure 1(b), there is an infinity of planes touching c at T, all containing the tangent line to c at T.

The circles need not lie in a plane perpendicular to p. The centres

20

of the 5 cm circles are all 5 cm from T so that they lie on a sphere of radius 5 cm with its centre at T.

The intersections of l and c are shown in the two cases of Figure B. In case (a), $l \cap c = \{R\}$; (b) $l \cap c = \varnothing$. (i) A tangent line to a circle is defined to be a line in the plane of the circle such that $n(l \cap c) = 1$. Note that l is not called a 'tangent' to c if l and c are not coplanar, nor when l cuts c in more than one point. (ii) A tangent plane to a circle is defined to be a plane such that $n(p \cap c) = 1$.

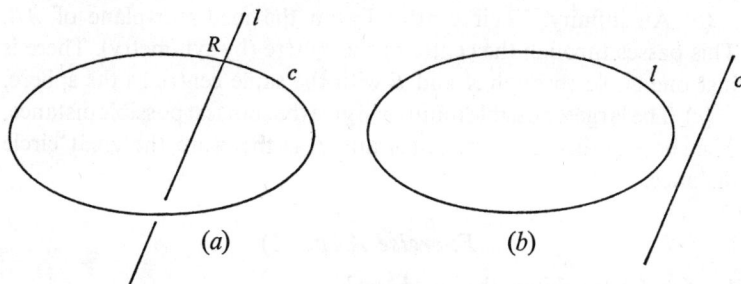

Fig. B

2. THE SPHERE

The definition of a sphere differs from that of a circle only in that the latter includes the words 'in a plane'. The set s partitions space into a bounded inside and an unbounded outside; in set language

$$\{P: OP < r\} \quad \text{and} \quad \{P: OP > r\}.$$

Since $\angle OQX = 90°$, $QX^2 = r^2 - d^2 \Rightarrow QX = \sqrt{(r^2 - d^2)}$

and this is independent of the position of X. The distance of X from the fixed point Q is therefore fixed and so c is a circle. The 'appearance' of the sphere is its intersection with a plane perpendicular to a line from the eye to the centre, see Figure C. All sections of a

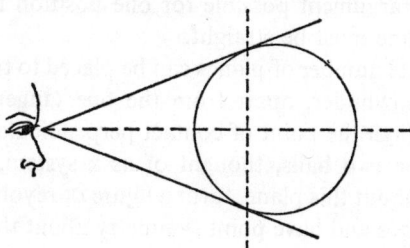

Fig. C

sphere are circles. A sphere has bilateral symmetry about any plane through its centre, rotational symmetry about any diameter and point symmetry about its centre.

2.1 The shortest distance along the surface between points on a sphere

(a) An infinity of circles. The shortest arc will have the largest radius. In the limit the radius is infinite, the arc straight.

(b) An infinity. Their centres lie on the mediator-plane of AB. This passes through the centre of the sphere (by symmetry). There is just one circle through A and B with the same centre as the sphere.

(c) The largest possible radius will give the shortest possible distance. The shortest distance between A and B is therefore the great circle distance.

Exercise A (p. 31)

1. (a), (c) touching; the word 'on'.
   (b), (d) cutting; the words 'in' or 'into'.

2. They are in the same straight line. This is intuitive. If a formal proof is requested this can initiate an interesting discussion on an indirect proof. Either the three points are collinear or they are not. If not, there is a straight line joining the centres that does not pass through the point of contact. The distance between the centres is therefore smaller than the sum of the radii and so at least one point of one sphere must be inside the other. This is nonsense. It has to be admitted that the original assumption must have been wrong, since nothing is wrong with the logic. Another line of argument is to enquire, if the three points are not in a straight line, in which direction the line bends. Since there is no argument possible for one position rather than another, the line must be straight.

   An infinite number of planes can be placed to touch both, they envelope a cylinder, apart from the one tangent plane which passes through the point of contact perpendicular to the line of centres. The two balls, thought of as a system, have bilateral symmetry about this plane, form a figure of revolution about the line of centres and have point symmetry about the point of contact.

The answers are similar, but the envelope of the tangent planes is a cone (apart from the perpendicular plane). The system does not have bilateral symmetry about this, nor has it point symmetry.

3. Yes. In this case, both the sphere and the hemisphere have rotational symmetry of all orders about the line joining their centres; it follows that their figure of intersection has the same. It is not a sphere and it must be a circle. The radius of the scoop. When the two spheres touch, the intersection is a point circle.

4. $3\sqrt{2}$ or 4·24 cm; twice this distance, $6\sqrt{2}$ cm; 11·3 cm.

5. (a) $\sqrt{5}+\sqrt{12}$ or 5·70 cm approximately; (b) $\sqrt{7}$ or 2·65 cm. No. A point circle of radius zero.

6. 4·47 cm.

7. See Figure D(a). The compasses must be set to a width of $\sqrt{80}$ or 8·94 cm. Yes, provided the length of arm of the compasses is greater than the radius of the sphere. See Figure D(b). In practice it needs to be a good deal larger.

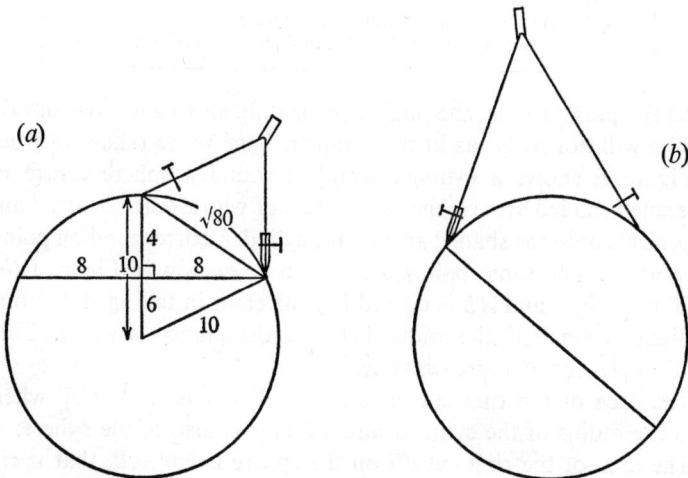

(a)

(b)

Fig. D

23

3. THE AREA OF A SPHERE

The proof of Archimedes's discovery depends on a knowledge of the calculus. His own proof stopped short of this. It is, however, both interesting and instructive to go through it with a group of pupils. The demonstration is an approximate one but leads to an exact answer. This is the fundamental sort of work in the calculus. It is worth spending some time on the idea. A flow diagram is as follows:

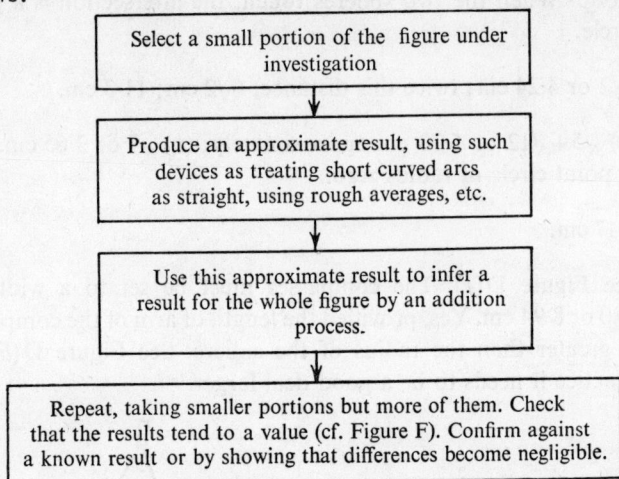

> Select a small portion of the figure under investigation

↓

> Produce an approximate result, using such devices as treating short curved arcs as straight, using rough averages, etc.

↓

> Use this approximate result to infer a result for the whole figure by an addition process.

↓

> Repeat, taking smaller portions but more of them. Check that the results tend to a value (cf. Figure F). Confirm against a known result or by showing that differences become negligible.

At the present time, the final check is difficult to conceive and the results will normally, as in this chapter, have to be taken on trust.

Figure E shows a cylinder wrapped round a sphere centre O. The small shaded area on the sphere, two of whose vertices are A and B, projects onto the shaded area on the cylinder, corresponding points A' and B'. The same points are shown in section in Figure E(b). $A'B'$ is straight and AB is curved but the error in taking AB also as straight is small if the width between the planes is small. Then $A'B' = AB \cos \theta°$ approximately.

The area of the ring cut off on the cylinder is $2\pi R . A'B'$ where R is the radius of the cylinder and, of course, also of the sphere.

The area of the ring cut off on the sphere is $2\pi r . AB$, that is circumference × width. Some explanation will be required here. The radius r is the average of PA and QB, that is CT. A rectangular

24

piece of sellotape of this length and width AB would cover the ring with only very slight stretching and wrinkling so long as AB is small. This is the nature of the justification for saying that the area of the ring can be found by a rectangle law.

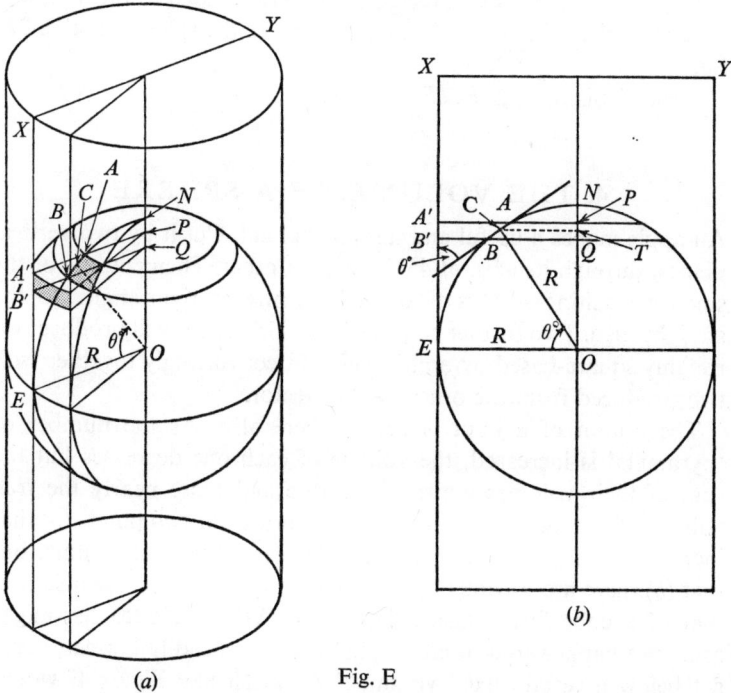

(a)   Fig. E

(b)

From the triangle OCT, $r = R \cos \theta°$.

Putting these results together we argue like this.

Area of ring on sphere, approximately,

$$= 2\pi r . AB$$

$$= 2\pi . (R \cos \theta°) . AB$$

$$= 2\pi R . AB \cos \theta°$$

$$= 2\pi R . A'B'$$

$$= \text{area of ring on cylinder.}$$

What is more, the narrower the strip AB, the better the approximation becomes, and it can be shown that the error is negligible when we take the very large number of strips required to add up to any required width. In fact it is true that the area of the sphere between any two horizontal slices is exactly equal to the area of the cylinder between the same slices.

In particular, the total area of the sphere is equal to the area of a section of the cylinder of the same height as the sphere, that is, $2R$. So,

Area of sphere $= 2\pi R \cdot 2R = 4\pi R^2$.

4. THE VOLUME OF A SPHERE

An apple makes a useful and tasty visual aid. Cut it by two vertical planes, through its axis, at 45° with each other. Then cut one of the smaller resulting sectors through its centre at right-angles to the straight edge. Two further cuts at 45° to this last cut will produce two roughly square-based pyramids which fit convincingly together with two produced from the other smaller sector.

The notion of a limit is present here also. As the number of 'pyramids' is increased, the volume of each one decreases but the sum of their volumes approaches more and more nearly the true volume of the sphere. Discussion might bring out two points (a) that increasing the number of pyramids decreases the total volume, but that (b) there are obvious lower bounds to the volume, for instance, that of a cube fitting inside the sphere. 'What', the teacher might ask, 'can happen to a number that decreases steadily but can never get below a certain fixed volume?' A sketch like Figure F would help.

Exercise B (p. 33)

1. 380 cm²; 697 cm³.

2. 21·2 m.

3. 21·8 cm³.

4. Wrap the ball in a cylinder of stiff paper, making the height the same as the diameter of the sphere. Remove and divide the height of the rectangle into three equal lengths. Replace and prick through the paper into the sphere. Remove and cut the marzipan. No.

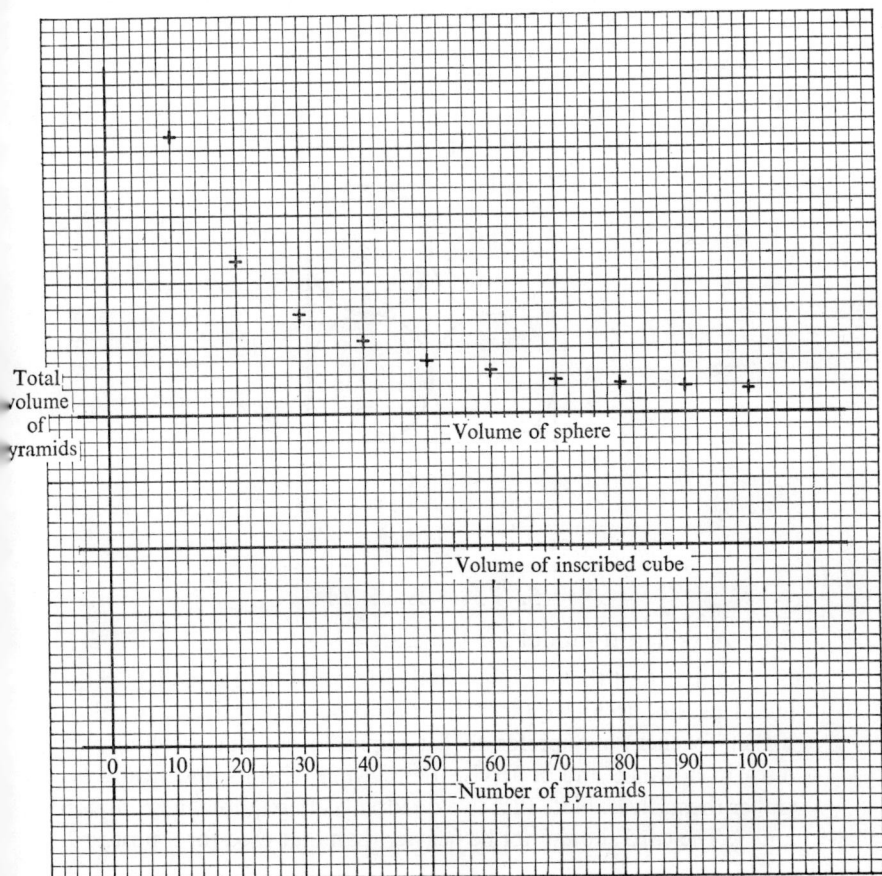

Fig. F

5. $2 \cdot 01 \times 10^8$ square nautical miles.

6. See Figure G. The lower level only is shown. The upper layer is the same. The volume wasted is 823 cm³ which is (unexpectedly?) the same as that wasted if a single ball of radius 6 cm is packed in the same box.

7. $A = 3d^2$; $V = \frac{1}{2}d^3$. 1:2 in each case.

8. $r = 9.85$ m, $s = 1220$ m^2.

9. 3 cm.

10. 225 cm^2.

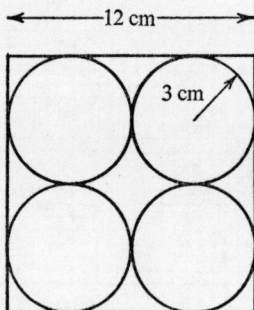

Fig. G

5. THE EARTH

5.1 A skeleton model for the Earth

It is important that each boy and girl should have a model for the initial part of this chapter. It is not absolutely straightforward to make. Teachers may prefer to get pupils to cut out the circles on discs in advance and supervise the cutting of slots and fitting together themselves. Note that two quadrants are required in Sections 6 and 7. The card should not be heavier than that used for a postcard.

5.2 Meridians and longitude

A Geographer's Globe should be to hand if possible. Each circle can then be found on this as well as on the cardboard models.

There are four meridians on the model. It does not matter since, from the definition of the angle between two planes, any point will give the same result. Yes, every point in the Northern (and in the Southern) hemisphere lies on one and only one meridian. The longitude of Greenwich is 0°. There is one in the Northern and one in the Southern hemisphere. Since 90° alone would be ambiguous; it could be east or west.

28

5.3 Parallels and latitude

No, it has a small radius unless it is laid on the equatorial plane where it would be of no use. Any meridian cuts the small circle ABC and the circle of the Equator in two points P and Q, such that $\angle POQ = \phi°$. The symmetry of the sphere and the fact that the two circles lie in parallel planes make all such lines equivalent. C can be seen to be approximately half way from F to N.P. on the circle (S.P., F, N.P.) which is seen in elevation. Therefore $\phi° \approx 45°$. The latitude of the N.P. is $90°$. A latitude of $100°$ would indicate a point whose latitude is $80°$ on the Antimeridian (see Question 1 of Exercise C). It is convenient to consider that $-90° \leqslant \phi° \leqslant 90°$.

5.4 Specifying position on the Earth's surface

The Earth is very nearly a perfect sphere, quite near enough for purposes of navigation, see Question 11 of Exercise C.

Greenwich is east of the centre of London.

Exercise C (p. 37)

1. 180° E or W; 130° E, 65° W.

2. N.P. is 90° N, S.P. is 90° S. Longitude is measured by rotating a plane about a line (the axis) and so varies from 180° E to 180 °W, i.e. through 360°. Latitude is measured by translating a plane parallel to a plane (the equatorial plane) and so varies from 90° N to 90° S, i.e. through 180°. This is a hard question to answer. The N.P. and S.P. are defined by the axis of rotation of the Earth. It does not rotate about an E–W line.

3. It has no longitude since no meridian is defined by it.

4. New York   40° 45′ N, 74° 0′W
   Naples   40° 43′N, 14° 18′ E
   Bogota   4° 38′ N, 74° 15′ W

5. (a) No; by observing the rotation he could tell the poles; he could not tell which was which; the ice-caps might not help him if he was from Mars.
   (b) Yes, in the plane perpendicular to the axis.
   (c) No.

29

(*d*) No, he could not distinguish 30° N from 30° S, but could estimate the approximate position of the one or the other having found the Equator.

(*e*) No.

6. (*a*) The 40° North parallel.
(*b*) The 170 °W meridian.
(*c*) The point of intersection of these, or 40° N, 170° W.
(*d*) The great circle comprising the 27° W meridian and the 153° E meridian.
(*e*) The region approximately within the Arctic Circle.

7. (*a*) On the Equator.
(*b*) 10000 km.
(*c*) Yes, at S.P.
(*d*) Yes, at S.P., the directions specify that they travel South.

8. (*a*) (i) {Stuttgart, St Helier}, d. long. 11° on 49° N.
(ii) {Milan, Bordeaux}, d. long. 10° on 45° N.
(*b*) (iii) {Stuttgart, Milan}, d. lat. 4°.
(iv) {St Helier, Aberdeen}, d. lat. 8°.

The candidates are either (i) or (iv). This question should make the point that distances on a parallel are generally less than distances with the same separation on a meridian. In fact (iv) is greatest as can be verified when Section 7 has been tackled.

9. He would fly in a spiral course called a Rhumb Line, see Figure H.

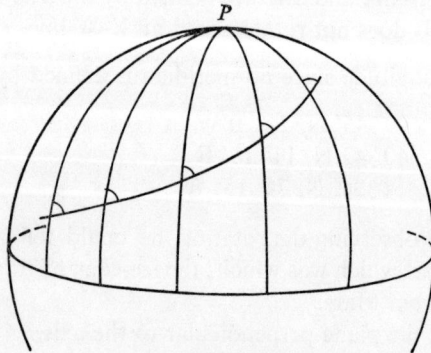

Fig. H

If the angle is not a right-angle the path spirals towards one of the poles. A Rhumb Line is followed when keeping to a constant course. In practice, a whole journey is composed of a number of Rhumb Line sections with alterations of course between one section and the next. He would finish at the North Pole since his 'Northing' is continually increasing.

10. Nearly $\frac{1}{3}$%. About $\frac{1}{3}$ cm. Only detectable with very accurate measuring instruments. Everest; just over 9 km. The Mariana Trench in the Pacific ocean is nearly 11 km deep and the Challenger Deep may be even more. These would result in blemishes of at most 2 mm depth in the 1 m sphere which would certainly be 'smooth'.

11. Height, measured from the centre of the Earth. Adding the third coordinate (θ, ϕ, h) gives a system known as spherical polar coordinates.

6. NAUTICAL MILES

The metre is a geodetic unit. It was taken to be one ten-millionth of a meridian quadrant and its utility was geared to the proposed subdivision of a full turn into 100 or 1000 parts instead of 360. This arrangement never came into general use and it seems likely that the nautical mile will continue in use despite metrication.

Meridians are parts of Great Circles like the Equator.

Exercise D (p. 39)

1. 21 600 n.m.; 3437 n.m.

2. 1851·9 m.

3. 15 702 n.m.

4. See Figure I.
   (*a*) 30°, 1800 n.m.
   (*b*) 90°, 5400 n.m.
   (*c*) If the places are in the same hemispheres, then

   $$\text{d. lat.} = |\phi_1 - \phi_2|.$$

31

(d) If the places are in different hemispheres, then
$$\text{d. lat.} = \phi_1 + \phi_2.$$

5. (a) See diagram in Figure J.
$$\text{d. lat.} = 101° 34';$$
distance = 6094 n.m.

   (b) 11290 km.

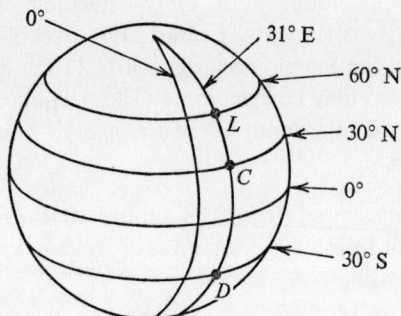

Fig. I

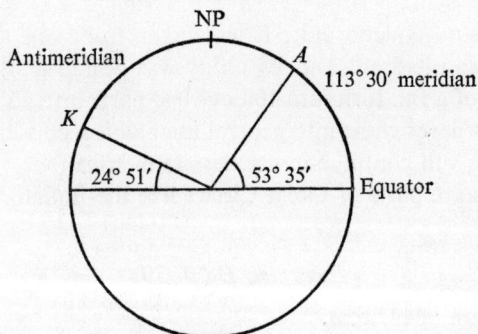

Fig. J

6. 80° S; New Zealand.

7. Entebbe.

8. (a) 2140 n.m.   (b) 960 n.m.   (c) 1640 n.m.

9. Yes. This is an important question. There is only one Great Circle between two points since, in general, the two points and the centre of the sphere define a unique plane cutting the sphere

32

in just one circle. The exception is when the two points are at opposite ends of a diameter; then there is an infinity of Great Circles joining them. The Great Circle distance is always taken to be the least distance and so is unique. In the case of the infinity of ways, the distance is always the same and so is still unique.

10. (*a*) 33° 20′ N, 160° E; (*b*) 0°, 166° 40′ W; (*c*) 0°, 126° 40′ E.

11. (*a*) 9°. (*b*) 18°. (*c*) 45°. (*d*) 9*x*°. *x* km → $(\frac{9}{1000}x)°$.

7. DISTANCE ON A PARALLEL
OF LATITUDE

The demonstration of the expression for a distance on a parallel is a little complicated but should be worked through as an excellent example of trigonometry in three dimensions. It should be pointed out that the cosine of an angle is always less than, or equal to, unity which links with the Great Circle, Small Circle idea and provides a ready check that the relation has not been written the wrong way round.

Exercise E (*p. 41*)

1. (*a*) 300 n.m.   (*b*) 519·6 n.m.
Neither, for $\cos \frac{1}{2}x° \neq \frac{1}{2} \cos x°$.

2. 10620 n.m. Because each point is on the antimeridian of the other

3. See Figure K.
(*a*) 10150 n.m. (£507);   (*b*) 8400 n.m. (£420), 17 %.

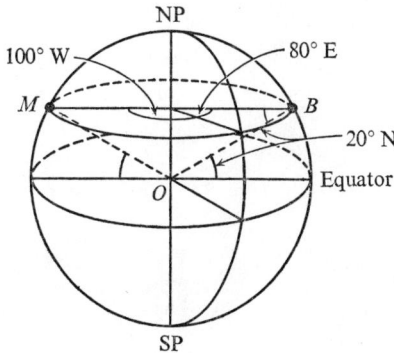

Fig. K

4. It should be explained that 'north of due east' is not intended to be the compass point 'north of east'.

   South of due east.

5. (a) 142° 42' W;   (b) 127° 18' E;   (c) 145° 22' W.

6. 15°. 900 knots due west. Slower, at 554 knots.

7. In the days of sail, the speed of a ship was found by throwing overboard a log attached to a knotted rope. As the log fell astern the number of knots passing through the seaman's hands during a certain time was counted and this measured the speed. The operation was equally effective at night.

8. A magnetic compass points to the magnetic pole whose position relative to the true pole varies. A gyro compass can be set either to the magnetic or to the true pole. It is unaffected by the magnetism of the earth but needs a power supply to keep it going.

9. The North Pole.

10. Helicopter 2 finishes in position 9° N, 9° E (relative to the starting point). Helicopter 1 finishes in position 9° N, 9° 7' E. They are hence nearly 7 nautical miles apart and can easily see each other.

4

QUADRATIC FUNCTIONS

This chapter is intended to revise graphing and algebraic manipulation and to take a first look at techniques for solving quadratic equations.

We should not regard it all as being essential for the average O-level student. We should expect him to know that a function of the form $x \rightarrow ax^2 + bx + c$ gives rise to a certain type of graph, and that it is possible to solve an equation $ax^2 + bx + c = d$ from this graph. But the technique of completing the square is a specialized one. It is difficult to justify the solution of quadratics by completing the square (or its generalized version, the 'formula') from the point of view of practical usefulness. Physicists are hard put to it to give examples of its necessity at O-level: the distance-time relation $s = ut + \frac{1}{2}at^2$ is usually the only example, and involved questions about this have been asked because, in the past, the mathematical techniques have been available. The physics of the situation can be examined without this. (The Nuffield course, for example, does not demand it.)

We should prefer to delay the formal techniques until the A-level course. For most O-level candidates we should suggest that Section 2, Exercise B, and Exercise C, Questions 10–13 are omitted.

1. FUNCTIONS AND GRAPHS

This section is intended to contrast quadratic equations with linear and cubic equations and to make the point that a quadratic equation has at most two solutions.

Graphing functions of this complexity has previously been done in *Book* 4, Chapter 2 and this section provides useful revision.

(*a*) $x = 2$.

(*b*) (i) It is a straight line.

(ii) Its gradient is *a*.

(iii) It intercepts the line $x = 0$ at $y = b$.

One solution (provided that $a \neq 0$).

(c) It is a curve (a parabola) and not a straight line. See Figure A.
  (i) Two solutions $x = 2$ and $x = {}^-2$.
  (ii) No solutions in the set of real numbers.

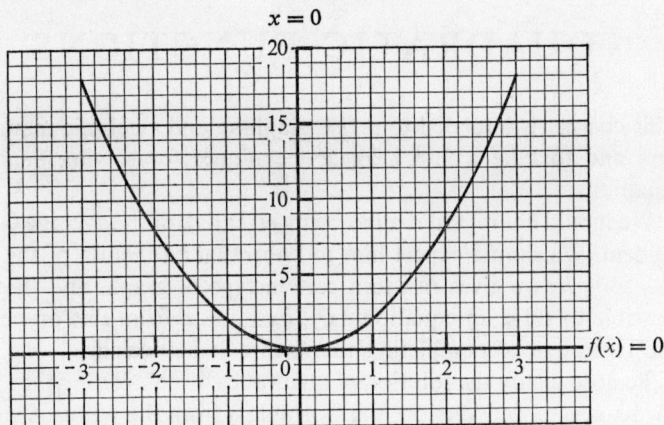

Fig. A

(d) (i) $x = {}^-1$ or $-\frac{1}{2}$.
  (ii) $x = {}^-2$ or $\frac{1}{2}$.
  (iii) No solutions in the set of real numbers.

(e)

x	-3	-2	-1	$-\frac{1}{2}$	0	1	2	3
x^3	-27	-8	-1	$-\frac{1}{8}$	0	1	8	27
$-x^2$	-9	-4	-1	$-\frac{1}{4}$	0	-1	-4	-9
$-2x$	6	4	2	1	0	-2	-4	-6
x^3-x^2-2x	-30	-8	0	$\frac{5}{8}$	0	-2	0	12

See Figure B.

$$x = {}^-1 \quad \text{or} \quad x = 0 \quad \text{or} \quad x = 2.$$

No: one, two or three real and distinct solutions.

Exercise A (p. 46)

1. (a) See Figure C.

  (b) (i) $x = {}^-1;$ (ii) $x = 7;$ (iii) $x = 2.$

2. See Figure D.

   (i) $x = {}^{-}1{\cdot}4$ or $x = 1{\cdot}4$ (to 2 s.f.).

   (ii) No solution in the set of real numbers.

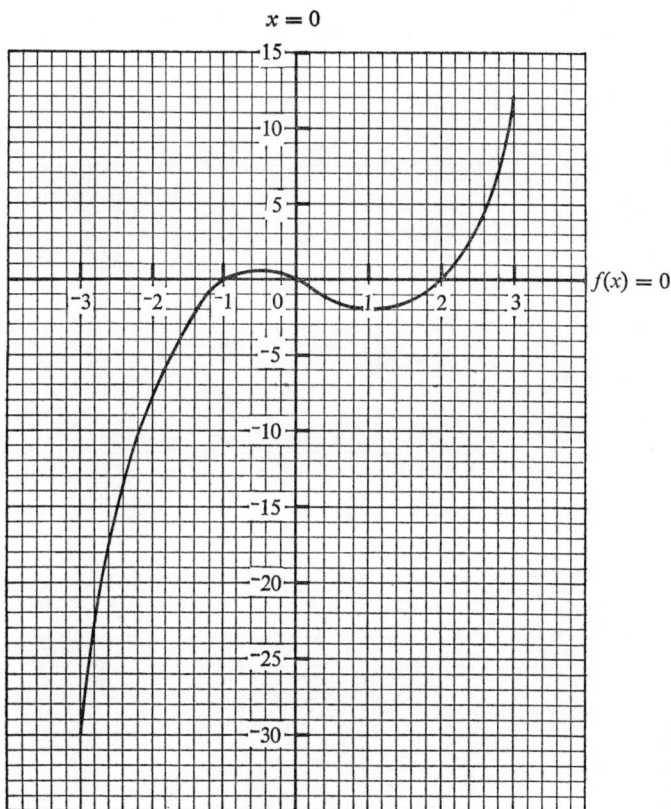

Fig. B

3. See Figure E.

   (a) A translation $\begin{pmatrix} 0 \\ 1 \end{pmatrix}$.

   (b) Reflection in the line $y = 0$ (or $f(x) = 0$).

$x = 0$

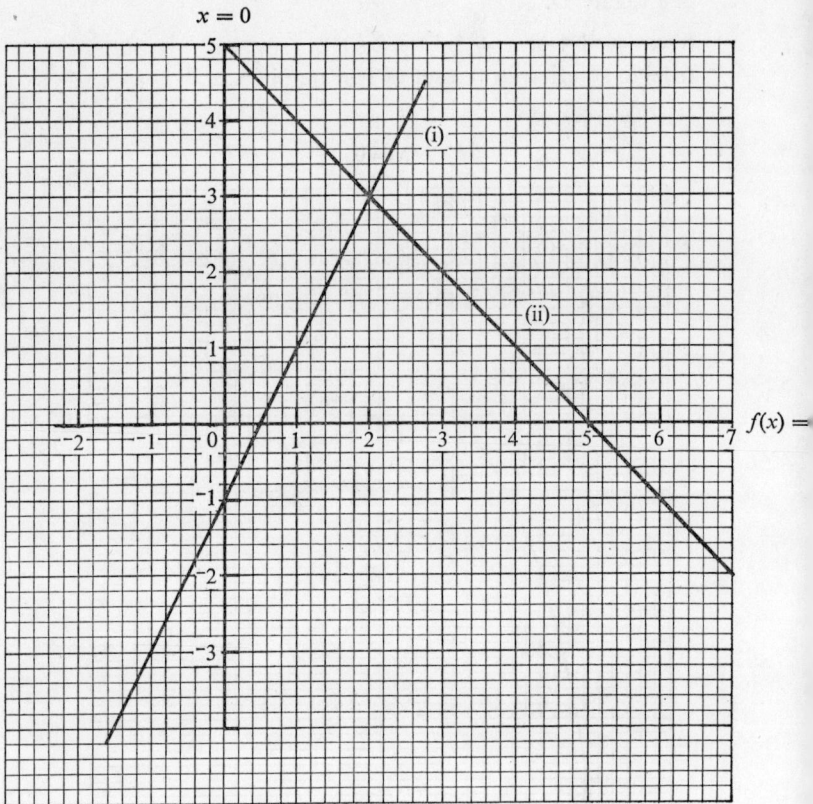

Fig. C

4. 4·6 s (to 2 S.F.).

5.

x	$^-2$	$^-1$	0	1	2	3	4
x^3	$^-8$	$^-1$	0	1	8	27	64
$-3x^2$	$^-12$	$^-3$	0	$^-3$	$^-12$	$^-27$	$^-48$
^-x	2	1	0	$^-1$	$^-2$	$^-3$	$^-4$
3	3	3	3	3	3	3	3
x^3-3x^2-x+3	$^-15$	0	3	0	$^-3$	0	15

See Figure F.

$$x = {}^-1 \quad \text{or} \quad x = 1 \quad \text{or} \quad x = 3.$$

$3{\cdot}1 \geqslant c \geqslant {}^-3{\cdot}1$ (answer correct to 2 S.F.).

38

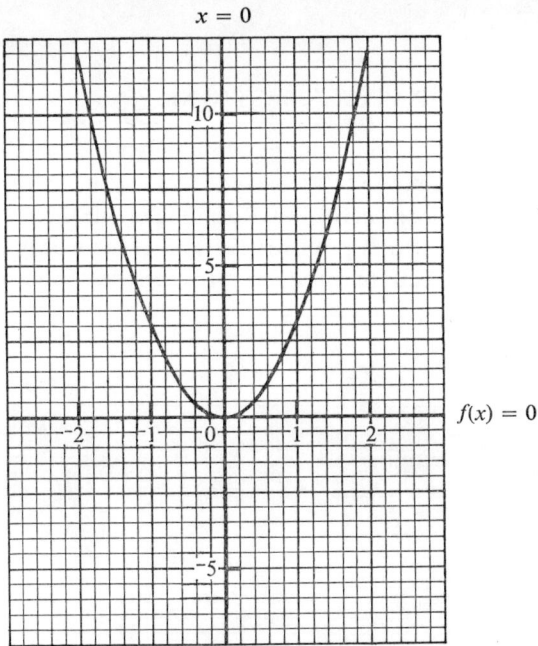

$x = 0$

$f(x) = 0$

Fig. D

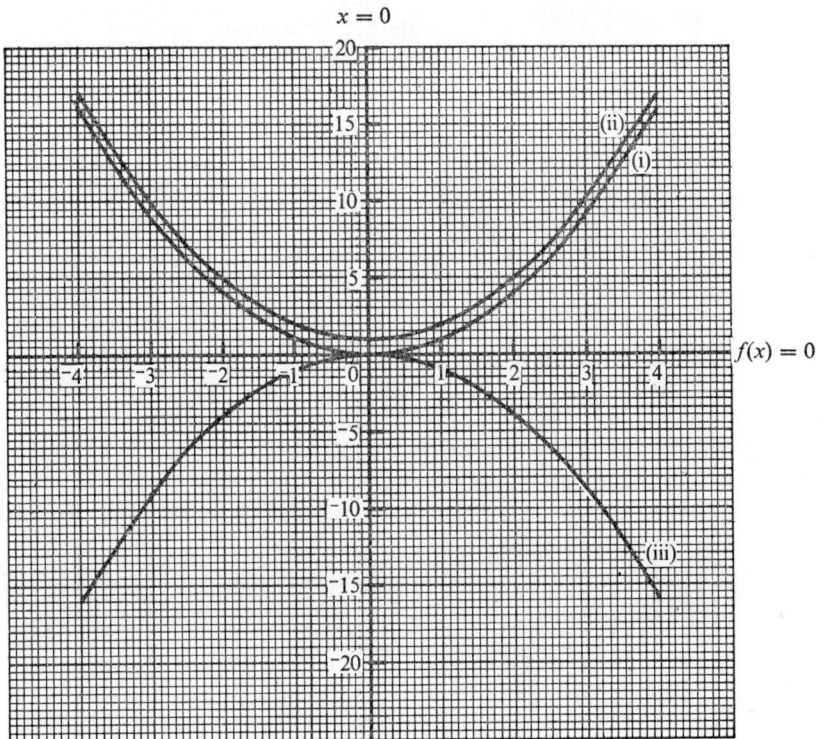

$x = 0$

$f(x) = 0$

Fig. E

39

6. This is an open-ended question intended for the more able students. A group of them could work on it together. The curve is a parabola, a curve always bending in one direction; the 'cup' is upwards if a is positive; the line of symmetry is $x = {}^-b/2a$; as x increases (a positive) or decreases from zero, so $f(x)$ increases.

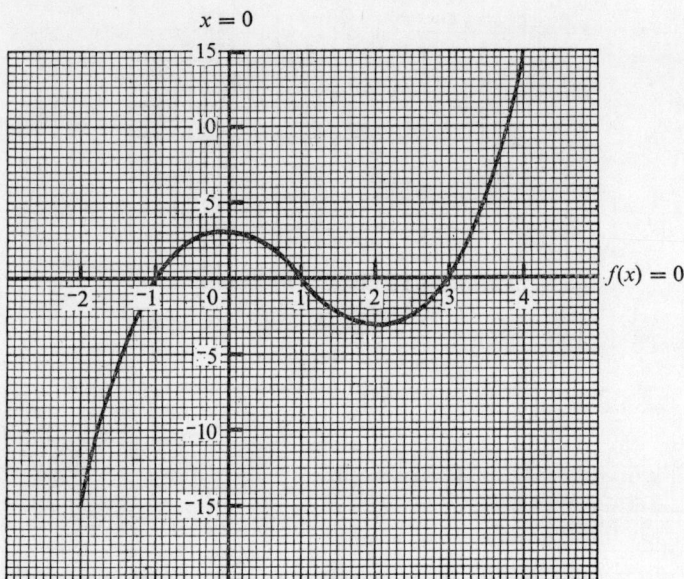

Fig. F

2. QUADRATIC FUNCTIONS

This section is concerned with the method of completing the square. It is the familiar treatment except that it is expressed in terms of functions and uses the 'machine' idea for breaking up a function and for finding the inverse.

It can be extended to the general case $x \rightarrow ax^2 + bx + c$ by splitting it up into

$$x \rightarrow x^2 + \frac{b}{a}x + \frac{c}{a} \text{ followed by } x \rightarrow ax.$$

The first of these can be written

$$x \to \left(x + \frac{b}{2a}\right)^2 - \frac{b^2 - 4ac}{4a^2}.$$

The flow diagram is

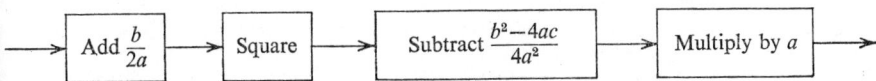

| → | Add $\frac{b}{2a}$ | → | Square | → | Subtract $\frac{b^2-4ac}{4a^2}$ | → | Multiply by a | → |

The flow diagram for the inverse is,

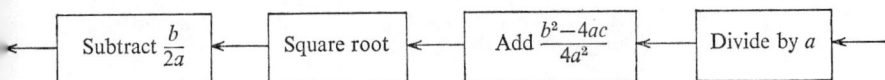

| ← | Subtract $\frac{b}{2a}$ | ← | Square root | ← | Add $\frac{b^2-4ac}{4a^2}$ | ← | Divide by a | ← |

Thus, putting 0 into this inverse machine gives

$$\pm \sqrt{\left(\frac{b^2 - 4ac}{4a^2}\right)} - \frac{b}{2a},$$

or, as it is usually written,

$$\frac{-b \pm \sqrt{(b^2 - 4ac)}}{2a}.$$

2.1 The inverse of a quadratic function

(a) (i)

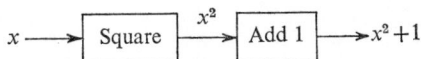

$$x \longrightarrow \boxed{\text{Square}} \xrightarrow{\ x^2\ } \boxed{\text{Add 1}} \longrightarrow x^2 + 1$$

(ii) $x \to x^2 + 1$.

(iii) Either $^-2$ or 2.

(iv)

$$\pm\sqrt{(x-1)} \longleftarrow \boxed{\text{Square root}} \xleftarrow{\ x-1\ } \boxed{\text{Subtract 1}} \longleftarrow x$$

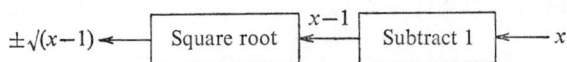

It does not represent a function because there is not a unique answer ($\pm$).

(b) (i) No. Because two functions have the same value for one element of the domain, it does not follow that they have the same value for all elements of the domain.

(ii)

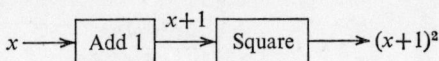

$$x \to (x+1)^2.$$

(iii)

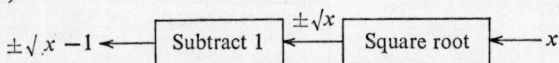

(c) (i) The difficulty is that although you can subtract 1, you cannot subtract twice the number thought of because you do not know it.

(ii) $x \to x^2 + 2x + 1$.

2.2 The solution of quadratic equations by inverse functions

The numbers could be $^-5$ or 3.

(a) (i)

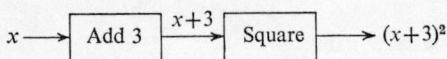

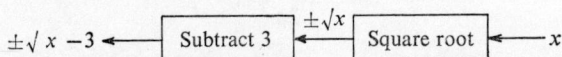

(ii)

		x	3
x		x^2	$3x$
3		$3x$	9

(iii) $(x+3)^2 = x^2 + 6x + 9$.

(iv) $x \to \pm\sqrt{x} - 3$.

(b) (i) The last step is to add 4 instead of 1.

(ii) $x \to (x+1)^2 + 3$.

(iii)

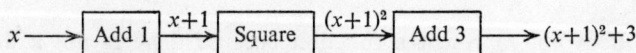

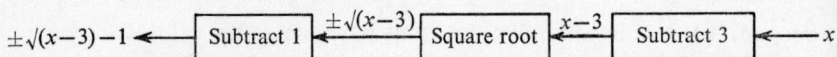

(iv) (a) $^-4$ or 2.   (b) $^-1$.   (c) No real number.

(c) (i) The $10x$ is split into equal parts. The x^2 and $10x$ are thereby accounted for in $(x+5)^2$.

It is then necessary to add 1 to make the 5^2 into 26.

(ii) $x \rightarrow \pm \sqrt{(x-1)}-5$.

Exercise B (p. 50)

1. (a) $^-4$ or 4.

(b)

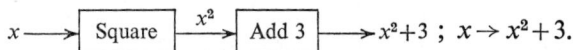

$x \longrightarrow \boxed{\text{Square}} \xrightarrow{x^2} \boxed{\text{Add 3}} \longrightarrow x^2+3 \; ; \; x \rightarrow x^2+3.$

(c)

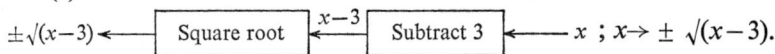

$\pm\sqrt{(x-3)} \longleftarrow \boxed{\text{Square root}} \xleftarrow{x-3} \boxed{\text{Subtract 3}} \longleftarrow x \; ; \; x \rightarrow \pm \sqrt{(x-3)}.$

2. (a) $^-8$ or 2.

(b)

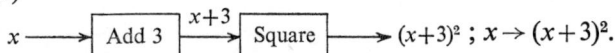

$x \longrightarrow \boxed{\text{Add 3}} \xrightarrow{x+3} \boxed{\text{Square}} \longrightarrow (x+3)^2 \; ; \; x \rightarrow (x+3)^2.$

(c)

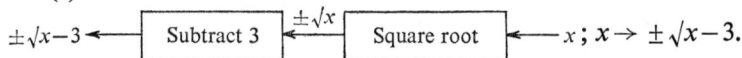

$\pm\sqrt{x}-3 \longleftarrow \boxed{\text{Subtract 3}} \xleftarrow{\pm\sqrt{x}} \boxed{\text{Square root}} \longleftarrow x \; ; \; x \rightarrow \pm\sqrt{x}-3.$

3. $x \rightarrow \pm \sqrt{(x)}-2.$

4.

	x	2			x	3			x	$^-2$
x	x^2	$2x$		x	x^2	$3x$		x	x^2	^-2x
2	$2x$	4		3	$3x$	9		$^-2$	^-2x	4

(a) x^2+4x+4;   (b) x^2+6x+9;   (c) x^2-4x+4.

5. (a) $x \rightarrow \pm\sqrt{x}-2$;   (b) $x \rightarrow \pm\sqrt{x}-3$;   (c) $x \rightarrow \pm\sqrt{x}+2$.

6. (a) $x \rightarrow (x+2)^2-1.$
   $x \rightarrow \pm \sqrt{(x+1)}-2.$
   $x = ^-3$ or $^-1.$
   (b) $x = ^-5$ or $^-1.$
   (c) $x = 5$ or $^-1.$

43

7. $x \to (x+2)^2+2$.

The difficulty arises in finding the square root of a negative number. This question could lead to a discussion of complex numbers.

8. (a)

	x	$\frac{9}{4}$
x	x^2	$\frac{9}{4}x$
$\frac{9}{4}$	$\frac{9}{4}x$	$\frac{81}{16}$

(b) $x \to (x+\frac{9}{4})^2 + {}^-\frac{49}{16}$.

(c) $gf: x \to 2x^2+9x+4 = 2[(x+\frac{9}{4})^2 + {}^-\frac{49}{16}]$.
Inverse of gf is $x \to \pm\sqrt{(\frac{1}{2}x+\frac{49}{16})} - \frac{9}{4}$.

(d) $x = {}^-4$ or $-\frac{1}{2}$.

9. $x \to 3x^2+12x$ can be split into $x \to x^2+4x$ followed by $x \to 3x$. The first of these can be written $x \to (x+2)^2-4$. The flow diagram is

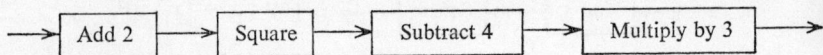

Add 2	→	Square	→	Subtract 4	→	Multiply by 3

and the inverse flow diagram is

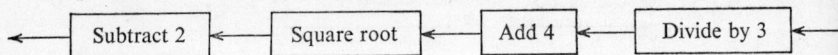

Subtract 2	←	Square root	←	Add 4	←	Divide by 3

$x = {}^-6$ or 2.

10. 4 seconds. (The negative answer has no meaning in this physical situation.)

3. FACTORS

3.1 $ab = 0$

Section 3 is concerned with an important property of the set of real numbers: an algebraist would say that this set possesses no zero divisors (see Birkhoff and MacLane).

This property enables some equations to be solved easily. As Question 10 suggests this is not always the most convenient method.

The last three questions of Exercise C are intended to stretch able students.

(*a*) At least one of *a* and *b* must be 0.

(*b*) Either, at least one of *a* and *b* is 0; or $a = 3, b = 4$, or $a = 4, b = 3$; or $a = 2, b = 3$, or $a = 3, b = 2$.

(*c*) $\begin{pmatrix} 0 & 0 \\ 0 & 0 \end{pmatrix}$.

It does not follow that either **A** or **B** is a zero matrix.

(*d*) No. P and Q could be any disjoint sets.

3.2 The solution of quadratic equations by factors

(*a*) Either $x+2 = 0$ or $x+4 = 0$ (they cannot *both* be zero for the same value of x).

$$x = {}^-2 \quad \text{or} \quad x = {}^-4.$$

(*b*)

	x	2
x	x^2	$2x$
4	$4x$	8

$(x+2)(x+4) = x^2+6x+8.$

(*c*) $x = {}^-4 \quad \text{or} \quad x = {}^-2.$

(*d*)

	x	3
x	x^2	$3x$
1	x	3

$x^2+4x+3 = (x+3)(x+1).$
$x = {}^-3 \quad \text{or} \quad {}^-1.$

(*e*)

	x	a
x	x^2	ax
b	bx	ab

$\left.\begin{array}{l} a \times b = 14 \\ a+b = 9 \end{array}\right\} \Rightarrow \begin{array}{l} a = 7, b = 2 \\ \text{or} \\ a = 2, b = 7. \end{array}$

$x = {}^-7 \quad \text{or} \quad {}^-2.$

Exercise C (p. 52)

1. (*a*) $x = 0$.

(*b*) X is not necessarily the zero matrix. A more positive statement can be made: if the matrix is $\begin{pmatrix} a & b \\ c & d \end{pmatrix}$ where not all a, b, c, d are zero, then $a+d = 0$ and $a^2+bc = 0$.

2. Both P and Q are empty sets.

3. Either at least one of a and b is 0;

$$\text{or} \quad a = 2, \quad b = 6 \quad \text{or} \quad a = 3, \quad b = 4$$
$$\text{or} \quad a = 3, \quad b = 8 \quad \text{or} \quad a = 4, \quad b = 6$$
$$\text{or} \quad a = 4, \quad b = 9 \quad \text{or} \quad a = 6, \quad b = 6$$
$$\text{or} \quad a = 6, \quad b = 8 \quad \text{or} \quad a = 6, \quad b = 10$$
$$\text{or} \quad a = 8, \quad b = 9$$

or any of these with a and b interchanged.

4. (a) and (b) (i) $x = {}^-2$ or ${}^-1$; (ii) $x = 1$ or 2;
   (iii) $x = {}^-2$ or 1; (iv) $x = {}^-1$ or 1.

5. (a) $x+4$; (b) $x+3$; (c) $x+2$; (d) $x+5$; (e) $x-3$;
   (f) $x-6$; (g) $x+2$; (h) $3x-1$; (i) $4x-3$; (j) $2x+\frac{3}{2}$.

6. (a) $x+2, x+3$; (b) $x+5, x+5$; (c) $x-1, 2x+3$;
   (d) $x-1, x-4$; (e) $2x+3, 3x-1$; (f) $5x+1, 6x-5$.

7. (a) $x = {}^-6$ or ${}^-3$; (b) $x = 2$ or 3;
   (c) $x = {}^-3$; (d) $x = 6$ or ${}^-1$;
   (e) $x = {}^-5$ or 1; (f) $x = {}^-6$ or 0;
   (g) $x = \frac{1}{2}$ or 2; (h) $x = 3$ or ${}^-3$;
   (i) $x = \frac{{}^-5}{2}$ or $\frac{5}{2}$.

8. (a) $x = 1$ or 2; (b) $x = {}^-1$ or 4;
   (c) $x = {}^-2$ or 1; (d) $x = 1$ or 2;
   (e) $x = 0$ or 1; (f) $x = 0$ or $\frac{2}{3}$.

9. (a) $x = 1$ and $x = 3$ are solutions. Hence $x-1$ and $x-3$ are factors. The function is

$$x \to (x-1)(x-3) = x^2 - 4x + 3.$$

(b) Translate the graph of (i) by $\begin{pmatrix} 0 \\ 1 \end{pmatrix}$.
Hence $x \to x^2 - 4x + 4$.

(c) Translate the graph of (ii) by $\begin{pmatrix} 0 \\ 1 \end{pmatrix}$.
Hence $x \to x^2 - 4x + 5$.

10. The difficulty arises in finding two numbers whose sum is 5 and whose product is 5. They exist, but not in the set of integers.

$$(x+\tfrac{5}{2})^2 - \tfrac{5}{4} = 0.$$

$$x = \pm\sqrt{\tfrac{5}{4}} - \tfrac{5}{2}.$$

11. (*a*) (i) x^2+6x+8.   (ii) x^2+6x+8.

It is not ambiguous—the associative law holds.

(*b*) (i) x^2+6x+8; (ii) x^2+6x+8; (iii) x^2+6x+8.

(*c*) 3   (i) ⁻1;   (ii) 0;   (iii) 15.

(*d*) The pattern of the numbers in the matrix is the same as in the area table.

12. The matrix is

$$\begin{pmatrix} 1 & 3 \\ 5 & 15 \end{pmatrix} \quad \text{or} \quad \begin{pmatrix} 1 & 5 \\ 3 & 15 \end{pmatrix}.$$

The factors are $x+3$ and $x+5$.

It is not suggested that this is a convenient method for finding the factors of a quadratic, but it is included because it shows yet another appearance of a matrix. This method of writing a quadratic expression is of considerable importance in linear algebra (see Birkhoff and MacLane) and finds application in mechanics.

$$(x+a)(x+b) = x^2+(a+b)x+ab = (x \quad 1)\begin{pmatrix} 1 & a \\ b & ab \end{pmatrix}\begin{pmatrix} x \\ 1 \end{pmatrix}$$

and the determinant of the matrix is 0.

13. It is necessary that *both* determinant **A** and determinant **B** are 0. For, suppose determinant $\mathbf{A} \neq 0$, then $\mathbf{A}^{-1}$ exists, and hence

$$\mathbf{A}^{-1}\mathbf{A}\mathbf{B} = \mathbf{A}^{-1}\mathbf{0},$$

$$\mathbf{B} = \mathbf{0}.$$

This contradicts the statement that **B** is non-zero.

Hence determinant $\mathbf{A} = 0$.

A similar argument gives determinant $\mathbf{B} = 0$.

5

PRACTICAL ARITHMETIC

1. HEATING A HOUSE

It should perhaps be pointed out that some at least of the money apparently saved by more efficient fires and insulation will, in practice, be used up in greater comfort!

The section is best dealt with after the Physics department have handled the theory of the transfer of the heat.

The formula, $H = U \times A \times (\theta_i - \theta_0)$ kJ/h per house could be approached on a commonsense basis arguing that the loss will depend on the area and temperature difference in direct proportion and also on how good an insulator or conductor the material is; then with the right choice of units, this formula follows.

Answers are given to two significant figures.

Exercise A (p. 60)

1. (a) 1000 kJ/h.
   (b) 4700 kJ/h.
   (c) 5600 kJ/h.
   (d) 15000 kJ/h. (Door 300, windows 4000, walls 10700.)

2. (a) 3000 kJ/h;   (b) 510 kJ/h.;   (c) 7500 kJ/h.

Exercise B (p. 60)

1. 110000 l/h or 110 m³/h.

2. 170 m³/h.   3. 1400 m³/h.

4. (a) 2(·2);   (b) 3(·4);   (c) 29.

Exercise C (p. 62)

1. 1700 kJ/h.   4. 100 % increase.

Exercise D (*p. 65*)

1. (*a*) £94;   (*b*) £69;   (*c*) £59;   (*d*) £51;   (*e*) £91;
(*f*) £120;   (*g*) £110.

2. A coal merchant will provide the local figures.

Exercise E (*p. 65*)

1. 8 rolls; £8; 11 000 MJ; £12.

2. 29 %.   3. 7350 MJ; £8·40.

4. *B* better after 2500 MJ.

5. 88 new pence per square metre per year.

6. *A*, £($70 + 220 \, n$). *B*, £($200 + 90 \, n$). *C*, £($400 + 106 \, n$). *D*, £($450 + 114 \, n$). *E*, £($550 + 64 \, n$). *F*, £($450 + 74 \, n$). *G*, £$138 \, n$. *H*, £($90 + 81 \, n$).
(*a*) 2·6 years;   (*b*) never;   (*c*) 3·6 years;   (*d*) 7 years;
(*e*) 7 weeks.

2. INVESTMENT

At least a few members of any form will enjoy the exercise of investing an imaginary £100 for one year as they like. More ambitious pupils may try £1000 in say 10 different securities. Shares and Government stocks are quoted in many papers. Assume that a $\frac{1}{2}$ % charge is made when Government Stocks are bought or transferred and a 3 % charge in other cases. Not everyone realizes that Government Stock may be easily bought and sold through any Savings Bank Post Office.

2.1 The value of money

The variation in the purchasing power of the pound is not an easy concept for children to grasp. Discussion may help. For example, 'How many oranges could be bought for £1 in 1860, 1917, 1938, 1950 or now?' Use the graph as a basis. Or, 'How many pounds were needed to buy the same bicycle in different years?'

Figure 4 does not show tax deducted from the Corporation loan as young persons are unlikely to have to pay tax on this. Tax is inevitably deducted at source and cannot be reclaimed from Building Society interest payments. The first £15 of interest on Post Office

Savings is free of tax. Tax has, however, been shown deducted from the Unit Trust so that too much weight is not given to this and also because equity investment is more likely to take place later in life when tax will be paid. 6 % British Savings Bonds may be bought through Post Offices: if these Bonds are left for 5 years, then £102 is repayable for each £100 held, making, for non-income-tax payers, an effective rate of 6·4 % per annum. (It is a useful exercise to add a graph for these Bonds to Figure 4.) Premium Bonds pay out as prizes $4\frac{5}{8}$ % of the money deposited. Is this investment or speculation? Unit Trusts are not as satisfactory as Investment Trusts for non-income-tax payers, but, as they are more easily purchased, are perhaps easiest for a start to investment in shares.

There are many forms of endowment insurance policy. All aim to provide money for dependents on the death of the insured person. The with-profits endowment assurance policy is a sound investment. This is for a fixed period of time, for example, 15 or 20 years. Some endowment assurance policies are now linked to the changing value of shares as an added counter to inflation.

A 'family man's policy' provides protection for dependents relatively cheaply but, should the insured person outlive the agreed period, he obtains no return.

In this chapter, money answers are best given only to the nearest pound and only slide rule accuracy is expected.

Exercise F (p. 70)

1. (b) £23; (c) £25; (d) £24; (e) £27.

2. £24.   3. (a) £70; (b) £42.

4. (a) 48 %; (b) 37 %.

5. 1·9 % equivalent to an annual rate of 5·7 %.

6. Purchasing power in 1968 was only 26 % of that in 1938, that is, prices have risen by an average of $\frac{100}{26} = 3\cdot85$ times compared with the rise in the price of beef of 4 times.

D7. The last section shows *how* the value of money has varied in Britain: the aim of this question is to start a discussion on *why* this should happen. It is hard to find an answer: at least some of the following points might be mentioned.

The value of money depends upon the relation between the amount of money and the quantity of goods that are available. This value remains stable when the total national income (the sum of the wages and salaries of individuals) equals the total national output of goods. When there is more than enough money or if there is a shortage of goods, then prices will rise, money be exchanged for fewer goods and the value of the money be said to fall. The following are some examples of the circumstances which generate more than enough money (but it should be noticed that they are not necessarily independent of each other): an increase in wages and salaries (over the country as a whole) faster than an increase in production at a time of full employment; an excess of personal or industrial spending and a withdrawal of savings; high government spending, for example, on social service grants, the expansion of education or of building programmes; when it is easy to borrow money at low rates of interest; an increase in the general level of industrial investment. A shortage of goods may be the result of a failure in the supply of raw materials or of a restriction of sales.

After the First World War, the countries of Europe were in debt and in need of reconstruction. Governments at that time, did not have the techniques nor the theory necessary for the control of their countries' economy (even now these theories do not seem to be very effective), but they did try to control the movement of money between countries. In Britain, after the War there was a reconstruction boom, but in 1920, the Government decided to reduce the amount of money leaving the country by raising the Bank Rate and thus increasing the amount to be charged on loans. Unfortunately this had the second effect of reducing the possibility that industries could borrow and made them cut back their activities. Men were unable to find employment, their earnings became lower, money became scarce and its value went up. (This disastrous effect of mass unemployment might have been avoided had the country been economically strong at the time; but there had been too little investment in industry for years past and also, during the war, other countries had built up some of their industries to replace the goods that we had failed to supply: our cotton and ships were less in demand and oil was beginning to replace coal.)

After the Second World War, countries devised methods by which they hoped to control their economies and they determined to take no measures to restrict world trade so that prosperity could return to Europe. Money was provided by the United States of America for reconstruction, mutual aid and for the development of world trade (particularly under the International Monetary Fund within the United Nations). In Britain, the social services were developed and taxation organized with the aim of maintaining a high level of employment and this remained possible with the expansion of world trade. More than enough money became available and so its value tended to diminish.

3. GROWTH OF MONEY

Because of the exponential nature of curves b, d and e (and also of the curves of Figure 5) these can be used to estimate growths over longer periods than 10 years. For example, the 6 % graph, (e) in Figure 4 shows an increase of 1·62 % in eight years, so, after 40 years

$$£100 \text{ becomes } £(1·62)^5 \times 100 = £1100,$$

and after 45 years

$$£(1·62)^5 \times 1·35 \times 100 = £1500.$$

(1·35 is the growth factor for 5 years.)

Exercise G (p. 73)

1. £91.

2. £33.

3. £180.

4. £230.

5. £240. The difference between 1·791 and 1·82 corresponds to the difference between adding interest annually and monthly at 6 % per annum.

6. £1400.

7. £3800.

8. £3900.

9. £640.

4. HIRE PURCHASE

Over the relatively short period of hire purchase loans, compound interest has been ignored as almost insignificant and simple interest has been used instead.

Exercise H (p. 76)

1. £3·6, (£3 repayment, plus £0·6 interest); £94·4.
2. £84. (£84·50).   3.   £8·64; 23·4 %.
4. £4 repayment plus 40p interest. Effective rate of interest 18·5 %.

5. BUYING A HOUSE

The determination of interest payment and repayment of loan is too involved and only results are quoted.

We should like to suggest that at some moment during this chapter, and this would be a good time, there should be some discussion on the need for expert advice before investing or before committing even small initial amounts of money in, for instance, mortgage payments, insurance or hire purchase. The approachability of bank managers and solicitors and the existence of various brokers might be mentioned.

Concerning mortgage payments which consist partly of capital repayment and partly of interest payment, the income tax allowance is on the latter part only. It is worth investigating the advantages of taking out an endowment policy for the full amount of the mortgage and not repaying any part of the loan until the end of the period when the policy matures and provides the money. This has the advantage of safeguarding dependents but also, in the present situation, it turns out that, although the interest is higher, the whole arrangement is more economical for the individual especially if he takes out a with-profits policy.

Exercise I (p. 77)

1. (a) £80; (b) £46.   2.   £8600.
3. (a) £240; (b) £2400.

6. INCOME TAX

6.1 Allowances

The method of calculation is the same as that used in the Coding Allowance by the Inland Revenue authorities.

53

Example 6

Part (i). Only $\frac{7}{9}$ of the premium is allowed for superannuation because the rest—$\frac{2}{9}$—is already allowed for under earned income allowance.

Example 6

Part (vi). Family allowances are regarded as earned income and so $\frac{2}{9}$ of the amount could appear under coding allowance and the whole of Family allowances be deducted in this item. However, $\frac{7}{9}$ deducted under this item is simpler to do, though not perhaps to understand.

Exercise J (*p. 80*)

(*a*) (i) £242; (ii) £536; (iii) £176·76; (iv) £14·73.

(*b*) (i) £626; (ii) £152; (iii) £35·60; (iv) £2·97.

(*c*) (i) £258; (ii) £520; (iii) £170·20; (iv) £14·18.

(*d*) (i) £208; (ii) £570; (iii) £190·70; (iv) £15·89.

(*e*) (i) £516; (ii) £262; (iii) £68·60; (iv) £5·72.

7. RATES
Exercise K (*p. 82*)

1. (*a*) £156500; (*b*) £5450.

2. (*a*) £0·56; (*b*) £0·42.

3. (*a*) (i) £29·80; (ii) £31·50.
   (*b*) (i) £43·80; (ii) £46·30.

6

INVARIANTS IN GEOMETRY

The study of invariants under transformations of one kind and another is an underlying theme in mathematics and shows through very clearly in the 'motion geometry' of this course. Each transformation can be classified by the geometrical properties which it leaves invariant and in going, for example, from a translation where almost everything is invariant to a topological transformation where at first nothing seems fixed, there has been a large reduction in the number of constraints and consequently fewer invariants. Between these two extremes there are many intermediate transformations with different sets of invariants.

The isometries keep distance invariant and in so doing keep length, angle and area constant. As the constraints are released the properties which become significant change so that by the time we reach the topological transformations it is the incidence properties which are important.

This chapter begins to show the link between the geometrical invariants and the matrix algebra which we have used to describe them. To do this fully would be beyond the scope of the course, for it would need familiarity with, for example the scalar product, so we have singled out the properties which can most easily be handled algebraically. If this seems to be the tail wagging the dog it is because in many ways the chapter is on matrix algebra which happens to find a geometrical representation useful to illustrate its properties.

The structure of the chapter is then:

1. A study of the invariant properties of geometric transformations with

(i) a brief classification of the known transformations based on their invariants, and

(ii) their application to investigating the properties of figures.

2. An algebraic approach to the geometric transformations which can be represented by
$$\begin{pmatrix} x \\ y \end{pmatrix} \to \begin{pmatrix} a & b \\ c & d \end{pmatrix} \begin{pmatrix} x \\ y \end{pmatrix} + \begin{pmatrix} h \\ k \end{pmatrix}.$$

3. An investigation of the 'points' which stay fixed under a matrix transformation.

4. An extension of Section 3 and the beginnings of an algebraic classification of the affine transformations.

A useful reference for anyone interested in pursuing the ideas in this chapter is

Matrices and Transformations, by A. J. Pettofrezzo.

1. GEOMETRIC INVARIANTS

(*a*) (i) Position, direction.

  (ii) Area, angles, lengths of sides.

(*b*) Corresponding sides parallel.

  Angles equal.

  Ratio of lengths of corresponding sides equal.

(*c*) Order of points on a line.

  Number and types of nodes.

  Number and types of regions.

(*d*) This transformation might be described as a 'disintegration'. Area is invariant in this case.

(*e*) Yes. This comes back to the rigidity of a triangle (or the SSS case of congruence).

The converse is not true. An enlargement always preserves angle but not length.

Exercise A (p. 86)

The first four questions in this exercise are concerned with investigating the invariant properties of different transformations while Questions 5–9 give some ideas on their application.

1. It is important to appreciate that in this question the deductions are being made from a single figure in each case and that it is impossible to generalize—the transformations have not been defined so the answers are really about the common properties of *ABCD* and *A'B'C'D'*.

  (*a*) *c, d, f*;   (*b*) *a, d*;
  (*c*) *a, b, c, d, f*;   (*d*) *b, d, e, f*;
  (*e*) *d*.

2. See Figure A.

    (*a*) Translation;   (*b*) 90° rotation;   (*c*) 180° rotation;

    (*d*) 270° rotation;   (*e*) reflection;   (*f*) (*g*), (*h*) glide reflections.

As the transformations concerned are all isometries, they all have area, length and angles between lines as invariants.

Direction is an invariant only of the translation (*a*), while sense is an invariant of the four direct isometries (*a*), (*b*), (*c*) and (*d*).

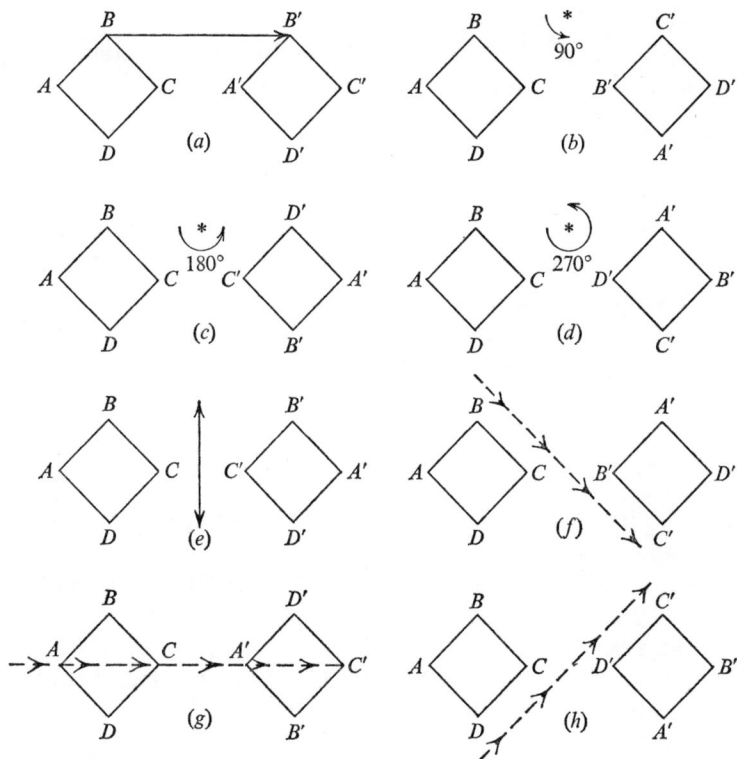

Fig. A

D3.   An equilateral triangle can be mapped onto itself in an infinite number of ways by dissecting it and rearranging the pieces. The only property which is invariant for all these possibilities is then area. However, we could imagine a mapping in which some parts of the triangle were enlarged and other parts shrunk so that even area then goes. Having seen the possible scope to this question, it only becomes realistic if the answer is confined to the isometries when there are 6 transformations:

the direct isometries—identity; 120° rotation about centre and 240° rotation about centre;

the opposite isometries—reflection in each median.

All the isometries preserve length, angle and area but only the direct isometries preserve sense.

Because the triangle is mapped onto itself we now have the additional possibility of points themselves being invariant in the sense that they are mapped onto themselves.

*4. Anyone with a background of sixth form geometry will recognize this transformation as an *orthogonal projection* and they may remember how useful it was in deducing properties of ellipses to see them first as properties of a circle which was then projected into an ellipse.

The image plane π' has been drawn to appear horizontal in the belief that the diagram is more easily appreciated this way.

Orthogonal projection is closely related to a one-way stretch where l is the invariant line. Compare the figure with

$$\begin{pmatrix} x \\ y \end{pmatrix} \rightarrow \begin{pmatrix} \cos\alpha° & 0 \\ 0 & 1 \end{pmatrix} \begin{pmatrix} x \\ y \end{pmatrix}.$$

Needless to say, a model will help in visualizing this transformation.

(a) Yes. The perpendiculars from a line in π form a plane which intersects π' in a line.

(b) Yes.

(c) No. Only line segments like AB parallel to l map onto segments of equal length.

(d) Yes.

(e) A rectangle.

(f) The question assumes a constant scale factor. This is justified if one considers any shape in π covered by thin rectangles running at right angles to l. These rectangles map onto rectangles of the same width but whose length is reduced by a scale factor $\cos\alpha°$, where $\alpha°$ is the angle between the planes. The area scale factor is $\cos\alpha°$.

(g) No, the diagonals of a rectangle are not perpendicular. In general, angle is not an invariant.

(h) An ellipse.

This is an affine transformation (parallel lines map onto parallel lines).

5. $A \to B, \quad X \to Y.$

Hence $AX \to BY$ and as length is an invariant of a rotation, and all lines turn through the angle of the rotation:

(i) $AX = BY$,

(ii) the angle between AX and BY is 40°.

6. (a) Use angle sum of a triangle.

(b) See Figure B. (This shows the inverse transformation.)

Reflection in CB.

Rotation about C through $\tan^{-1} \frac{4}{3}$ clockwise.

Enlargement centre C, scale factor $\frac{5}{3}$.

$$BN = \tfrac{3}{5} \times 4 = \tfrac{12}{5}. \quad CN = \tfrac{3}{5} \times 3 = \tfrac{9}{5}.$$

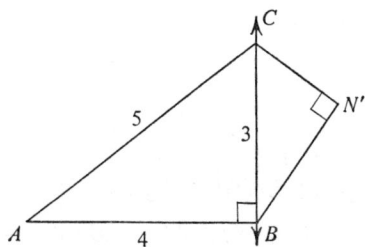

(a)

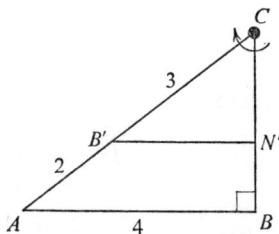

(b)

Fig. B

7. (a) $p = r = q = 30°$ (angle of rotation).

Length is an invariant hence $\triangle ABB'$ and $\triangle ACC'$ are isosceles. $s = t = 75°$.

(b) $\triangle ACC' \to \triangle ABB'$.

Several other pairs look possible but need a change of sense, that is, a reflection would have to be introduced.

8, 9. Many interesting constructions can be made by seeing clearly the invariants of different transformations. Both these questions rely on drawing a square satisfying all but one of the conditions and then enlarging from A until S comes on BC (or arc BC).

2. INVARIANTS IN MATRIX GEOMETRY

This section gives some leads into the way in which the geometrical properties of the general affine transformation may be studied. Many of the special cases discussed could be readily turned into general proofs by inserting letters for numbers but the abstract nature of this would be beyond the majority of the pupils.

2.1 Some general properties

$$A'(6, 4), \quad B'(22, 16).$$
$$M(1, 3), \quad M'(14, 10).$$

Another way to prove that 'straight lines' are always mapped onto 'straight lines' is to express the general equation of a line in parametric form:

$$x = p(t),$$
$$y = q(t),$$

where p and q are linear functions of a parameter t. Then

$$\begin{pmatrix} x \\ y \end{pmatrix} \to \begin{pmatrix} a & b \\ c & d \end{pmatrix} \begin{pmatrix} p(t) \\ q(t) \end{pmatrix} = \begin{pmatrix} a.p(t)+b.q(t) \\ c.p(t)+d.q(t) \end{pmatrix} = \begin{pmatrix} P(t) \\ Q(t) \end{pmatrix},$$

where $P(t)$ and $Q(t)$ are also linear functions of t and hence the equations

$$\begin{cases} x = P(t) \\ y = Q(t) \end{cases} \quad \text{are those of a straight line.}$$

For example, to find the effect on $y = 2x+3$ of the transformation

$$\begin{pmatrix} x \\ y \end{pmatrix} \to \begin{pmatrix} 3 & 9 \\ 4 & -1 \end{pmatrix} \begin{pmatrix} x \\ y \end{pmatrix},$$

we can express the line by the parametric equations

$$\begin{cases} x = t \\ y = 2t+3, \end{cases}$$

[Note the connection with

$$\begin{pmatrix} x \\ y \end{pmatrix} = t\begin{pmatrix} 1 \\ 2 \end{pmatrix} + \begin{pmatrix} 0 \\ 3 \end{pmatrix}$$

which is the vector equation of the line.]

And then
$$\begin{pmatrix} x \\ y \end{pmatrix} \rightarrow \begin{pmatrix} 3 & 9 \\ 4 & -1 \end{pmatrix} \begin{pmatrix} t \\ 2t+3 \end{pmatrix}$$

$$= \begin{pmatrix} 21t+27 \\ 2t-3 \end{pmatrix}$$

from which, by eliminating t,

$$\frac{x-27}{21} = \frac{y+3}{2},$$

$$21y = 2x - 117.$$

(*c*) See Figure C. Both the sense and the area are changed.

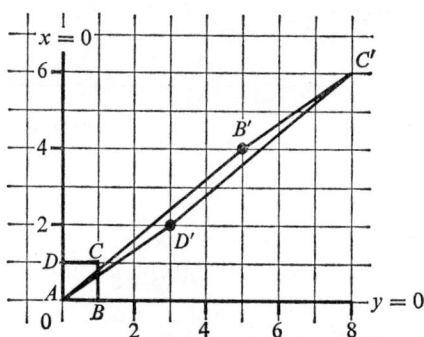

Fig. C

(*d*) $\triangle = {}^-2$. This tells us that the area has been doubled and the sense changed.

Exercise B (p. 91)

1. (*a*) **AB** $= \begin{pmatrix} 3 \\ -1 \end{pmatrix}$. **BC** $= \begin{pmatrix} 6 \\ -2 \end{pmatrix} = 2\begin{pmatrix} 3 \\ -1 \end{pmatrix} = 2\textbf{AB}.$

As **BC** $= 2\textbf{AB}$ then the line segments AB and BC are parallel which in turn implies that A, B, C are collinear.

(*b*) $AB : BC = 1 : 2.$

61

2. $A'(1, 16)$, $B'(11, 6)$, $C'(31, -14)$.

$$\mathbf{A'B'} = \begin{pmatrix} 10 \\ -10 \end{pmatrix}; \quad \mathbf{B'C'} = \begin{pmatrix} 20 \\ -20 \end{pmatrix};$$

hence $\qquad\qquad \mathbf{B'C'} = 2\mathbf{A'B'}$.

(a) and (c) are true. (b) is not true.

No matter what matrix is chosen, (a) and (c) will be true unless $\triangle = 0$, while in general (b) will be false.

3. There is a lot of work in the question but it acts as a useful revision of previous work on finding the distance between two points and conditions for two lines to be parallel or perpendicular.

	P	Q	R	S
Parallel	✓	✗	✗	✓
Equal length	✗	✓	✓	✓
Perpendicular	✗	✓	✗	✗

(b) Whereas the answers to the questions in (a) depended on the particular matrix and the line segment it is always true that matrices map parallel line segments onto parallel line segments.

A general proof of this is as follows:

Any line in the plane with gradient m can be put in the vector form

$$\begin{pmatrix} x \\ y \end{pmatrix} = \begin{pmatrix} 0 \\ k \end{pmatrix} + \lambda \begin{pmatrix} 1 \\ m \end{pmatrix},$$

where k is its intercept on the y axis and λ is a parameter capable of taking all values from $-\infty$ to $+\infty$.

The effect of the transformation

$$\begin{pmatrix} x \\ y \end{pmatrix} \rightarrow \begin{pmatrix} a & b \\ c & d \end{pmatrix} \begin{pmatrix} x \\ y \end{pmatrix}$$

on such a line is to map it onto

$$\begin{pmatrix} x \\ y \end{pmatrix} = \begin{pmatrix} a & b \\ c & d \end{pmatrix} \begin{pmatrix} 0 \\ k \end{pmatrix} + \lambda \begin{pmatrix} a & b \\ c & d \end{pmatrix} \begin{pmatrix} 1 \\ m \end{pmatrix}$$

$$= \begin{pmatrix} bk \\ dk \end{pmatrix} + \lambda \begin{pmatrix} a+bm \\ c+dm \end{pmatrix},$$

which is a line with gradient

$$m' = \frac{c+dm}{a+bm}.$$

As this formula for the gradient depends only on the elements of the transforming matrix and the gradient of the original line, it follows that any line with gradient m will be mapped onto a line with the same gradient m' as above.

4. S is a shear with invariant line $y = x$ and hence all points 'move' parallel to it. Any line parallel to $y = x$ will be invariant as a whole as it 'slides' along itself under the shear.

5. This transformation is equivalent to

$$\begin{pmatrix} x \\ y \end{pmatrix} \rightarrow \begin{pmatrix} 5 & 0 \\ 0 & 5 \end{pmatrix} \begin{pmatrix} \frac{3}{5} & \frac{-4}{5} \\ \frac{4}{5} & \frac{3}{5} \end{pmatrix} \begin{pmatrix} x \\ y \end{pmatrix} + \begin{pmatrix} 8 \\ -2 \end{pmatrix}$$

which can be thought of as a rotation about the origin through $\cos^{-1}(\frac{3}{5})$, followed by an enlargement from the origin with scale factor 5, followed by a translation.

Hence any line segment will be mapped onto a line segment 5 times its original length.

6. If $x = t$ and $y = 2t$, then it is always true that $y = 2x$.

$$\begin{pmatrix} 2 & 1 \\ 0 & -1 \end{pmatrix} \begin{pmatrix} t \\ 2t \end{pmatrix} = \begin{pmatrix} 4t \\ -2t \end{pmatrix}.$$

Hence $x = 4t$ and $y = -2t$ from which $y = -\frac{1}{2}x$.

V does not map all lines onto perpendicular lines as may be found by taking parametric equations of lines or, more easily, points defining the end points of line segments and determining their images.

7. This question is put in to prevent pupils getting the idea that $\triangle = 1$ always implies a rotation or a shear. It is an open-ended question which could lead to some interesting investigations.

A two-way stretch is one good example of a transformation for which $\triangle$ could equal 1 but which is not a rotation

$$\begin{pmatrix} x \\ y \end{pmatrix} \rightarrow \begin{pmatrix} k & 0 \\ 0 & 1/k \end{pmatrix} \begin{pmatrix} x \\ y \end{pmatrix}.$$

8. The area of the unit circle is π and, as $\triangle = 5$ the area scale factor of the transformation is 5 and it follows that the area of the ellipse is 5π square units.

*9. This is another form of the rotation matrix.

3. INVARIANT POINTS

In this section the emphasis is towards the algebra and the domain is now
$$\{(x, y): x \text{ and } y \text{ real}\}$$
which can be readily represented as the Cartesian coordinates of points in a plane.

The question under discussion is,

'When we perform a transformation of the form
$$\begin{pmatrix} x \\ y \end{pmatrix} \rightarrow \begin{pmatrix} a & b \\ c & d \end{pmatrix} \begin{pmatrix} x \\ y \end{pmatrix} + \begin{pmatrix} h \\ k \end{pmatrix}$$
are any elements (x, y) of the domain mapped onto themselves and if so what significance have they?'

In the process of answering this, a technique is given for finding such invariant elements and then put to use in further investigating the geometric transformations.

(*a*) Distances between points remain the same.

The sense of a figure is unaltered.

All points move in concentric circles through the same angle about the centre of rotation, which is the only point which does not move.

Every line turns through the same angle.

(*b*) (*c*) *G* is the centre of rotation and is thus mapped onto itself—the rest follows.

The worked examples show how the inaccuracies of drawing to find a centre of rotation can be replaced by an exact algebraic method and also how when a transformation is described geometrically it can be easily expressed algebraically.

The ability to change a geometric situation into an algebraic one and the converse with ease allows a person to see a problem from another perspective and often leads to a solution in one situation which is not at all clear in another.

Exercise C (p. 96)

1. (5, 2).

2. (a) $A(2, 0) \rightarrow A'(5, 6)$.
   $B(7, 0) \rightarrow B'(^-5, 6)$.
   $C(0, 4) \rightarrow C'(9, ^-2)$.

   See Figure D.

   Scale factor $^-2$.

   Centre at (3, 2).
   (b) (3, 2).

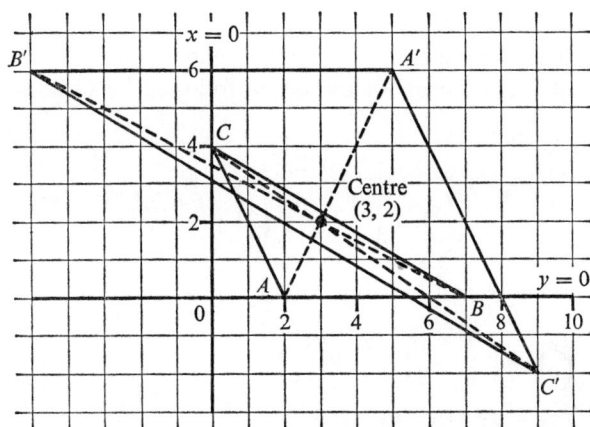

Fig. D

3. (a) $(^-5, 3)$, the centre of the enlargement.
   (b) $(^-\frac{7}{2}, ^-\frac{3}{2})$, the centre of the rotation.
   (c) $(^-2, 2)$, the centre of the two-way stretch.

4. (a) 90° rotation about the origin followed by the translation $\binom{3}{1}$.

$$\binom{x}{y} \rightarrow \begin{pmatrix} 0 & ^-1 \\ 1 & 0 \end{pmatrix} \binom{x}{y} + \binom{3}{1}.$$

This is equivalent to a 90° rotation about (1, 2).

65

(b) 90° rotation about the origin followed by the translation

$$\begin{pmatrix} -1 \\ 1 \end{pmatrix}.$$

$$\begin{pmatrix} x \\ y \end{pmatrix} \rightarrow \begin{pmatrix} 0 & -1 \\ 1 & 0 \end{pmatrix} \begin{pmatrix} x \\ y \end{pmatrix} + \begin{pmatrix} -1 \\ 1 \end{pmatrix}.$$

This is equivalent to a 90° rotation about (−1, 0).

(c) 270° rotation about the origin followed by the translation

$$\begin{pmatrix} -3 \\ 2 \end{pmatrix}.$$

$$\begin{pmatrix} x \\ y \end{pmatrix} \rightarrow \begin{pmatrix} 0 & 1 \\ -1 & 0 \end{pmatrix} \begin{pmatrix} x \\ y \end{pmatrix} + \begin{pmatrix} -3 \\ 2 \end{pmatrix}.$$

This is equivalent to a 270° rotation about $(^{-}\tfrac{1}{2}, 2\tfrac{1}{2})$.

(d) 180° rotation about the origin followed by the translation

$$\begin{pmatrix} 0 \\ -2 \end{pmatrix}.$$

$$\begin{pmatrix} x \\ y \end{pmatrix} \rightarrow \begin{pmatrix} -1 & 0 \\ 0 & -1 \end{pmatrix} \begin{pmatrix} x \\ y \end{pmatrix} + \begin{pmatrix} 0 \\ -2 \end{pmatrix}.$$

This is equivalent to a 180° rotation about (0, −1).

5. (a) $\begin{pmatrix} x \\ y \end{pmatrix} \rightarrow \begin{pmatrix} -1 & 0 \\ 0 & -1 \end{pmatrix} \begin{pmatrix} x \\ y \end{pmatrix} + \begin{pmatrix} 10 \\ 6 \end{pmatrix}.$

(b) $\begin{pmatrix} x \\ y \end{pmatrix} \rightarrow \begin{pmatrix} 2 & 0 \\ 0 & 2 \end{pmatrix} \begin{pmatrix} x \\ y \end{pmatrix} + \begin{pmatrix} -2 \\ 7 \end{pmatrix}.$

(c) $\begin{pmatrix} x \\ y \end{pmatrix} \rightarrow \begin{pmatrix} 0 & -1 \\ 1 & 0 \end{pmatrix} \begin{pmatrix} x \\ y \end{pmatrix} + \begin{pmatrix} -3 \\ 5 \end{pmatrix}.$

(d) $\begin{pmatrix} x \\ y \end{pmatrix} \rightarrow \begin{pmatrix} 5 & 0 \\ 0 & 2 \end{pmatrix} \begin{pmatrix} x \\ y \end{pmatrix} + \begin{pmatrix} -8 \\ -4 \end{pmatrix}.$

6. Centre of **H** at $P(-1, 2)$.

Centre of **K** at $Q(3, 4)$.

HK is equivalent to the translation with the vector

$$2QP = \begin{pmatrix} -8 \\ -4 \end{pmatrix}.$$

KH is equivalent to the translation with the vector

$$2\mathbf{PQ} = \begin{pmatrix} 8 \\ 4 \end{pmatrix}.$$

*7. Centre of E_1 is $C_1(3, -2)$.

Centre of E_2 is $C_2(2, 1)$.

The transformation $E_2 E_1$ is

$$\begin{pmatrix} x \\ y \end{pmatrix} \to \begin{pmatrix} -3 & 0 \\ 0 & -3 \end{pmatrix} \left\{ \begin{pmatrix} 4 & 0 \\ 0 & 4 \end{pmatrix} \begin{pmatrix} x \\ y \end{pmatrix} + \begin{pmatrix} -9 \\ 6 \end{pmatrix} \right\} + \begin{pmatrix} 8 \\ 4 \end{pmatrix}$$

$$= \begin{pmatrix} -12 & 0 \\ 0 & -12 \end{pmatrix} \begin{pmatrix} x \\ y \end{pmatrix} + \begin{pmatrix} 35 \\ -14 \end{pmatrix}$$

with centre $\qquad C_3 \left(\dfrac{35}{13}, \dfrac{-14}{13} \right).$

To test for collinearity it is sufficient to show that

the vector $\mathbf{C_1 C_2}$ is a scalar multiple of the vector $\mathbf{C_2 C_3}$.

Now $\mathbf{C_1 C_2} = \begin{pmatrix} -1 \\ 3 \end{pmatrix}$ and $\mathbf{C_2 C_3} = \begin{pmatrix} \dfrac{9}{13} \\ \dfrac{-27}{13} \end{pmatrix} = \dfrac{-9}{13} \begin{pmatrix} -1 \\ 3 \end{pmatrix}$

hence $\qquad \mathbf{C_1 C_2} = \dfrac{-13}{9} \mathbf{C_2 C_3}.$

This question can easily be generalized to prove that when any two enlargements are combined they produce a third enlargement. The three centres are collinear and furthermore a formula can be found which gives the ratio of the distances between the centres.

*8. $\triangle ABC$ could be mapped onto $\triangle A'B'C'$ by a 90° rotation about *any* point followed by the scale 2 enlargement from an appropriate centre. The point about this question is that, if the centres are to coincide, this single centre will be an invariant point under the combined transformation.

The only satisfactory way to find such a point is to express the transformation algebraically and calculate its set of invariant points.

The enlargement is given by

$$\begin{pmatrix} x \\ y \end{pmatrix} \to \begin{pmatrix} 2 & 0 \\ 0 & 2 \end{pmatrix} \begin{pmatrix} x \\ y \end{pmatrix} + \begin{pmatrix} 7 \\ -4 \end{pmatrix}$$

and the 90° rotation by

$$\begin{pmatrix} x \\ y \end{pmatrix} \rightarrow \begin{pmatrix} 0 & -1 \\ 1 & 0 \end{pmatrix} \begin{pmatrix} x \\ y \end{pmatrix}.$$

Their combination gives

$$\begin{pmatrix} x \\ y \end{pmatrix} \rightarrow \begin{pmatrix} 0 & -2 \\ 2 & 0 \end{pmatrix} \begin{pmatrix} x \\ y \end{pmatrix} + \begin{pmatrix} 7 \\ -4 \end{pmatrix}$$

and this has an invariant point (3, 2).

It is instructive to draw Figure 19 and on it the result of a 90° rotation about (3, 2) followed by a scale 2 enlargement.

4. INVARIANT LINES

The examples in the previous section were carefully selected to have only one invariant point. Here we see that there are two other cases to consider, (i) a line of invariant points and (ii) no invariant points.

It is very important to note the difference between an invariant line and a line of invariant points. The technique employed here is for finding lines of invariant points and it does not give lines which are not pointwise invariant.

(*a*) A shear, a one-way stretch.

Combinations of shears, reflections and one-way stretches which have the same line of invariant points.

The results
$$\begin{cases} a+2b = 3, \\ \quad b = b, \end{cases}$$

in Example 1 may need careful discussion before a class is happy that this is equivalent to the line with equation

$$x+2y = 3.$$

(*c*) The equations which result are

$$x = y+3,$$
$$y = x+5,$$

which cannot both be true together so there are no solutions and hence no invariant points.

(d)

	Invariant points			Value of Δ		
	One	Line	None	+1	$\neq \pm 1$	-1
Reflection		✓				✓
Glide reflection			✓			✓
Rotation	✓			✓		
Translation			✓	✓		
Shear		✓		✓		
Enlargement	✓			✓	✓	
One-way stretch		✓			✓	✓
Two-way stretch	✓			✓	✓	✓

The identity transformation with $\Delta = 1$ and all points invariant is not included in the table.

Exercise D (p. 100)

1. (a) Translation—all lines parallel to the displacement.

Shear—all lines parallel to the direction of the shear other than the invariant line.

Glide-reflection—the glide axis.

(b) Reflection—mirror line.

Shear—the invariant line.

One-way stretch—the invariant line.

(c) Enlargement—all lines through the centre.

Half-turn rotation—all lines through the centre.

Reflection—all lines perpendicular to the mirror line.

One-way stretch—all lines perpendicular to the invariant line.

2. (a) $y = x - 5$; (b) $x = 2$; (c) $2y = 3x + 1$.

3. (a) $\begin{pmatrix} x \\ y \end{pmatrix} \rightarrow \begin{pmatrix} 1 & 0 \\ 0 & -1 \end{pmatrix} \begin{pmatrix} x \\ y \end{pmatrix} + \begin{pmatrix} 0 \\ 6 \end{pmatrix}$; $y = 3$.

(b) $\begin{pmatrix} x \\ y \end{pmatrix} \rightarrow \begin{pmatrix} -1 & 0 \\ 0 & 1 \end{pmatrix} \begin{pmatrix} x \\ y \end{pmatrix} + \begin{pmatrix} -5 \\ 0 \end{pmatrix}$; $x = \dfrac{-5}{2}$.

(c) $\begin{pmatrix} x \\ y \end{pmatrix} \rightarrow \begin{pmatrix} 0 & 1 \\ 1 & 0 \end{pmatrix} \begin{pmatrix} x \\ y \end{pmatrix} + \begin{pmatrix} 3 \\ -3 \end{pmatrix}$; $y = x - 3$.

If the transformations are combined in the reverse order

(a) $\begin{pmatrix} x \\ y \end{pmatrix} \rightarrow \begin{pmatrix} 1 & 0 \\ 0 & -1 \end{pmatrix} \left[\begin{pmatrix} x \\ y \end{pmatrix} + \begin{pmatrix} 0 \\ 6 \end{pmatrix} \right]; \quad y = -3.$

(b) $\begin{pmatrix} x \\ y \end{pmatrix} \rightarrow \begin{pmatrix} -1 & 0 \\ 0 & 1 \end{pmatrix} \left[\begin{pmatrix} x \\ y \end{pmatrix} + \begin{pmatrix} -5 \\ 0 \end{pmatrix} \right]; \quad x = \frac{5}{2}.$

(c) $\begin{pmatrix} x \\ y \end{pmatrix} \rightarrow \begin{pmatrix} 0 & 1 \\ 1 & 0 \end{pmatrix} \left[\begin{pmatrix} x \\ y \end{pmatrix} + \begin{pmatrix} 3 \\ -3 \end{pmatrix} \right]; \quad y = x + 3.$

4. $y = -\frac{1}{2}x.$

5. (a) $y = -\frac{1}{2}x - \frac{3}{4}.$ (b) No solutions.

When $d = -3$ the translation $\begin{pmatrix} 6 \\ -3 \end{pmatrix}$ is parallel to the direction of the shear and has the effect of mapping one line back onto itself. When $d = 4$ the translation is not parallel to the direction of the shear and consequently no points are invariant.

6. For **M** to be a reflection the transformation must have a line of invariant points. Hence the equations,

$$x = -y + k$$

and $$y = -x + 7$$

must represent the same condition. This is the case when

$$k = 7.$$

When k has any other value **M** will represent a glide-reflection.

7. (a) $\triangle = 16$. Invariant point, $(-1, -\frac{1}{3})$. Enlargement.
   (b) $\triangle = 1$. Invariant points, $x + y = 2$. Shear
   (c) $\triangle = 5$. Invariant points, $x = -1$. One-way stretch.
   (d) $\triangle = -1$. No invariant points. Glide-reflection.
   (e) $\triangle = -1$. Invariant points, $8y = 6x + 25$. Reflection.
   (f) $\triangle = 1$. Invariant point $(17\frac{1}{2}, 22\frac{1}{2})$. Rotation.

8. This question in itself is easy to answer but it should encourage many questions about transformations in 3 D.

Invariant point $(1, -1, 2)$.

7

PLANS AND ELEVATIONS

This is another chapter designed to help pupils 'think in three dimensions'—which some of them find very difficult. Some pupils may enjoy the elementary examples here, and the opportunity to do some drawing, but it is not expected that everybody will be able to cope successfully with the whole chapter.

Some teachers may feel that the absence of traditional Euclidean geometry from the S.M.P. course has led to an undesirable reduction in the amount of accurate construction work required. If that is the case, there is plenty of scope for remedying the deficiency whilst tackling this chapter. The latter half of the chapter also gives much practice with trigonometry, Pythagoras's Theorem, and computation generally.

The knowledge of Plans and Elevations required for the O-level syllabus is not very great, and here we go beyond the minimum examination requirements. There are, of course, two conventions for the drawing of plans and elevations in general use, and much thought was devoted to whether or not both of them should be dealt with in this book. To avoid confusion we came down in favour of pursuing one of them only, the Third Angle method. We feel that it should be mentioned that the First Angle convention is still used—and may be encountered by some pupils later; but it is not necessary to go into detail. Further information about First Angle drawings may be found, if desired, elsewhere.

There are plenty of books available which deal with the subject of technical drawing, among which may be mentioned:

Engineering Drawing Practice, BS 308 or (abridged) BS 308a (British Standards Institution, 1964).

Solid Geometry in 3D for Technical Drawing, by A. G. J. Davies.

The latter makes use of anaglyphs, i.e. stereoscopic drawings requiring the use of red and green spectacles (provided).

In many of the questions the answer is not unique. Most projection lines have been omitted so that they do not obscure the clarity of the drawings.

1. PROJECTION

Exercise A (p. 112)

1. (*a*) Cuboidal box (could be a wedge).
   (*b*) Cylinder.   (*c*) Sphere, ball.
   (*d*) Square-based pyramid.   (*e*) Torus, ring, quoit.
   (*f*) Hollow tube.   (*g*) Bottle-stopper.
   (*h*) Triangular prism, roof, bar of Toblerone.
   (*i*) Roof.   (*j*) Cuboidal box.
   (*k*) Square-based pyramid.
   (*l*) Truncated square pyramid, pedestal.

2. *Construction lines are omitted*

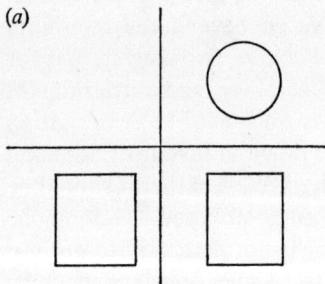

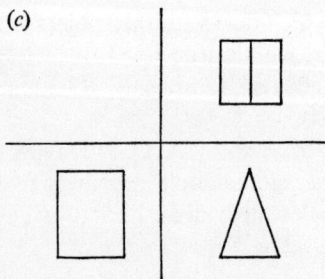

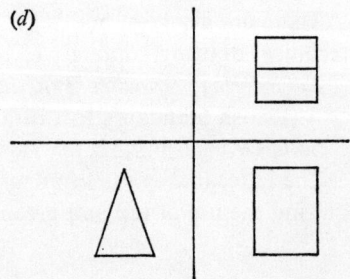

(*a*)

(*b*)

(*c*)

(*d*)

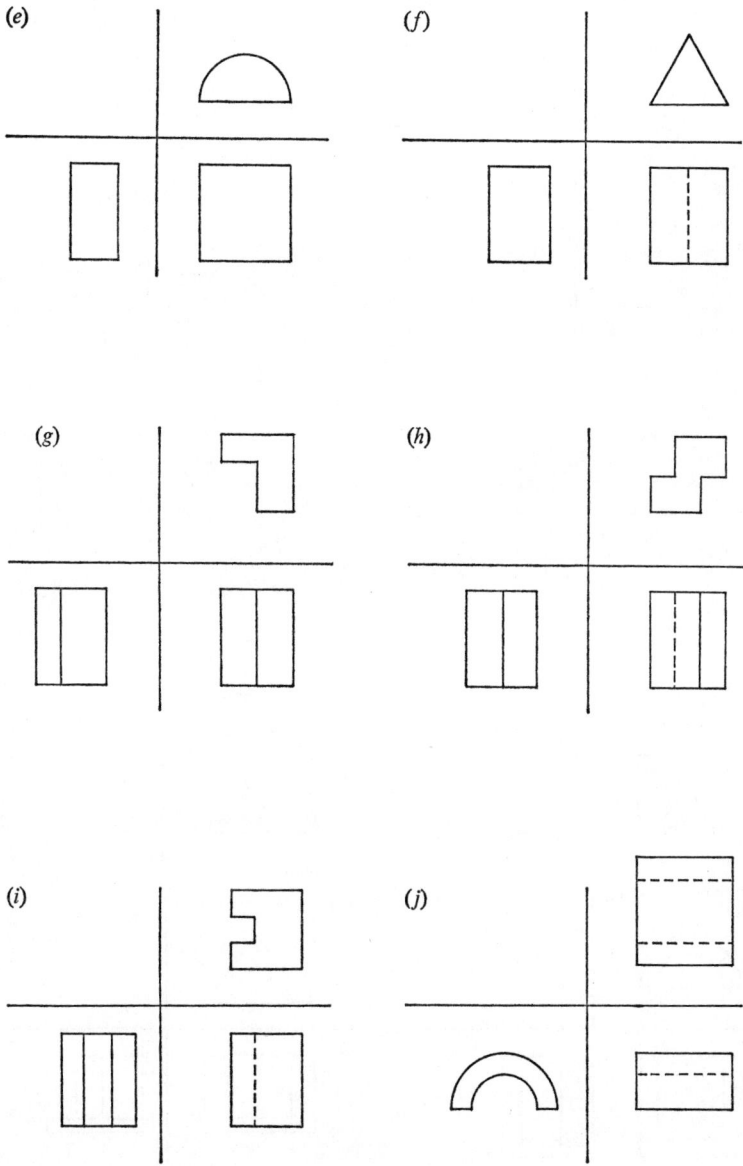

Fig. A

CH. 7. PLANS AND ELEVATIONS

3. *Construction lines are omitted*

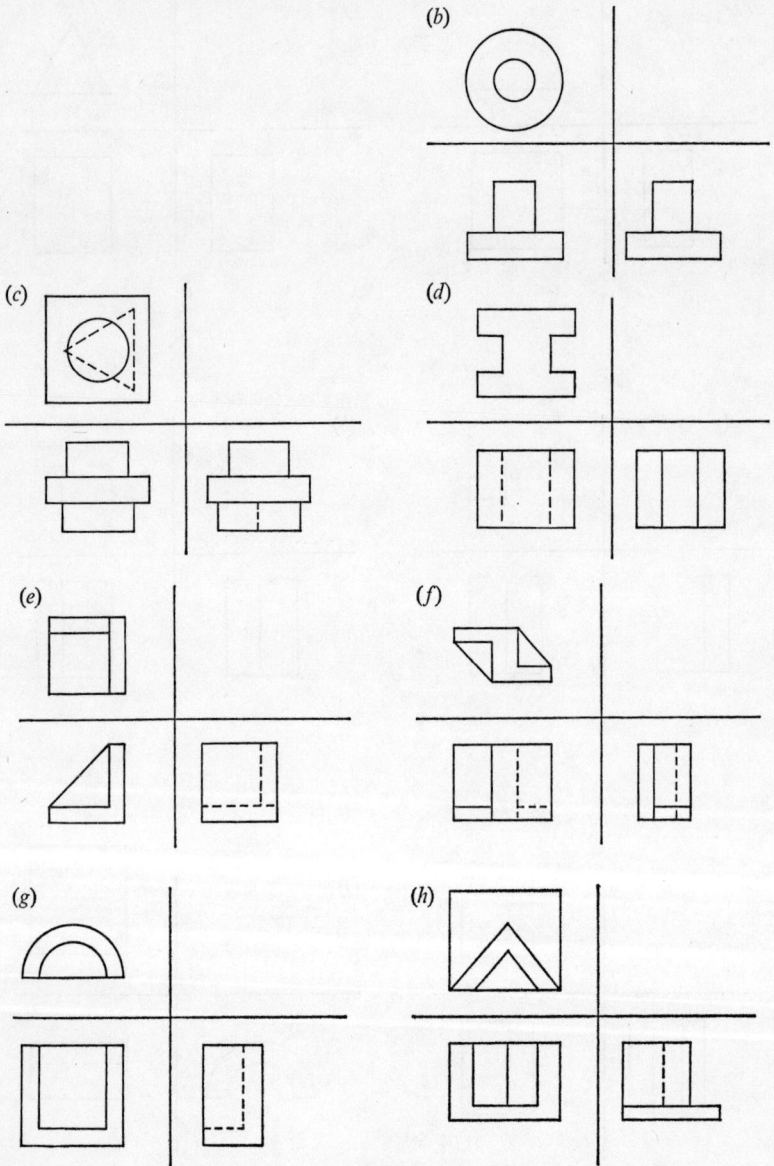

Fig. B

Exercise B (p. 119)

1.

(a)

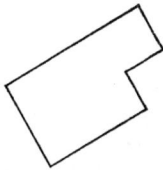

(b)

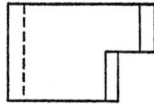

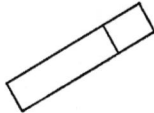

(c)

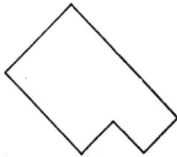

(d)

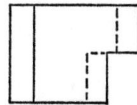

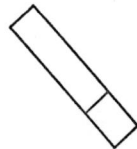

Fig. C

2.

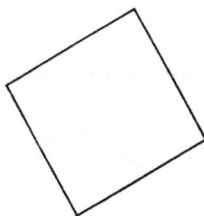

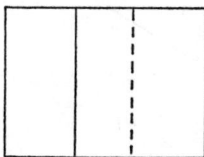

Fig. D

3.

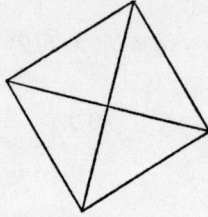

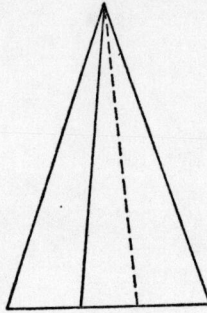

Fig. E

4.

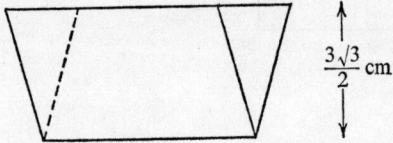

$\dfrac{3\sqrt{3}}{2}$ cm

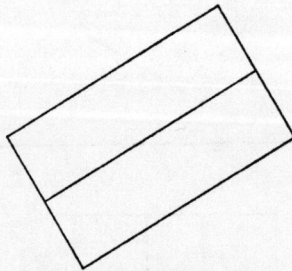

Fig. F

1.

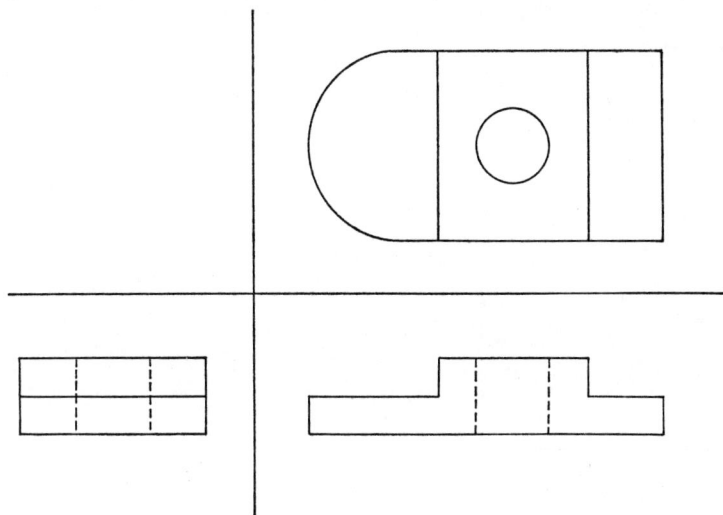

Fig. G

2.

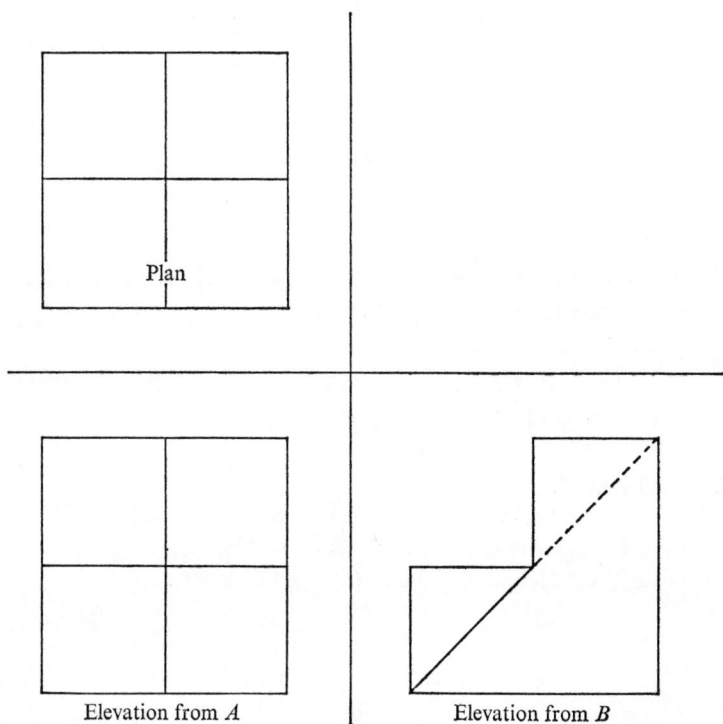

Plan

Elevation from *A*   Elevation from *B*

Fig. H

3. See Figure I.

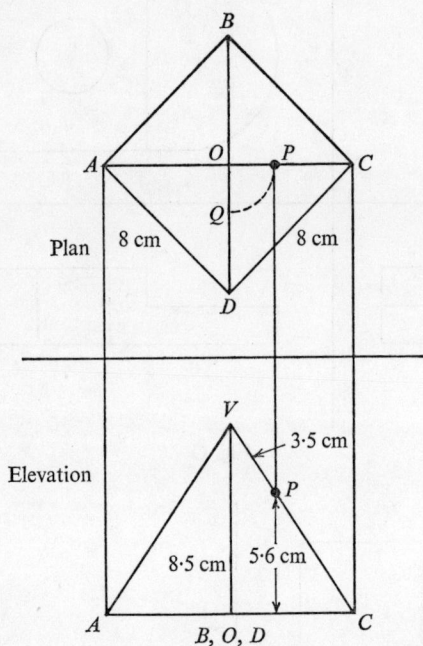

Fig. I

Begin by drawing outline of plan (giving AC), hence elevation. Mark P on the elevation (VP is given), hence on plan. Use compasses to construct Q.

Height of $P \approx 5.6$ cm (measured on elevation); length of $PQ \approx 2.7$ cm (measured on plan).

4. See Figure J.
Construct plan with AC parallel to vertical plane VP. AC can then be drawn in elevation, hence sloping edges (using compasses). (a) Height ≈ 4.1 cm. (b) $\angle AVC \approx 69°$.

78

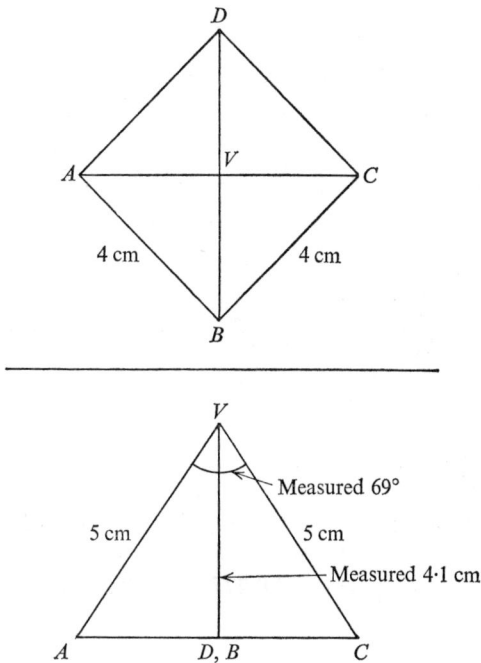

Fig. J

2. OTHER METHODS OF SOLVING 3-D PROBLEMS

Exercise D (p. 125)

Only a selection of the examples from this exercise need be worked by the average pupil.

For convenience, inverse trigonometrical ratios are used in giving the answers—but of course this notation is not expected of the pupil.

1. (*a*) $AE = 5$ cm; $VA = \sqrt{41}$ cm $= 6 \cdot 40$ cm (3 s.f.).

    (*b*) $\angle VME = \tan^{-1} \frac{4}{3} \approx 53°$.

2. (*a*) $OP = \sqrt{50}$ units $= 7 \cdot 07$ units (3 s.f.).

    (*b*) (i) $\sin^{-1} \dfrac{3}{\sqrt{50}} = 25 \cdot 1°$,   (ii) $\sin^{-1} \dfrac{4}{\sqrt{50}} = 34 \cdot 5°$,

       (iii) $\tan^{-1} 1 = 45°$.

79

3. $AF = 70 \sin 30°$ m;
   $TF = AF \tan 45° = 70 \times \frac{1}{2} = 35$ m.

4. $AF = 70 \tan 60° = 70\sqrt{3}$m;
   $TF = AF \tan \alpha° = 210$ m;
   $BF = 70/\cos 60° = 140$ m;
   $BF \tan \beta = TF \Rightarrow \tan \beta = 1\cdot5 \Rightarrow \beta = 56\cdot3°.$

5. (a) 12 cm;
   (b) $\cos^{-1} \frac{5}{13} = 67\cdot4°$;
   (c) $\tan^{-1} \frac{12}{3} = 76\cdot0°.$

6. DB makes angle $\sin^{-1} \frac{2}{10} = 11\cdot5°$ with horizontal; bearing of B from D is $\tan^{-1} \dfrac{6}{\sqrt{60}} = 037\cdot7°$

7. $2 \sin^{-1} \dfrac{\frac{1}{2}\sqrt{8}}{\sqrt{5}} = 78\cdot5°$; yes.

8. (a) 2 cm; (b) $\tan^{-1} 2 = 63\cdot4°$; (c) $\sin^{-1} \frac{2}{3} = 41\cdot8°.$

9. (b) $\cos^{-1} \dfrac{2}{\sqrt{(6^2+4^2)}} = \cos^{-1} 0\cdot277 = 73\cdot9°$; (c) $2\sqrt{3}$ cm; about 13·9 cm³.

10. $\sin^{-1} (\sin 40° \cos 30°) = 33\cdot8°.$

11. (a) Tetrahedron;   (b) six, E and F;
    (c) $CD = \sqrt{18} = 4\cdot24$ units (3 s.f.), $AE = 5$ units;
    (d) $AF = 5$ units, $FC = \sqrt{18}$ units;
    (e) 90°;
    (f) before: $2 \sin^{-1} \frac{3}{5} = 73\cdot8°$; after: $2 \sin^{-1} 0\cdot424 = 50\cdot2°.$

12. M is 5 m from both BC and AB; E is 10 m from BC. Total area of roof is 800 m². Area of each tile is 1200 cm² or effectively 800 cm². Hence about 10 000 tiles are required.

13. 18·4 cm;   25·6 cm.

14. $PE = 27\cdot4$ m; elevation of pole top is
$$\sin^{-1} \frac{20}{27\cdot4} = 46\cdot9°.$$

8

LINEAR PROGRAMMING

1. MATHEMATICAL MODELS

The idea of a mathematical model is not particularly easy to grasp. It is better to talk round the subject and offer examples than to attempt to give a definition. All work on a practical problem with pen and paper is, in a sense, making a model of the real situation. The numbers measuring length, breadth, mass, weight, cost, etc., represent more or less concrete attributes and so are models of them.

As soon as problem-solving starts, some facts are discarded as unnecessary or as too difficult to deal with. The first section of this chapter takes a problem concerning a journey and seeks to make explicit the nature of the model used in the simplest case and then in a slightly more complex one. In neither case is it necessary to try to picture the vehicle as having size, mass, temperature, etc., although these may affect the answers to some small degree and would become of considerable importance if the questions were different. The questions posed in the text are rhetorical and are answered in subsequent sentences.

For further reading see Battersby, *Mathematics in Management*; Hammersley and Handscomb, *Monte Carlo Methods* (more advanced).

Exercise A (p. 131)

1. (a), (c), (e).

   (b) See Figure A. A weightless beam with a force of 800 N acting downwards at a point determined by the position of the saddle and supported at its two ends.

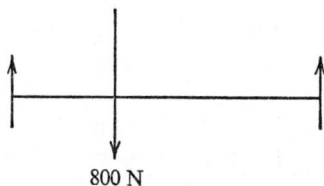

800 N

Fig. A

   (d) A displacement of length 1·8 units being translated in its own direction through a distance of (15 + 1·8) m at 18 km/h.

CH. 8. LINEAR PROGRAMMING

2. Many questions suggest themselves for the first two models.

   (a) If the radius of the record is 15 cm, how fast is the fly moving linearly?

   (b) What effect would the mass of the fly have on the stability of a rotating record?

   To find a question for which neither of these models will do requires more imagination. For instance:—

   (c) The fly is facing the spindle and its front four legs lose adhesion, given that its mass is 0·02 g make an estimate of its minimum dimensions if it is thrown over on its back.

3. (a) The total cost of the pencils.

   (b) The number of rulers with no pencils to go with them. Or a more elementary model would do, for example, the difference between the number of pencils and the number of rulers.

   (c) The cost of the pencils and rulers in pounds (£).

   (d) The number of pencils that could be bought for the price of one ruler. Or the ratio of the price of a ruler to that of a pencil. In that the letters stand for numbers of concrete objects, either pencils, rulers or the number of pence symbolizing their cost. The letters are being manipulated in place of actual objects or piles of coins.

4. (a) $R = 3x - 4$; (b) $R = \dfrac{xy}{5}$;

   (c) $R = x^2 + x^3$; (d) $R = \dfrac{x}{y+z}$;

   (e) $R = \frac{1}{2}y(x + 3y + 7z)$.

5. $C = \dfrac{px}{100}$; $p = \dfrac{100C}{x}$. If 30 litres of petrol cost £2·10, find the cost in pence per litre.

6. The sum of any number of consecutive integers, starting from 1, is obtained by multiplying half that number by that number increased by 1.

7. (a) Let l be the number of units in the length, w be the number of units in the width, then $l = 2w$.

82

It is worth insisting that the word 'number' appears in every definition of a letter in examples of this type. It is asking for trouble to accept a statement such as 'Let l be the length', since this is only one place removed from 'Let c be a cow'—a classic source of muddle since c is being used as an abbreviation for a word rather than a number.

(b) Let D be the number of units of density, M of mass and V of volume, then $D = M/V$ (the units must be compatible).

(c) Let x be the number of horses, y the number of cows, then $y = 2x$. If z is the total number of animals, then $z = x+y = 3x$, etc. It is advisable not always to use the initial letters of the objects under discussion.

(d) Let m be the number of men and w the number of women, then $m \geqslant 10$ and $w \geqslant 12$. If p is the number of people then $p \geqslant 22$. The danger in this question is that pupils will write statements concerning '$10m+12w$'. This is another howler of the 'Let c be a cow' type. A careful definition of the meanings of m and w should avoid this.

8. The following sentences are possible examples.

(a) The number of pupils present is the number in the class less the number absent.

(b) The volume of the box in litres is the product of the number of centimetres in the length, breadth and height divided by 1000.

(c) A certain boy's mark was better than the average of his three friends'.

(d) The number of square units in the area of a square is the square of the number of units in its side.

9. Let a, b, c be the number of units of length in the sides of a triangle, then $a < b+c$, $b < c+a$ and $c < a+b$. A triangle is a set of points satisfying certain conditions. A drawing is a model of this in the sense that it is an approximation (to an ideal triangle) which will be used as a visual aid in planning the work to be done. Measurements could provide a rough check on calculations, visual observations could check whether points could be collinear, etc.

10. Let x be the number of kilograms of oranges, then there will be $2x$ lemons, $2x$ kg of sugar and $2x$ litres of water. Let y be the number of kilograms of marmalade, then $y \geqslant 4x$.

11. $|x^2 + y^2 - (x+y)^2| = 2xy$. True. The vertical lines indicate 'difference between', that is, that no account is to be taken of sign.

12. (a) Assuming that the test is sound, the marks could be used to order the boys. Without other evidence it would not be possible to say where dividing lines between sets should come.

(b) Much more problematic. One set of marks would not be a good enough model of ability to make predictions like this.

(c) All prizes are a lottery to a large extent. This is probably as good as any other!

(d) Only useful in relation to the boys' known ability.

There would be many other considerations besides mark scores.

2. LINEAR PROGRAMMING

2.1 A haulage problem

The conditions are $x \leqslant 7$, $y \leqslant 4$, $x+y \leqslant 9$, $4x+5y \geqslant 30$. The last ordering has been simplified. Pupils should be shown the importance of reducing all conditions to their simplest form before starting their plotting. The regions are identified in Figure B.

In this book the convention previously employed whereby regions which contain their boundaries are distinguished from those that do not by the use of solid or broken lines will still be used. In other texts a solid line is used in both cases and this must be interpreted in the light of the data of the question.

The dots represent solutions that satisfy the conditions. The smallest number of drivers is seven, split in any one of the ways $(5, 2)$, $(4, 3)$ or $(3, 4)$. The last arrangement moves most coal as can be seen by calculating the capacity in each case.

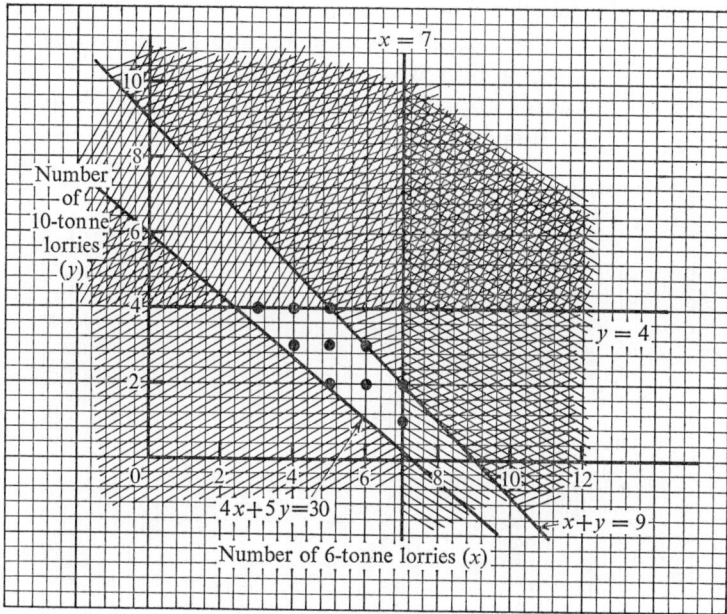

Fig. B

2.2 Lines of equal cost

In this section a new idea of great importance in linear programming is introduced. This introduction usually takes time, and, with slow groups of pupils, it might be advisable to duplicate Figure C, unlabelled, to use as the basis of a detailed discussion, after the pupils have plotted their own lines which may not all be entirely accurate. The vital ideas are (a) that lines on which the cost stays constant form a set of parallel lines and (b) that the distance of these lines from the origin is proportional to the constant cost.

There are no combinations costing £6 per 10 km run other than those mentioned; $x+2y = 6$; fractional solutions are not meaningful since lorries cannot be divided.

The solutions are (10, 0), (8, 1), (6, 2), (4, 3), (2, 4), (0, 5);

$$x+2y = 10;$$

the points (6,2) and (4, 3) are 'dotted' points. Some teachers might like to reverse the order of this section and ask first for the equation

85

expressing the fact that x 6-tonne lorries and y 10-tonne lorries cost £10 per 10 km. The 'dotted' points which also lie on this line are (a) solutions of the problem which (b) cost £10 per 10 km run.

The solutions are (12, 0), (10, 1), (8, 2), (6, 3), (4, 4), (2, 5), (0, 6); $x+2y = 12$; (6, 3) and (4, 4) are 'dotted' points. The line nearest

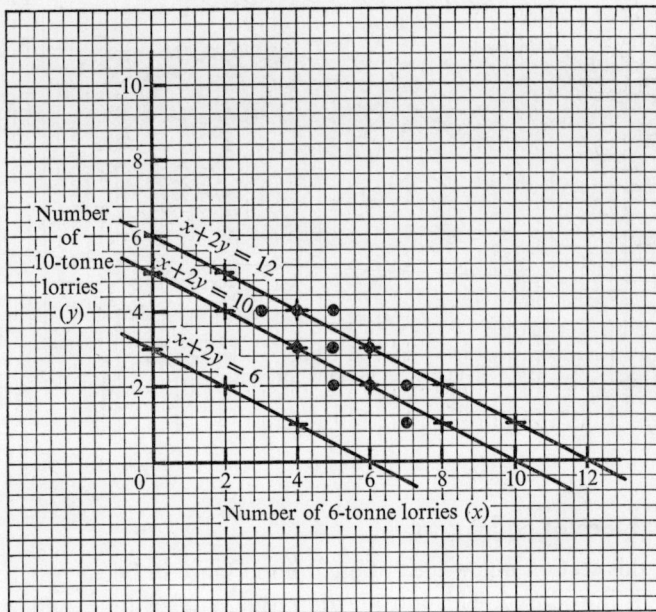

Fig. C

to (0, 0) represents the least cost; $x+2y = 10$. There is a better line that passes through a feasible solution, this is $x+2y = 9$. It is easily checked from the graph by sliding a ruler along the page. It includes the solutions (7, 1) and (5, 2).

2.3. Lines of equal profit

It is advisable that Example 2 be worked through in detail.

Example 2

The top right-hand vertex is not a point with positive integral co-ordinates and so cannot give a solution.

Exercise B (p. 136)

1. See Figure D.

(2, 0) and (3, 0); for example, $(2, \frac{1}{2})$, (1·6, 0·7), etc.

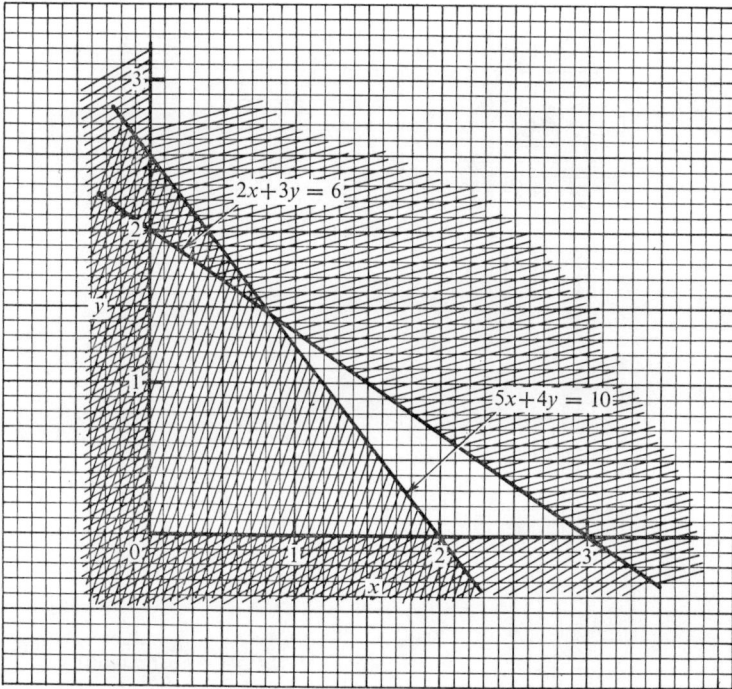

Fig. D

2. $x > 4$, $x < 15$, $y > 0$, $y < 10$, $x+y < 20$, $4x+5y > 40$. All of them, since they are in regions hatched only in one direction. 4 conditions.

3. The gradient of each is $\frac{-13}{11}$; or the intercepts are $(\frac{51}{13}, 0)$, $(0, \frac{51}{11})$; and $(\frac{56}{13}, 0)$, $(0, \frac{56}{11})$. With the point (0, 0), these points form a pair of triangles, the larger is an enlargement of the smaller, with scale factor $\frac{56}{51}$, and hence corresponding sides are parallel. Any point on $13x+11y=k$ where $51 < k < 56$.

87

4. See Figure E. Any number from 2 to 7 inclusive.

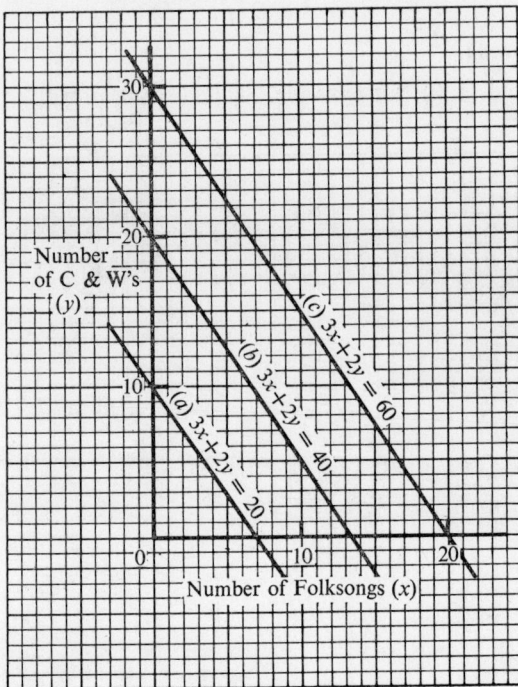

Fig. E

5.

	No. built	Cost (£)	Area (hectares)
Dorset	x	6000	$\frac{1}{2}$
Somerset	y	3000	$\frac{1}{8}$

$2x+y \leqslant 10$, $4x+y \leqslant 16$; $3x+y = $ constant.

See Figure F. It should be pointed out that in a case like this where the regions not required are obvious, it is possible to shade them all out at once using only one type of hatching. The lines of equal profit are shown as broken lines. (3, 4), that is 3 'Dorset' and 4 'Somerset' houses.

6. $2w+k \leqslant 10$, $7w+6k \leqslant 42$, $3w+4k \leqslant 24$. (a) Total number of hectares is $w+k$; no; 6·6 hectares.
(b) 3·6 hectares of wheat, 2·8 hectares of kale.

7. 14 X's and 6 Y's; no, two requirements would have to be relaxed.

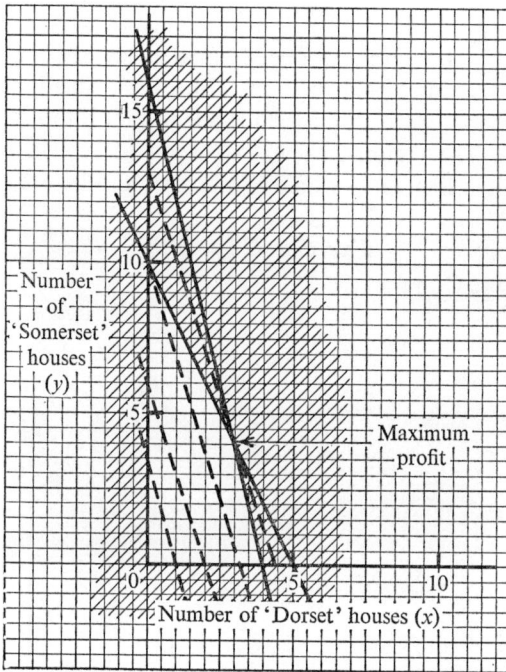

Fig. F

8. Fred works $4\frac{5}{6}$ h, Bill $3\frac{5}{6}$ h; the rise must be more than 25p per hour.

9. $x = 12{\cdot}9$, $y = 5{\cdot}7$; ratio $2{\cdot}25{:}1$.

10. 5 faces with machine A and 5 faces with machine B.

3. NON-LINEAR CONDITIONS

Example 3

The coordinates given to one decimal place are the only non-exact ones, the exact point being ($\sqrt{120}$, $\sqrt{120}$). This is the 'vertex' of the curve and hence an important one to plot if the drawing is to be accurate. The region $2x+y \leqslant 40$ is on the origin side of the plotted straight line. Only whole numbers of hurdles are feasible.

Exercise C (p. 140)

1. See Figure G.
    $A' \cap B'$.

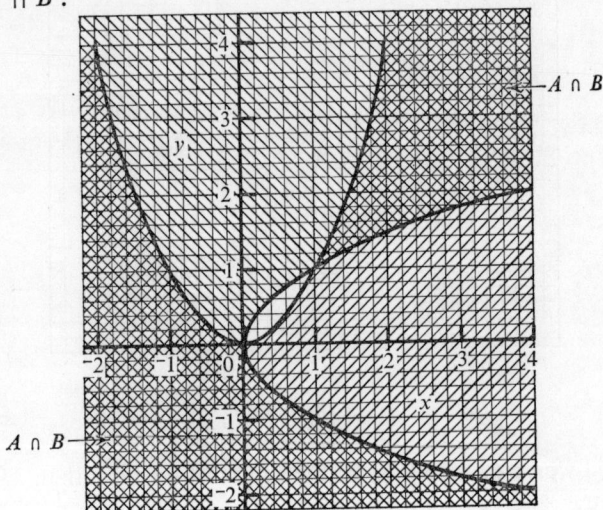

Fig. G

2.

Length	Breadth
12	2
8	3
6	4
4	6
3	8
2	12

See Figure H. 5; (*a*) 4, 8; (*b*) 3·5, 7·0 is easily read but more accurate answers may be estimated and checked by calculation.

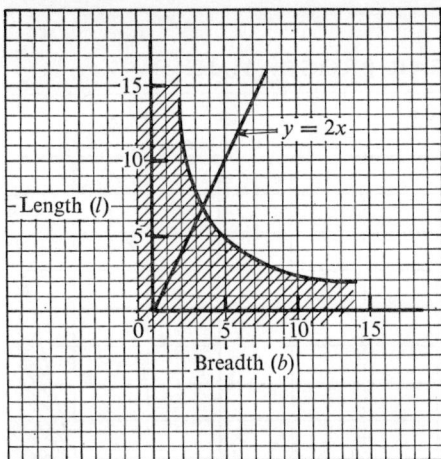

Fig. H

3. See Figure I.

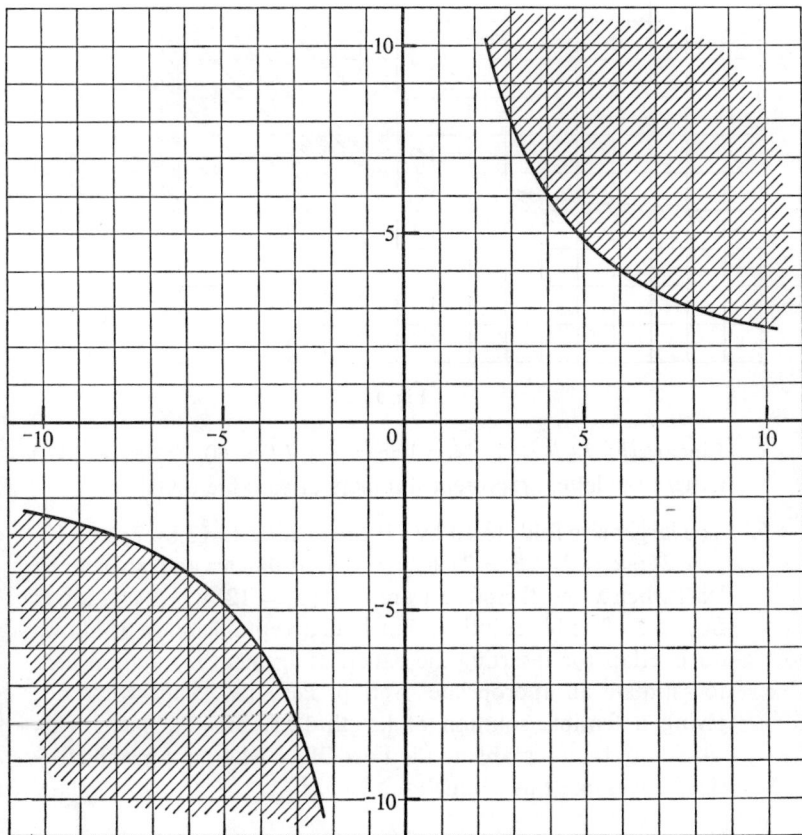

Fig. I

4. See Figure J.

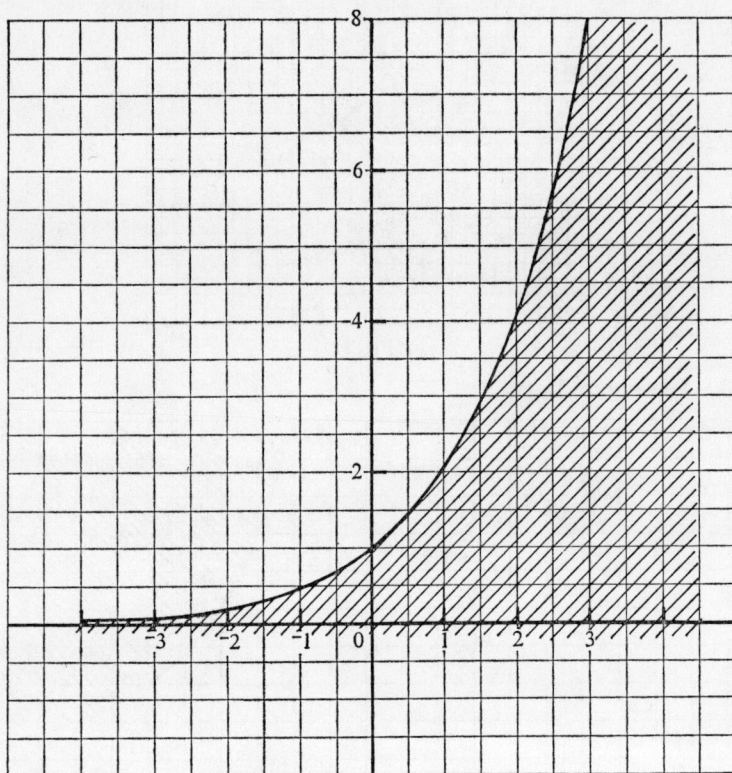

Fig. J

5. Linear (b) $l+b \leqslant 5$. Non-linear (a) $lA > 60$, (c) $vt < 1420$ (where the letters represent numbers of suitable units).

6. The larger size folds to 10 by $7\frac{1}{2}$, the smaller to 12 by 7; $x > 12$, $y > 7\frac{1}{2}$; $x \leqslant \frac{3}{2}y$; $P = 2x+2y$ which is linear and so will be least when x and therefore y are least; $x = 12$, $y = 8$ is a lower bound to feasible solutions but is unacceptable since it allows no overlap for inserting the paper. Judgement is required here to estimate an appropriate overlap. Perhaps 0·5 cm would do, giving a feasible solution of length 12·5, breadth 8 cm. This would not be acceptable to the Post Office who have a standard-sized envelope; this is much too small!

7.

v	0	1	2	3	4	5	6	7	8	9	10	11	12
d	0	11	20	27	32	35	36	35	32	27	20	11	0

At 12 km/h the distance is zero. Plainly the formula breaks down at this point and presumably for speeds near 12 km/h. It is likely that such speeds are unattainable; $d = 3v$; 27 km at 9 km/h; 36 km at 6 km/h, takes 6 hours.

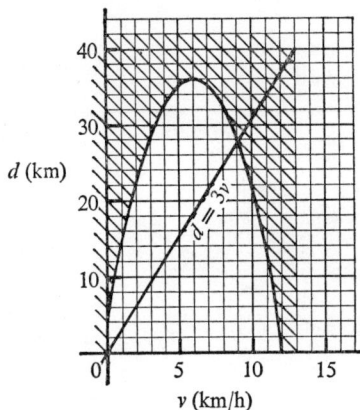

Fig. K

8.

θ	0	30	60	90	120	150
r	30	32·2	40	60	120	448

As θ tends to 180, $1+\cos\theta°$ tends to 0 and the receiving distance increases without limit, which is physically impossible; yes; by symmetry. See Figure L. It is a parabola; the outside. The one at (110,130), see the shaded areas in Figure L, in this case the sets are disjoint.

9. The curve passes through the points (0, 25), (10, 50), (20, 100), (30, 200), ... and so the law of growth is $n = 25 \times 2^{t/10}$. At some time between $t = 38$ and $t = 40$.

10. It shows that, as the price increases the demand falls off. It is justifiable to join up the points of such a curve and predict that intermediate prices would result in intermediate sales,

93   4-2

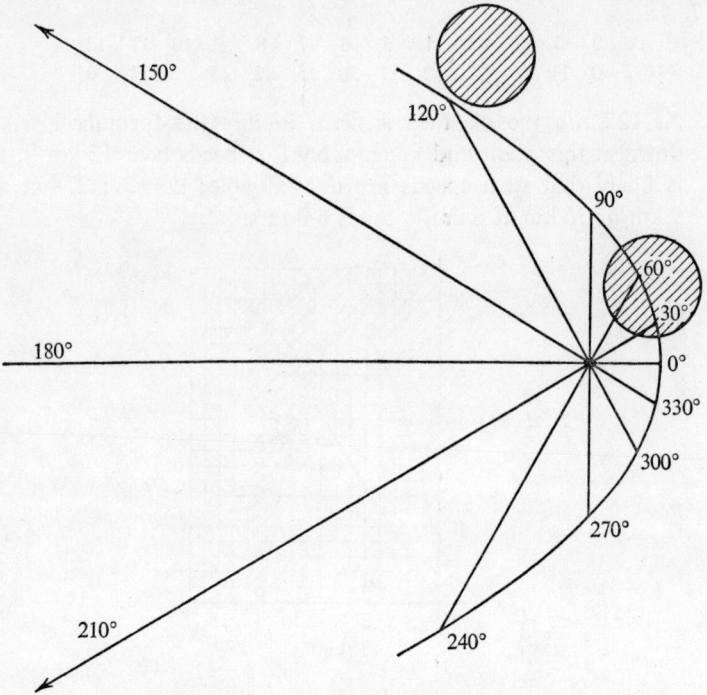

Fig. L

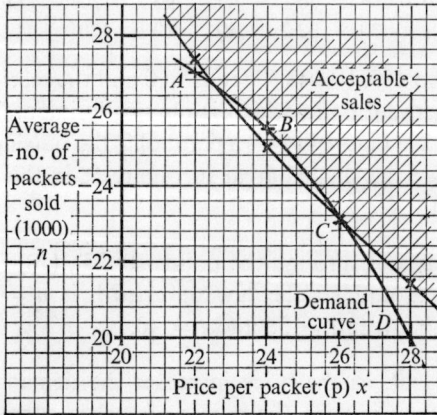

Fig. M

though the figures are unlikely to work out as neatly as in this example!

Price per packet (p)	x	22	24	26	28
Number to be sold to realize total (thousands)	n	27·3	25	23·1	21·4

$nx \geqslant 600$; only area B showed acceptable sales. Fix the price between 22·5p and 25·5p per packet. See Figure M.

REVIEW CHAPTERS

9

STRUCTURE

This chapter contains no new material. It is intended as private revision reading for some pupils who will begin to see the usefulness of looking at structure from a unified viewpoint, but it is hoped that it will contain useful material for written work and discussion also for all O-level pupils.

Section 1 provides a reminder of the ideas of element, operation and relation (including function) amid the details of the O-level course. Section 2 returns to the subject of operations and their properties, while Section 3 returns first to comparing orderings with equations to make pupils critically examine the rule, 'Do the same thing to both sides,' and then to discussing mappings and functions.

Section 4 shows how the similarities between different algebraic structures can be made precise and used as aids for solving problems and how the search for a systematic method of solving equations of the form $a \circ x = b$, in the various structures leads us naturally to consider the properties of Closure, Associativity, Identity and Inverse which characterize a Group. Finally, in Section 5 there is a mention of the structure necessary for the solution of equations involving two operations.

1. ELEMENTS, OPERATIONS AND RELATIONS

In Example 1, from $X * Y \rightarrow Z$, one can, of course, generally deduce $Y * Z \rightarrow X$ and various other valid statements. If the idea is thought worth pursuing, one could introduce small letter symbols for lines and a symbol ($\cap$ seems natural) for the meet of two lines. A possible exercise would be,

> '$A * B = c$; $B * C = a$; $b \cap c = D$; $b \rightarrow C$; any two lines or points with different letters are different. Draw and label a possible figure and make some more true statements about it'.

This is an exercise in inventing and using notation which could be applied to other common operations, e.g. 'take the average of' or 'find the H.C.F. of' for two numbers a and b.

In Section 1.3, the similarity between 'operation' and 'function' is stressed. In more advanced work the picture of the two-input 'addition machine' in Figure A (a) is replaced by that of a machine with the single input (x, y) in Figure A (b).

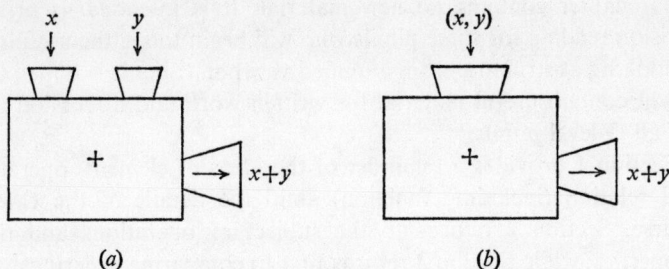

Fig. A

This means that addition is considered as a function whose domain is the set of all ordered pairs of numbers. Thus an operation is a special case of a function rather than, as here, the reverse.

2. OPERATIONS

This is a section of material familiar to the teacher but less so to the pupils. In it are made explicit the properties of operations that are needed for rearrangement within an expression (but not across a relation sign).

3. A LOOK AT RELATIONS

Sections 3.1 and 3.2 are mainly a reminder that the rules for manipulating orderings are more restrictive than those for equations. It could be used as a peg for discussing what 'equals' means, in view of the fact that the process by which we test the truth or falsity of an equation depends on the structure under consideration. Compare the meaning of '=' in each of the following:

$$`\tfrac{4}{5} - \tfrac{3}{4} = \tfrac{1}{20}`.$$

100

'In arithmetic modulo 7, $9 = 2$'.

'$\{3, 11, 12, 5, 1\} \cup \{9, 13, 11, 4, 5, 16, 2\}$
$$= \{12, 11, 9, 5, 4, 3, 2, 1, 16, 13\}'.$$

'If $\mathbf{M}$ is a reflection, $\mathbf{M}^2 = \mathbf{I}$'.

'The vectors $\mathbf{AB}$ and $\mathbf{CD}$ are equal in the figure'.

Section 3.3 deals with mappings.

4. THE USE OF STRUCTURE PATTERNS

The matrix example can be varied *ad lib* and leads to questions like 'Make up a matrix-and-vector equation with exactly the same pattern as $4(x-3) = 12$ and solve it', etc. The point to get over is that the technique learnt for one type of equation does equally well for the apparently more complex type (as long as one eschews the word 'divide'!); one should therefore demand that pupils check by substitution that the answers do work. The associative law is deliberately not mentioned and one goes straight from $\mathbf{Ax} = \mathbf{b}$ to $\mathbf{x} = \mathbf{A}^{-1}\mathbf{b}$.

4.3 Groups

The standard examples of groups are provided by

(*a*) the reals, the rationals, the integers, the finite arithmetics under $+$;

(*b*) the reals, the rationals, the prime finite arithmatics (all with zero excluded) under $\times$;

(*c*) various sets of linear transformations of the plane, such as:

   (i)   the isometries,   (ii)   the rotations about O,

   (iii) the translations,   (iv) the 'direct' isometries,

   (v)   the symmetry transformations of various shapes,

   (vi) the set of all shears with a given invariant line,

   each under the operation 'follows';

(*d*) the set of $m \times n$ matrices under addition, column vectors being one special case;

(*e*) various sets of matrices, usually representing sets of transformations, under multiplication.

Finite groups, where one can verify the properties by direct calculation, give useful examples for classwork. There follow a few techniques for constructing finite groups that are simple but not too stereotyped. They are amusing for the teacher and give scope for inventing examples.

If n is prime, the set $S = \{1, 2, \ldots, (n-1)\}$ under multiplication (mod n) is always a group. When n is inconveniently large, subgroups may be found, e.g. if $n = 17$, the set of powers of 4, $\{4, 16, 13, 1\}$, is a subgroup. If n is not prime, $(S, \times)$ is not a group but one can find subsets of S obeying some or all of the group properties, often with an identity which is different from 1. For instance, $\{3, 6, 9, 12\}$ (mod 15) is a group with 6 as the identity, whereas $\{1, 6, 9\}$ (mod 15) obeys Closure, Identity, and Associative law, with 1 as the identity. It is natural to compare $\{3, 6, 9, 12\}$ (mod 15) with $\{1, 2, 3, 4\}$ (mod 5), and indeed if p is prime and q any counting number, not a multiple of p, then $\{q, 2q, 3q, \ldots, (p-1)q\}$ is a group under multiplication (mod pq). Obviously its identity cannot be 1. Problem: find a general rule to find the identity.

Example

If $p = 5$, various values of q give the groups $\{2, 4, 6, 8\}$ (mod 10); $\{3, 6, 9, 12\}$ (mod 15); $\{4, 8, 12, 16\}$ (mod 20); and so on.

More important mathematically is the following: For *any* n, the set P_n of numbers from 1 to n–1 having no common factor with n, forms a group (multiplication mod n). This can be seen by drawing up the combination table for $\{1, 2, \ldots, (n-1)\}$. Zeros appear in various places. When one strikes out each row and column with a 0 in it, what remains is a group table, containing precisely the elements of P_n.

The function $n \rightarrow$ number of elements in P_n, is traditionally called ϕ, and is of great importance in number theory—as is P_n itself.

Simple examples of matrices which generate finite groups can be found easily by using the Cayley–Hamilton theorem that 'every square matrix **A** satisfies its characteristic equation det $(\mathbf{A} - \lambda \mathbf{I}) = 0$'. For a 2×2 matrix

$$\mathbf{A} = \begin{pmatrix} a & b \\ c & d \end{pmatrix}$$

this equation is

$$\det \begin{pmatrix} a-\lambda & b \\ c & d-\lambda \end{pmatrix} = 0$$

reducing to

$$\lambda^2 - (a+d)\lambda + (ad-bc) = 0.$$

The theorem states that

$$\mathbf{A}^2 - (a+d)\mathbf{A} + (ad-bc)\mathbf{I} = 0.$$

To find matrices satisying $A^n = I$ for $n = 2, 3$ and 4:

($n = 2$) Let the characteristic polynomial be $\lambda^2 - 1$. This implies

$$a + d = 0 \quad \text{and} \quad ad - bc = {}^{-}1.$$

($n = 3$) Let the characteristic polynomial be $\lambda^2 + \lambda + 1$, which is a factor of $\lambda^3 - 1$. This implies

$$a + d = {}^{-}1 \quad \text{and} \quad ad - bc = 1.$$

($n = 4$) Let the characteristic polynomial be $\lambda^2 + 1$, a factor of $\lambda^4 - 1$. (It could of course be $\lambda^2 - 1$ which has been dealt with.) This time,

$$a + d = 0 \quad \text{and} \quad ad - bc = 1.$$

The method only gives 'nice' matrices if one can find quadratic factors of $\lambda^n - 1$ with rational coefficients. It will work for $n = 6$ but not for $n = 5$ or any higher n, except to give quadratic factors found already.

Here are some matrices found by following the above rules: the reader may work out which rule applies to which matrix.

$$\begin{pmatrix} -1 & 1 \\ -1 & 0 \end{pmatrix}, \quad \begin{pmatrix} 0 & 1 \\ 1 & 0 \end{pmatrix}, \quad \begin{pmatrix} 3 & 4 \\ -2 & -3 \end{pmatrix},$$

$$\begin{pmatrix} 3 & 5 \\ -2 & -3 \end{pmatrix}, \quad \begin{pmatrix} 2 & -3 \\ 1 & -1 \end{pmatrix}, \quad \begin{pmatrix} -2 & -3 \\ 1 & 1 \end{pmatrix}.$$

A matrix A such that $A^n = I$ (but $A^m \neq I$ for any smaller m) generates, of course, the group $\{I, A, A^2, \dots, A^{n-1}\}$ with n elements: it is commutative. An interesting fact is that the matrices

$$A = \begin{pmatrix} -1 & 1 \\ -1 & 0 \end{pmatrix} \quad \text{and} \quad B = \begin{pmatrix} 0 & 1 \\ 1 & 0 \end{pmatrix}$$

(where $A^3 = I$, $B^2 = I$) generate a non-commutative group of order 6, isomorphic (as any such group of this order must be) to the symmetries of an equilateral triangle.

4.4 Simple equations

This section gives several examples (and there are plenty more in the exercises) to show that the four group properties are a sufficient condition for each simple equation to have a unique solution. They are not a necessary condition. This is not stated in the text but may be worth a mention. For example let $*$ be a subtraction: in the set of real numbers there are always unique solutions to $x-a = b$ and $a-x = b$. This is also true in finite arithmetics, where subtraction as well as addition tables are Latin Squares. What about division tables? There is scope for investigation here.

In Example 11, the associative law does not hold. For instance:

$$(1 * 1) * 2 = 0 * 2 = 2,$$
$$1 * (1 * 2) = 1 * 1 = 0.$$

The logical point is that, if we start from a false premiss (in this case, that for an x, either 0, 1 or 2, it is true that $1 * x = 2$), the conclusion may be true or false, especially when one of the steps in the reasoning (the application of the associative law) is also invalid.

5. EQUATIONS WITH TWO OPERATIONS

One way of reinforcing the inverse element technique is by solving linear equations in the prime finite arithmetics, which form the simplest examples of number fields. Suppose the modulus is 7. First the combination tables for $\{0, ..., 6\}$ under addition and multiplication are drawn up and kept handy (though most pupils prefer to do calculation mentally in simple cases). Next, the elements are listed in inverse pairs:

Addition: 0, 0; 1, 6; 2, 5; 3, 4;
Multiplication; 1, 1; 2, 4; 3, 5; 6, 6.

To solve the equation $3x+6 = 1.$
Add 1 (inverse of 6) $3x = 2.$
Multiply by 5 (inverse of 3) $x = 3.$

Such equations have the merit that even if one is able to solve them mentally, the inverse element method is the quickest and easiest way! From a simple start, one could develop the theme to: equations like $2(x+3) = 3(x+2)$; equations in arithmetic modulo 'a non-prime number', where multiplicative inverses do not always exist; one might be able to make up more-or-less convincing problems in which questions about days of the week are turned into equations modulo 7.

Exercise (*p. 168*)

1.

	Table no.	Equation	Set of solutions	Is there a solution?	Is it unique?
(a)	(i)	$x * 10 = 2$	{4}	Yes	Yes
(b)	(i)	$10 * x = 8$	{10}	Yes	Yes
(c)	(ii)	$5 * x = 3$	{2}	Yes	Yes
(d)	(ii)	$5 * (x * 4) = 3$	{4}	Yes	Yes
(e)	(iii)	$6 * x = 6$	{6}	Yes	Yes
(f)	(iii)	$0 * x = 0$	{0, 3, 6, 9, 12}	Yes	No
(g)	(iv)	${a} * X = {ab}$	{{b}, {a, b}}	Yes	No
(h)	(iv)	${a} * X = \varnothing$	$\varnothing$	No	—
(i)	(v)	${a} * X = {ab}$	{{b}}	Yes	Yes
(j)	(v)	${a} * X = \varnothing$	{{a}}	Yes	Yes
(k)	(viii)	$\mathbf{Q} * \mathbf{X} = \mathbf{I}$	{T}	Yes	Yes
(l)	(viii)	$\mathbf{T} * \mathbf{X} = \mathbf{Z}$	{W}	Yes	Yes
(m)	(vi)	$1 * x = 5$	{6}	Yes	Yes
(n)	(vi)	$5 * x = 1$	{4, 6}	Yes	No

Fig. B

2. (a) (i), (ii), (v), (vii), (viii).

(b) It must be a Latin Square.

3. (a) $x = 2$; (b) $x = 5$; (c) $X = {a}$; (d) $\mathbf{X} = \mathbf{W}$.

4. It is closed; the new identity is 1.

5. (i)   (ii)

	4	8
4	4	8
8	8	4

	2	4	8
2	4	8	4
4	8	4	8
8	4	8	4

(iii)

	1	2	4	8
1	1	2	4	8
2	2	4	8	4
4	4	8	4	8
8	8	4	8	4

(iv)

	1	5	7	11
1	1	5	7	11
5	5	1	11	7
7	7	11	1	5
11	11	7	5	1

Fig. C

All have identities except Table (ii).

(b) (i), (iv).

(c) $5 * x = 7 \Rightarrow 5 * 5 * x = 5 * 7 \Rightarrow x = 11.$

6. (a) The powers are **C, D, E, I** in that order.

(b)

	I	A	B	C	D	E
I	I	A	B	C	D	E
A	A	B	C	D	E	I
B	B	C	D	E	I	A
C	C	D	E	I	A	B
D	D	E	I	A	B	C
E	E	I	A	B	C	D

Fig. D

$\mathbf{A}^3 \times \mathbf{A}^4 = \mathbf{A}^7 = \mathbf{A}^6\mathbf{A} = \mathbf{A}$ since $\mathbf{A}^6 = \mathbf{I}.$

(c) Yes.   (d) $\mathbf{X} = \mathbf{C}.$

7. (a) This question is meant as a simple example of isomorphism. The clock-face can be drawn like Figure E. An alternative is to consider the unit vector $\mathbf{j} = \begin{pmatrix} 0 \\ 1 \end{pmatrix}$ as being the hand of a clock, initially at zero. The matrix $\mathbf{A}$ sends $\mathbf{j}$ to $\begin{pmatrix} 1 \\ 1 \end{pmatrix}$, then in turn to

$$\mathbf{A}^2\mathbf{j} = \begin{pmatrix} 1 \\ 0 \end{pmatrix}, \quad \mathbf{A}^3\mathbf{j} = \begin{pmatrix} 0 \\ -1 \end{pmatrix}, \dots, \mathbf{A}^6\mathbf{j} = \mathbf{j},$$

106

the complete 'revolution' taking six 'hours'. Of course any vector $\begin{pmatrix} x \\ y \end{pmatrix}$ would do as the 'starting position'. (See Figure F.)

(b) $\mathbf{ACE} = \mathbf{C}$, $\mathbf{ABCD} = \mathbf{D}$.   (c) $\mathbf{A}^{35} = \mathbf{E}$, $\mathbf{C}^{20} = \mathbf{I}$.

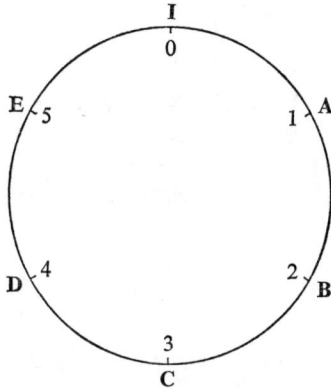

Fig. E

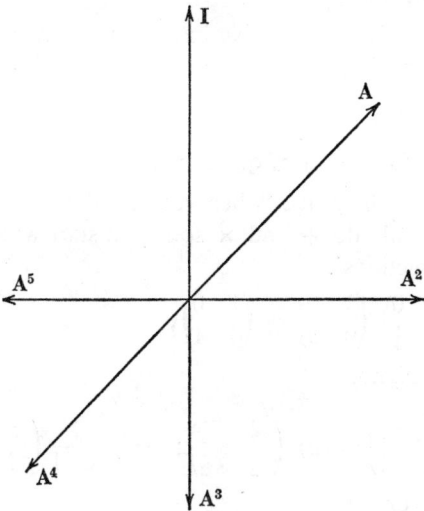

Fig. F

8. (a) Inverse pairs are:

$$\mathbf{I, I}; \quad \mathbf{P, Q}; \quad \mathbf{R, R};$$
$$\mathbf{S, S}; \quad \mathbf{T, T}.$$

107

(c) $\mathbf{X} = \mathbf{P}$.

	I	P	Q	R	S	T
I	I	P	Q	R	S	T
P	P	Q	I	T	R	S
Q	Q	I	P	S	T	R
R	R	S	T	I	P	Q
S	S	T	R	Q	I	P
T	T	R	S	P	Q	I

Fig. G

9. (a) $\mathbf{A(BC)} = \mathbf{(AB)\,C}$: 2 ways.

$$(\mathbf{A(BC))\,D} = ((\mathbf{AB)\,C)\,D} = (\mathbf{AB})\,(\mathbf{CD}) = \mathbf{A((BC)\,D)}$$
$$= \mathbf{A(B(CD))}: 5 \text{ ways.}$$

(b) $a * (b * c) = a * (c * b) = (b * c) * a = (c * b) * a$: 4 ways.

(c) Table (viii) is associative. $\mathbf{VQZ} = \mathbf{ZQV} = \mathbf{Q}$: all other arrangements equal $\mathbf{T}$.

(d) Table (vi) is commutative but not associative

$$5 * (3 * 2) = 5 * (2 * 3) = (3 * 2) * 5 = (2 * 3) * 5 = 4;$$

all other arrangements equal 0.

10. Nos. 10–14 form a set of questions.

(a) Yes: something like 'when you calculate a matrix multiplication you only do $+$ and $\times$ so if you start with integers you won't get fractions'.

(b) e.g. $\begin{pmatrix} 4 & 0 \\ 0 & \frac{1}{3} \end{pmatrix} \begin{pmatrix} \frac{1}{4} & 0 \\ 0 & 3 \end{pmatrix} = \begin{pmatrix} 1 & 0 \\ 0 & 1 \end{pmatrix}$;

(c) $\mathbf{N_1}$ yes; $\mathbf{N_2}$ no.

11. (a) (i) $\begin{pmatrix} 2 & -1 \\ -1 & 1 \end{pmatrix}$; (ii) $\begin{pmatrix} \frac{3}{2} & -\frac{1}{2} \\ -\frac{1}{2} & \frac{1}{2} \end{pmatrix}$; (iii) $\dfrac{1}{x-1} \begin{pmatrix} x & -1 \\ -1 & 1 \end{pmatrix}$.

(b) $x = 2$ or 0.

(c) $\dfrac{1}{y+4} \begin{pmatrix} 1 & 2 \\ -2 & y \end{pmatrix}$; $y = -5$ or -3.

12. The determinant must be 1 or -1. This condition is not only necessary but sufficient.

13. (*a*) The products are super-nice.

(*b*) The area scale factor of **A** and **B** is ± 1; hence that of **AB** is

$$(\pm 1) \times (\pm 1) = \pm 1.$$

(*c*) and (*d*) Shears and isometries have area scale factor equal to ± 1.

14. **S** is a group; **N**, satisfies Closure, Associativity, Identity, but not Inverse. The classical name for **S** is the Unimodular Group. It has uses in tesselations, elliptic functions, and number theory.

15. A puzzle-type question. (i) ? = 7 or 8; (ii) ? = $^-3$; (iii) impossible; (iv) surprisingly, just 14 different possibilities.

10

COORDINATES AND GRAPHS

1. COORDINATES AND MAPPINGS

In mathematics, relations are studied as sets of ordered pairs illustrated by arrow diagrams or graphs, and also as algebraic statements (and often as a mixture of the two). This O-level course has given much greater emphasis than has been usual to the former approach and to the easier methods used to obtain approximate algebraic expressions from the ordered pairs.

Notice that many questions can be answered at the non-algebraic level. For example, questions about intermediate evaluation, rates of change, the solution of equations, turning points: the accuracy of the answers is limited only by the accuracy of the data and by the time and skill of the person using these methods. In the A-level course, these points will be taken up again in the algebraic context and will naturally lead to the development of calculus.

On some graphs, the curves are marked with the notation

$$x \to f(x)$$

and the axes are marked x and $f(x)$. While on other graphs, the curves are marked

$$y = f(x)$$

and the axes are x and y. The difference might be one of emphasis or to indicate how the information graphed was obtained, from observations or from a formula. For example, if we had been given some observed readings for heights of men and their probabilities, then the axes might be marked h and p. If, on the other hand, we were using a probability function so that, knowing a height, we could work out (or look up in tables) the associated probability, then we might mark the axes h and $p(h)$.

When searching for an algebraic statement to express a relation known from given data, there are two main problems:

(i) to discover the real values beneath the errors of observation;

(ii) to find the algebraic expression that can act as model for these

110

accurately known readings. We have not dwelt upon the first problem: correlation is not part of the course. The second has been described as a process of finding two functions, f and l, such that,

$$x \to f(x) \quad \text{and} \quad f(x) \to l[f(x)] \quad \text{so that} \quad l[f(x)] = y$$

where l is linear. The function f is guessed (a process that is assisted if the functions for some of the common curves are known (see Section 1.1)). The soundness of the guess and the detail of the linear function are discovered by graphing $f(x)$ and y. Questions on this work appear as Questions 3, 4 and 5 in both Exercise A and B.

Although the logarithmic function has been introduced in *Book* 4, it seemed too early to use it in place of guessing the function. For the same reason, it was decided not to introduce log graph paper.

Because of problems of space in *Book* 5, it was not possible to show the graph of a function and of its inverse on axes with the same scales and therefore to show that each was the image of the other under a reflection in the line $y = x$. It is hoped that this point can be made in the pupil's work.

111

Exercise A (p. 186)

1.

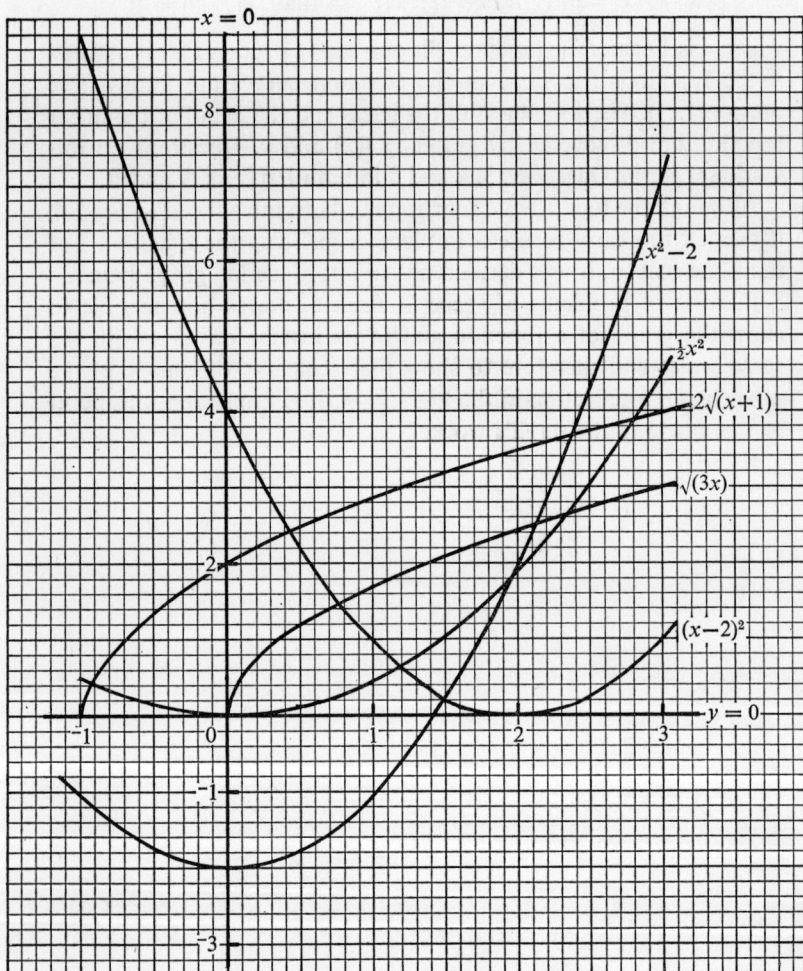

Fig. A (i) (Graphs *a–e*)

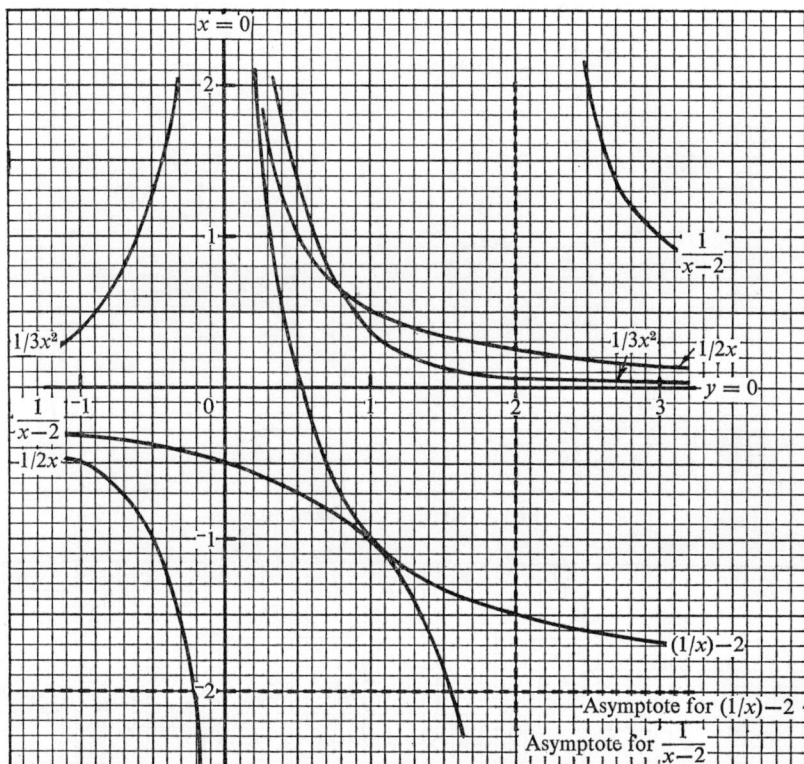

Fig. A (ii) (Graphs *f–i*)

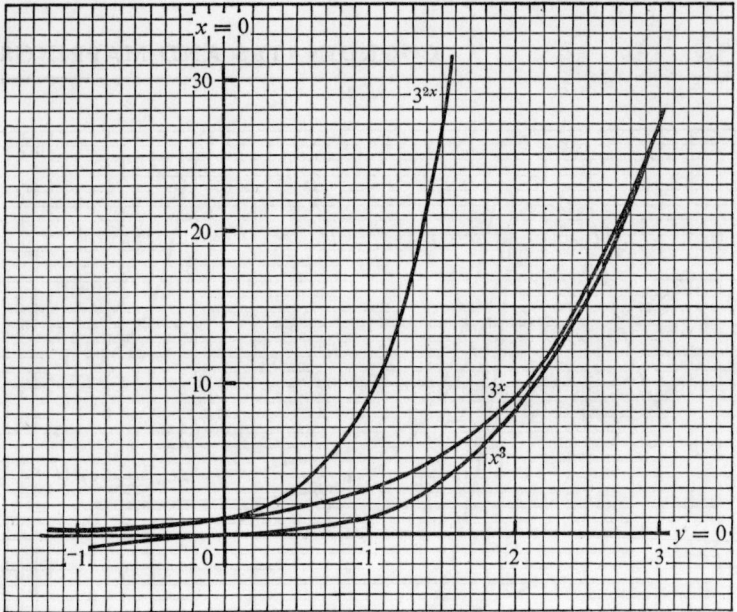

Fig. A (iii) (Graphs *j*, *k* and *m*)

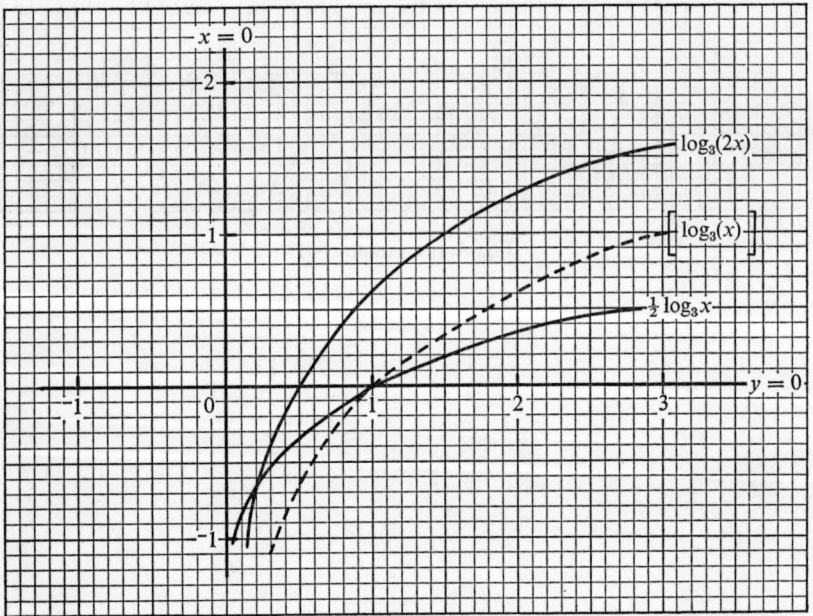

Fig. A (iv) (Graphs *l* and *n*)

114

2.

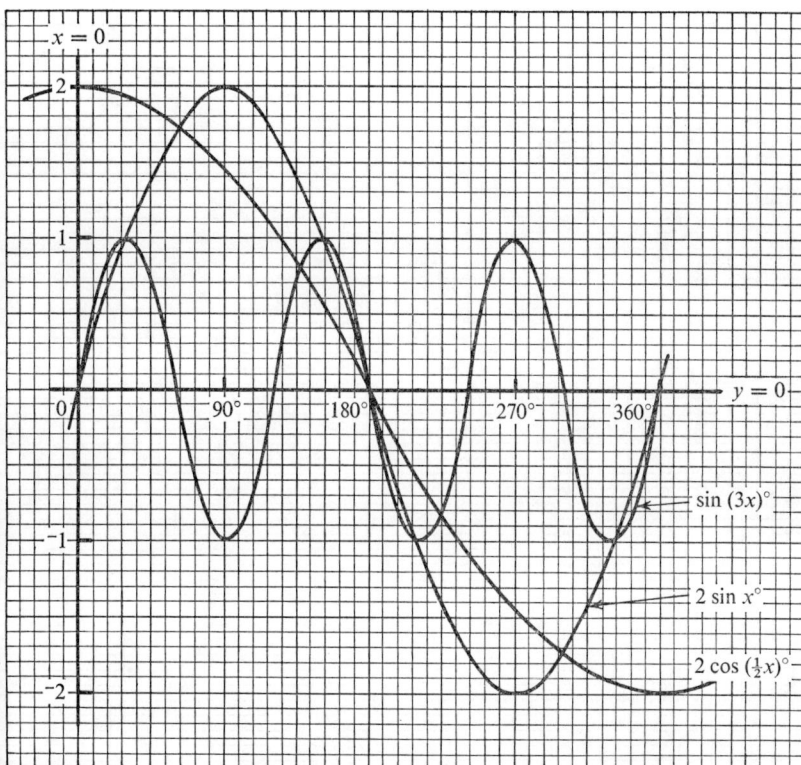

Fig. B

3.

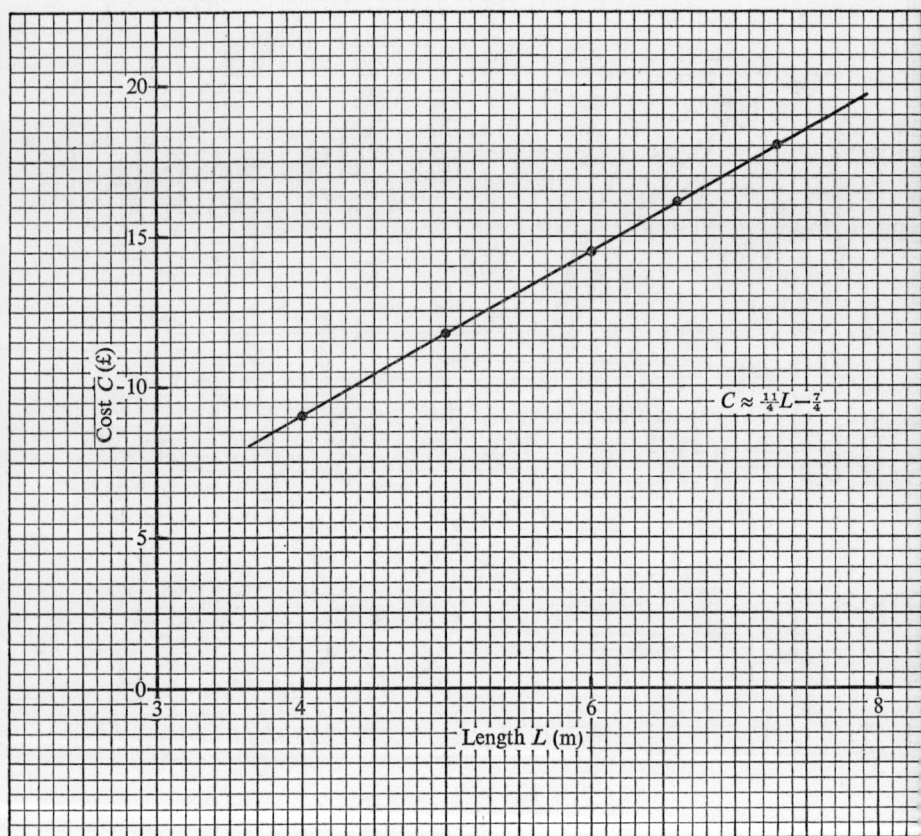

The graph shows Cost C (£) on the vertical axis and Length L (m) on the horizontal axis, with the line

$$C \approx \tfrac{11}{4}L - \tfrac{7}{4}$$

Fig. C

4.

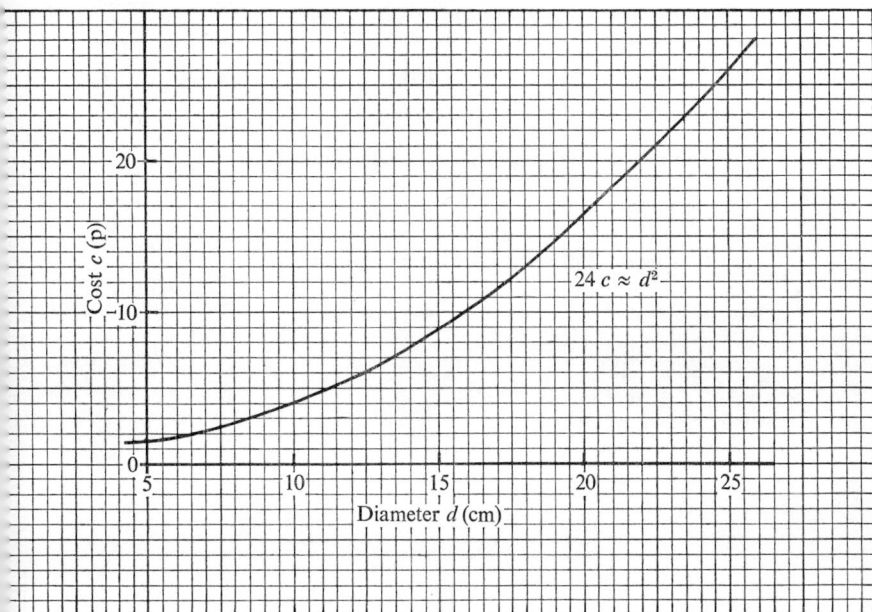

Fig. D

5.

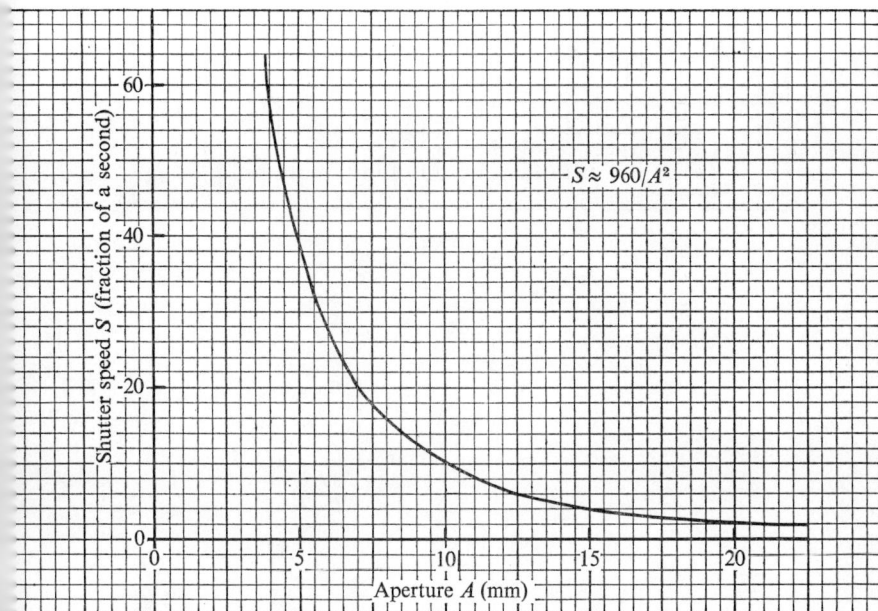

Fig. E

117

6. See Figure F.

   (*a*) 60 km/h;   (*b*) 40 km/h;

   (*c*) 100 km/h (between 10.45 and 11.00 hours);

   (*d*) 78 km/h;

   (*e*) 90 km/h; (between 10.43 and 11.23 hours).

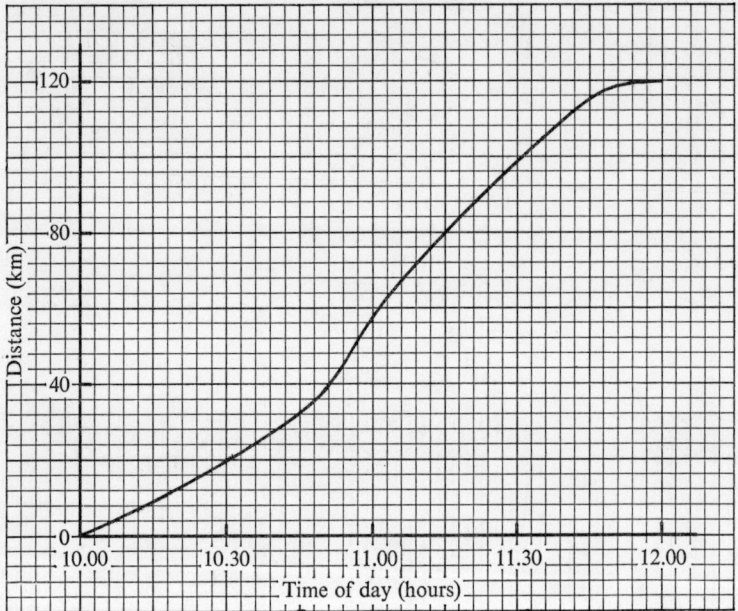

Fig. F

7.

Time	10.00	10.15	10.30	10.45	11.00	11.15	11.30	11.45	12.00 (h)
Speed	40	40	40	75	95	80	72	50	0 (km/h)

Area under graph represents 120 km, (trapezium rule), i.e. the distance covered by the car in the two hours.

8. See Figure G.

   (a) 9, ⁻3, 9;   (b) $x = 1$ and $x = 3$.

   (c) 16 square units (trapezium rule).

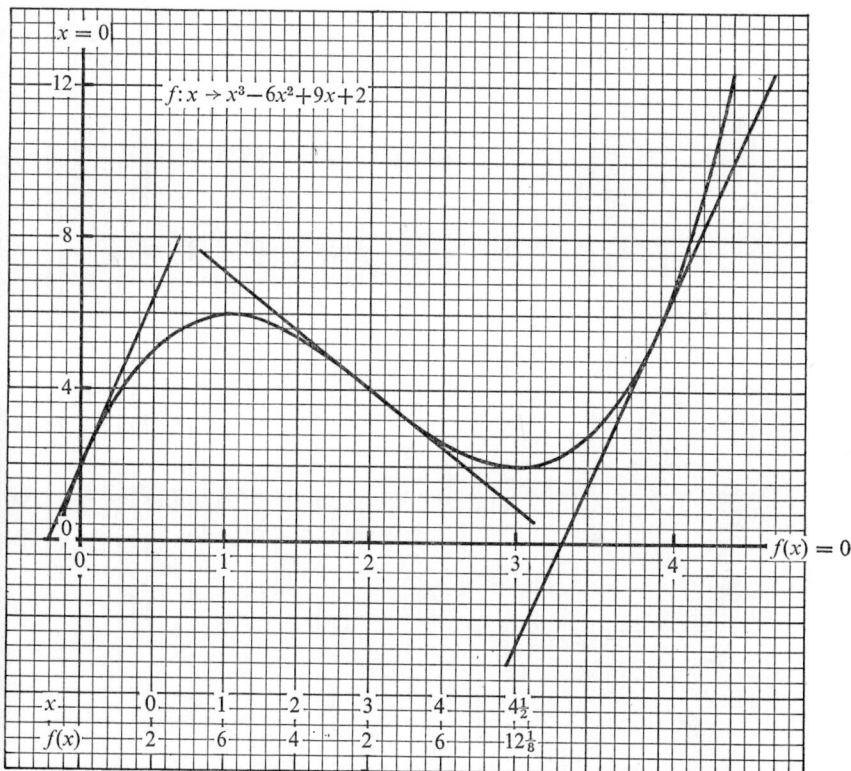

x	0	1	2	3	4	$4\frac{1}{2}$
$f(x)$	⁻2	6	⁻4	⁻2	6	$12\frac{1}{8}$

$f: x \to x^3 - 6x^2 + 9x + 2$

Fig. G

Exercise B (p. 187)

1.

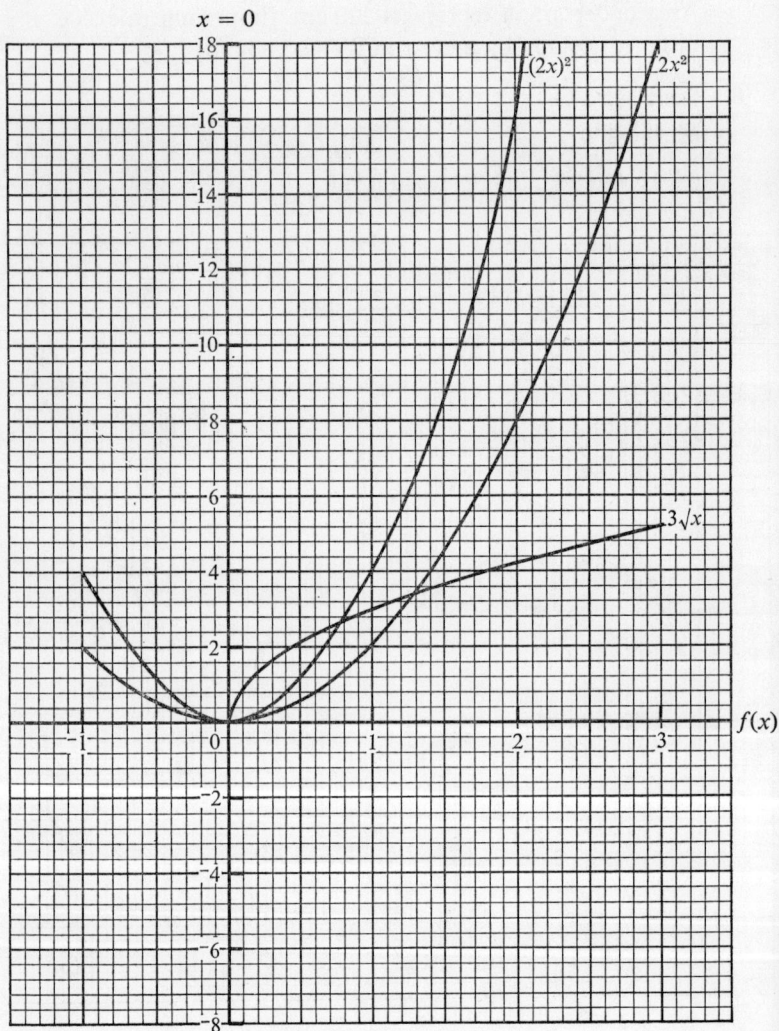

$x = 0$

$(2x)^2$

$2x^2$

$3\sqrt{x}$

$f(x)$

Fig. H (i) (Graph *a–c*)

120

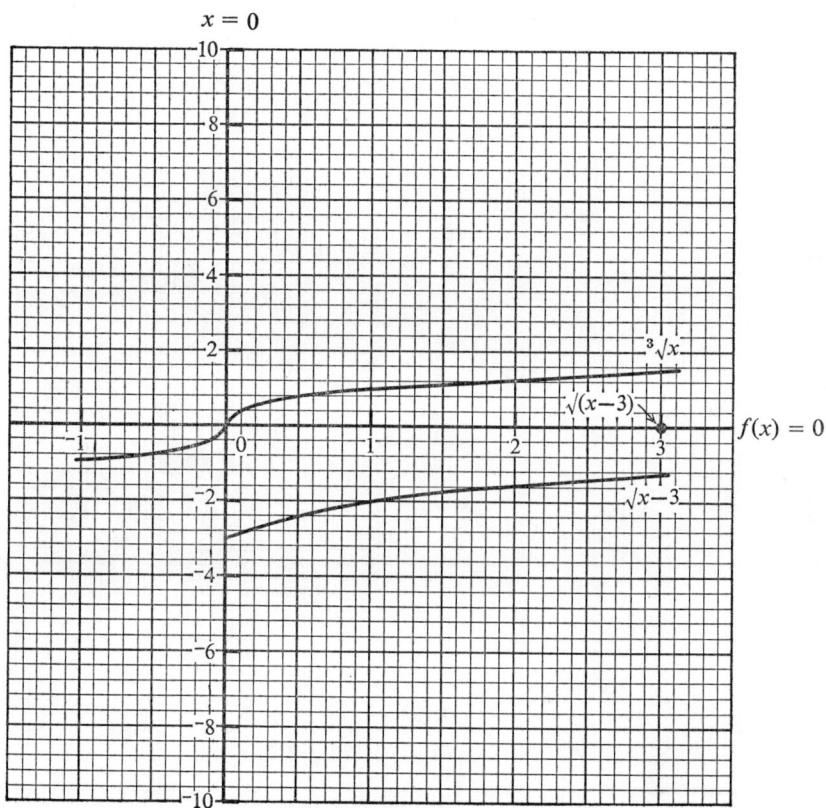

Fig. H (ii) (Graph *d–f*)

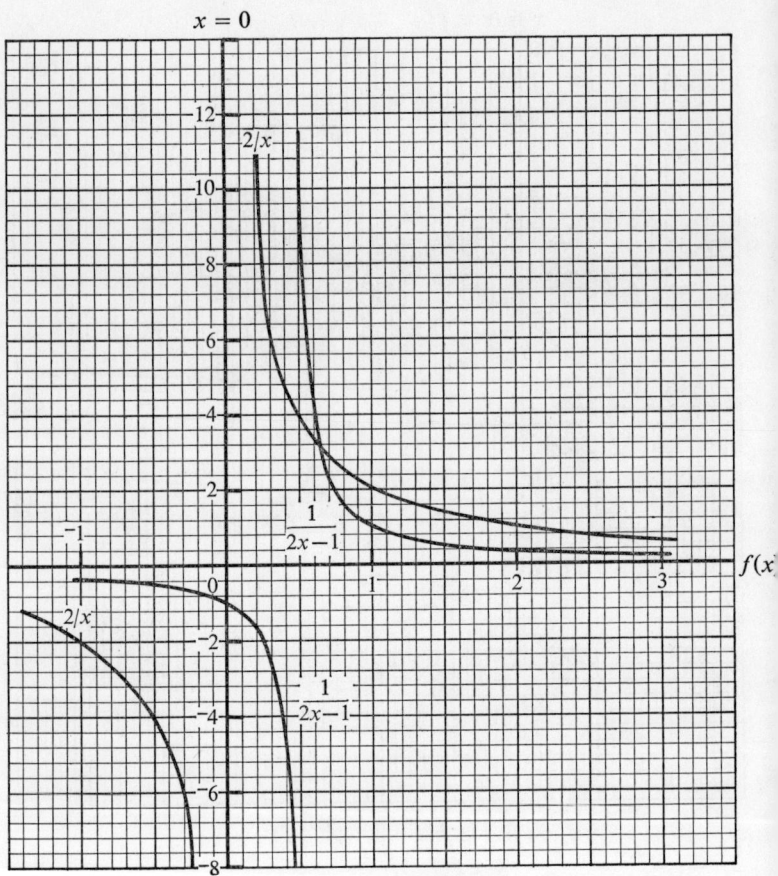

Fig. H (iii) (Graph g, h)

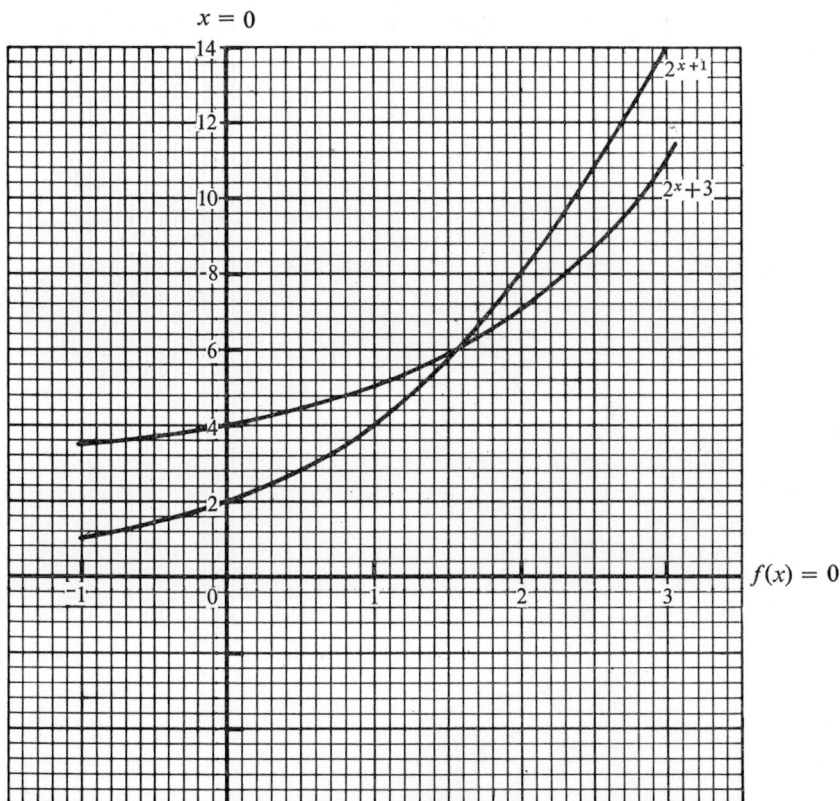

Fig. H (iv) (Graph i, j)

(k) When $x = 3$, $\log_2 (x-3) = -\infty$.

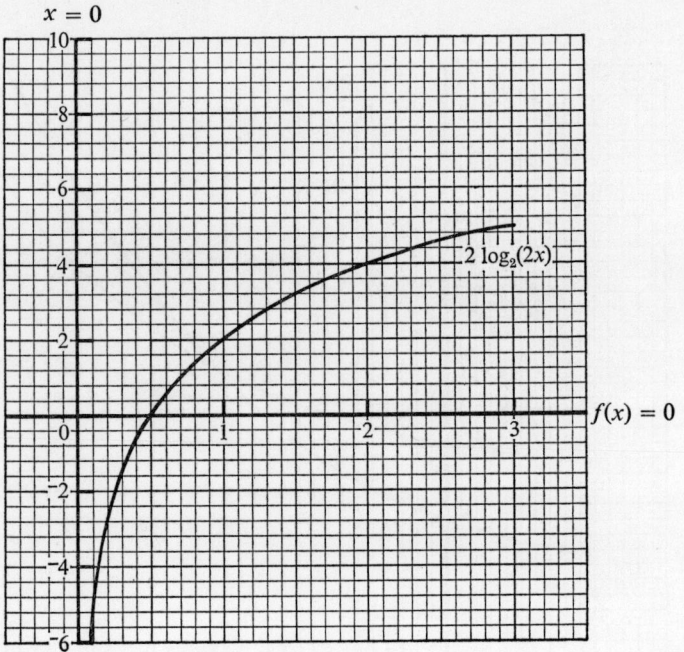

Fig. H (v) (Graph *l*)

2.

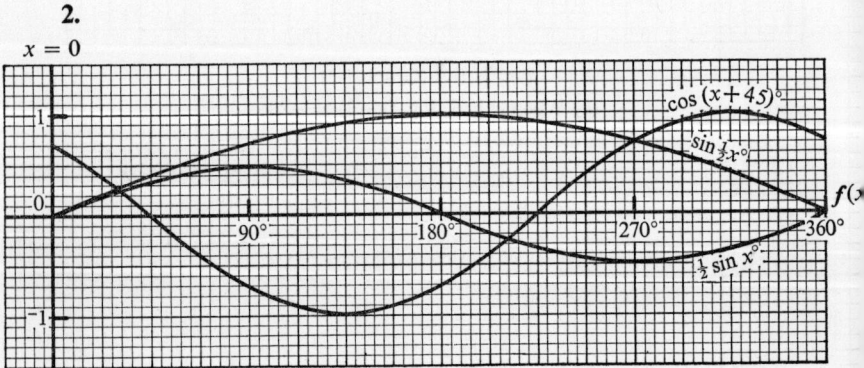

Fig. I

3.

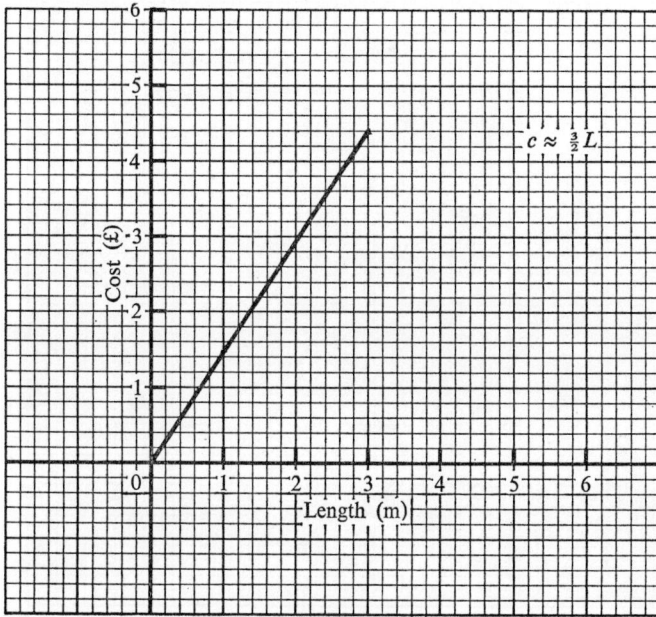

Fig. J

4.

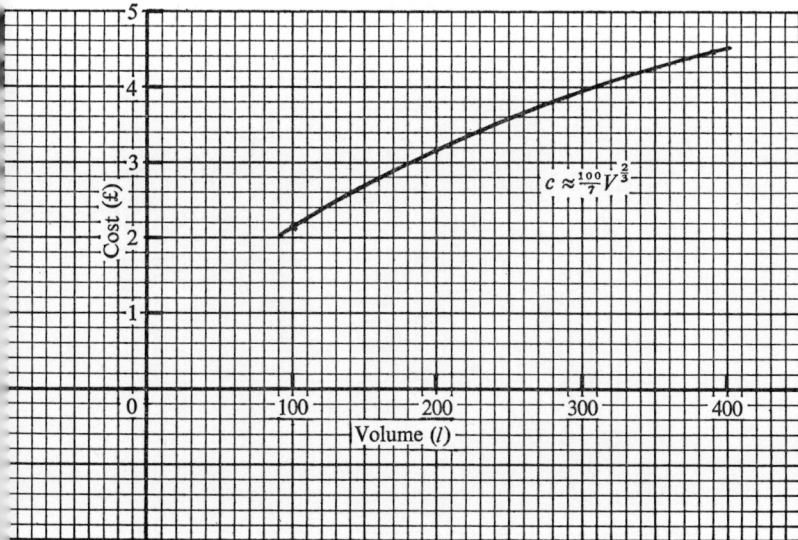

Fig. K

5.

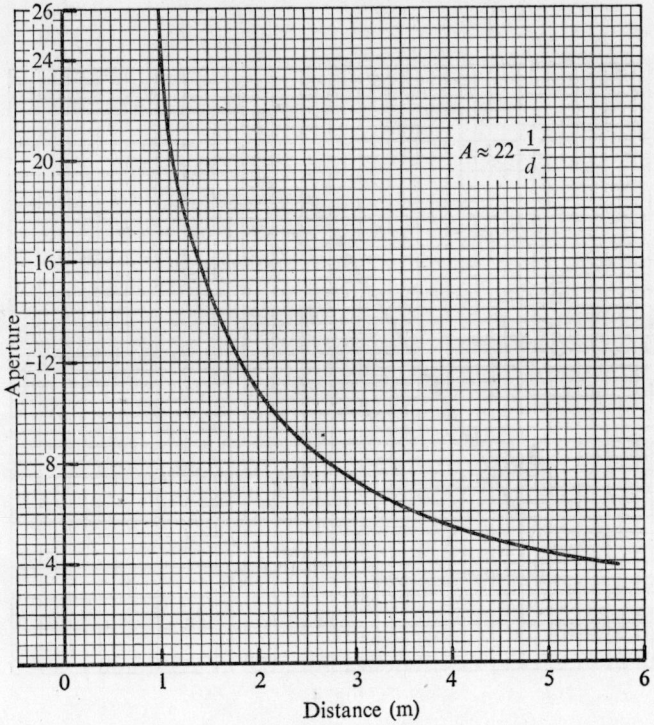

$$A \approx 22 \frac{1}{d}$$

Fig. L

6.

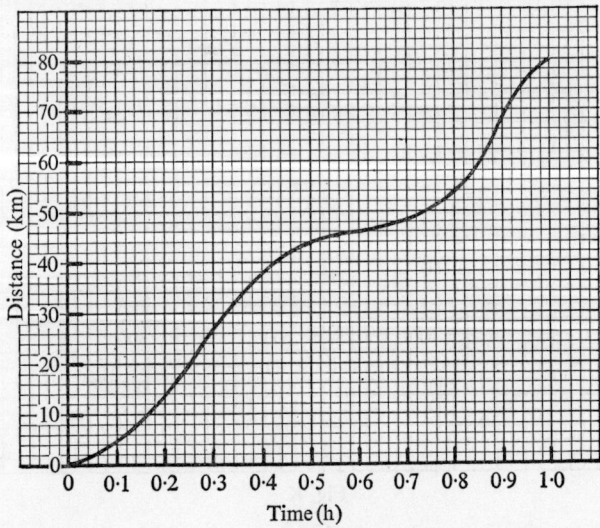

Fig. M

(a) Average speed over the first half-hour, 88 km/h.

(b) Speed when $d = 40$ km, 70 km/h.

(c) Maximum speed, 180 km/h.

7.

Speed (km/h)	40	60	100	160	80	40	10	30	90	180	60
Time (h)	0	0·1	0·2	0·3	0·4	0·5	0·6	0·7	0·8	0·9	1·0

The area under this curve represents the distance travelled by the trains in the hour, that is, 80 km.

8.

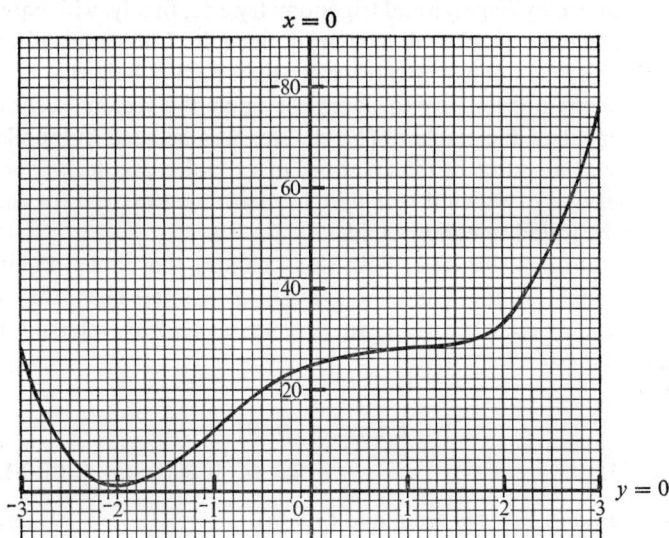

Fig. N

(a) When $x = {}^-2$, gradient is 0;

                  $x = 0$, gradient is 2;

                  $x = 2$, gradient is 16.

(b) The gradient is zero when $x = {}^-2$ and $x = 1$.

(c) The gradient is least when $x = {}^-3$ (within this domain); its value then is ${}^-64$.

(d) The area under the graph is $139\frac{1}{3}$ square units.

127

11

COMPUTATION

In this chapter are gathered together all those parts of the course which involve computation. It starts with an examination of the various number bases and moves on to methods of calculation and to questions of accuracy. It then deals with ratio, percentages and proportion, areas, Pythagoras and trigonometry and, finally, with equations and formulae (topics already mentioned in Chapter 9 where the emphasis was upon structure rather than manipulation).

It seems unnecessary to comment upon the various sections for the benefit of the teacher. The chapter will be used by pupils very largely as a source of information, of formulae and techniques, the background of which it would be burdensome to repeat for they are all to be found in earlier Guides.

The authors feel that, with this chapter, the pupils might very well benefit if the Guide was freely available. Then they could immediately see when their working was at fault by referring to the answers.

Exercise (p. 211)

1. 54.

2. (a) 10000_2; (b) $10000 \cdot 1_2$.

3. $3n + 4n^2$. Factors are n and $(3 + 4n)$.

4. 53_6.

5. 11_2.

6. (a) True; (b) true; (c) false; (d) true.

7. 5555_6. $[10000_6 - 1_6 = 6^4 - 1 = 5555_6 = 5 \times 1111_6$
$$= 5(1 + 6 + 6^2 + 6^3)].$$

8. (a) $1000a + 100b + 10c + d$.

(b) $^-999a + ^-90b + 90c + 999d = 9(^-111a + ^-10b + 10c + 111d)$.

(c) $9 \times 3 \times 37(d - a)$.

(d) $a(1 - n^3) + nb(1 - n) + nc(n - 1) + d(n^3 - 1)$ and this is divisible by $(n - 1)$.

9. (*a*) 2;   (*b*) 3;   (*c*) 1.

10. (*a*) (i) 5·2;   (ii) 450;   (iii) 0·096.
    (*b*) (i) 5·24;   (ii) 446·04;   (iii) 0·10.

11. 48. [2/1000 of 48·324 = 0·096648.]

12. (*a*) 0·91$\dot{6}$;   (*b*) 0·64;   (*c*) 0·1$\dot{8}$;   (*d*) 0·$\dot{4}$2857$\dot{1}$.

13. $3\frac{2}{7} \approx 3\cdot2857$.   [$3\frac{3}{11} \approx 3\cdot2727$.]

14. (*a*) 10;   (*b*) 100;   (*c*) 0·02;   (*d*) 0·009.

15. (*a*) $6\cdot30 \times 10^2$;   (*b*) $3\cdot8 \times 10^{-2}$;   (*c*) $6\cdot04 \times 10^{-4}$.

16. $2\cdot040 \times 10^3$.

17. (*a*) $3\cdot1 \times 10^{-2}$;   (*b*) $5\cdot0 \times 10^{-1}$;   (*c*) 6·1.

18. (*a*) 5^4;   (*b*) 3^4;   (*c*) 2^4.

19. $1\cdot28 \times 10^4$.   20. 10^{16}.

21. (*a*) 9·4;   (*b*) 0·32;   (*c*) 1·32.

22. Between 0·1 and 1.   [0·56].

23. 6.   24. £4·17.

25. (*a*) 52·25 cm $\leqslant$ true length $< 52\cdot75$ cm;
    (*b*) no; the smallest value is 156·0 cm;
    (*c*) 1380 cm² and 1350 cm².

26. 11·7 cm $\leqslant$ perimeter $< 12\cdot3$ cm.

27. $3 \leqslant t \leqslant 11$.   28. $x:y = 11:5$.

29. 5 km.   30. 128 cm².

31. 10^3.   32. 4·5 cm.

33. (*a*) 20 km due south (180°);   (*b*) 1/500000.

34. (*a*) 24 cm²;   (*b*) 9 cm;   (*c*) 54 cm².

35. 45°.   36. £7.

37. (*a*) £3·80;   (*b*) 71%;   (*c*) £82·80.

38. Original price was £45.   Sale price was £43·20.

39. 28%.

40. (a) 1·25%; (b) 0·029%.

41. p and q^2; $p = 75$.

42. 20 cm.

43. 1 cm.

44. 2·5 cm.

45. 38·2 m.

46. About 4 m.

47. 4 cm.

48. (a) False; (b) false; (c) impossible to tell from this data; (d) true.

49. 16·4 cm.

50. 5·2 m.

51. 4·2, 4·1 and 2·2 units. Area is 4·5 square units.

52. (a) False; (b) false; (c) true; (d) true.

53. (6·9, 4·0). [Or (⁻6·9, 4·0) or (6·9, ⁻4·0) or (⁻6·9, ⁻4·0).]

54. 7·7 cm.

55. $CD = 6$ cm. $BD:AC \approx 1·73:1$.

56. (a) $x = {}^-1$; (b) $x = \frac{5}{11}$; (c) $x = {}^-\frac{3}{8}$.

57. (a) $x > 6$; (b) $y \leqslant {}^-1$; (c) $x > 5$.

58. (a) $x = {}^-2, y = 3$; (b) $x = 0, y = 2\frac{1}{3}$.

59. $P = 48 - 18x$.

60. $t = 25W + 15$.

61. (a) $c = \dfrac{9}{T^2}$; (b) $c = \dfrac{x-b}{a}$; (c) $c = \dfrac{\sqrt{(a^2 - b^2)}}{a}$.

62. (a) True; (b) false $\left[W = \dfrac{2aT + a}{3} \right]$; (c) true; (d) true.

12

STATISTICS AND PROBABILITY

Sections 1–4 deal with descriptive statistics and, in the main, show the O-level range of statistical techniques being applied to one set of figures. These figures, though hypothetical, have a practical, realistic setting since it is felt that statistics is essentially a subject which should be studied against a practical background.

Fairly long, accurate calculations are needed at this stage and emphasis should be placed upon a tidy, systematic setting out of work. As is said in the text, this is not a chapter that can be glanced through: there are too many small points in it which would be missed by this approach. The examples and the tables should all be checked by the student.

Section 5 summarizes the basic work on probability. The work at this stage remains intuitive, and no attempt should be made to learn definitions or laws, but the basic ideas should be clear.

Section 6 ties together the previous work, and gives some clue as to where statistics leads. It is a bridge between descriptive and analytic statistics. But provided that the ideas are kept in concrete terms the student will not have difficulty understanding them.

2. AVERAGES

These three averages, as with the measures of spread which come later, are very simple ideas which could have been invented by almost anybody. Hours of calculation tend to hide their simplicity, but it should be this which the pupil grasps first.

Since any average attempts to summarize a set of figures by one figure it must be an approximation, and the last part of this chapter makes this point in some detail. Although figures in this example are given to one decimal place, the pupils should be taught to treat the third figure with scepticism. In particular, there seems to be no justification here for using linear interpolation to find the mode in a grouped frequency function; the modal group is sufficient, and its mid-point may be taken when a single figure is required.

The distinction between discrete and continuous variables is blurred over in this example because the discrete variable has such a wide range.

In forming grouped frequency functions with large class intervals the pupils should be encouraged to arrange their classes *symmetrically, or else a bias may be introduced into the calculations.*

Students are sometimes disappointed to find that there is not a golden rule which tells them which is the best average to use. It is important that they should see mathematics not as a mechanical instrument to solve all problems automatically, but rather as a tool to be guided by the skilled hand of the craftsman.

3. SPREAD

The inter-quartile range is not a very important measure, and not too much emphasis should be given to it, although it should be known. If the teacher wants to mention the standard deviation, there is a good approximate method of calculating it. Disregarding the top and bottom $2\frac{1}{2}\%$ of the ordered set, divide the range of the remaining elements by 6. This will be close to the true standard deviation.

The left-hand end of a cumulative frequency curve can present problems. It is necessary to look at each instance individually, and decide whether it is possible to establish a minimum value for the function (c.f. of 0). In this case the only possible answer is 0, which adds nothing to the curve, and so has been omitted.

4. GRAPHS

This is just a simple revision of the main terms. Of course, some frequency diagrams can also be bar charts. Notice that we have still not introduced the idea of a histogram where area is the relevant measure; at the moment it is only length which is important. This is basically true in the Pie Chart as well because area is proportional to angle alone, since the radius is held constant for any given set of figures.

The problem of discrete and continuous variables becomes explicit here in the discussion of line graphs. If the students are unclear about this, the teacher may need to provide a number of suggestions of figures which can be illustrated by line graphs, and those which cannot, and ask the students to choose between them.

No attempt has been made to state firm rules about which way round to draw axes. This is often found to be difficult, but pupils gradually improve. A comparison of different figures presented in different ways can often be instructive. In some cases it may be of use to state the convention that time is usually plotted across the page.

5. PROBABILITY

Most of the work here deals with finite universal sets, but the extension to infinite sets is not difficult, particularly when dealt with by tree diagrams. The example about ball-point pens is a transitional one which may need more explanation. In some cases, e.g. tossing dice, the probabilities obviously remain unaltered for the second event. In other cases, e.g. picking a team of 11 out of 14 candidates, they obviously change. In this case, if the child bought his second pen on the same day as the first one, then one might be justified in saying that the probability had changed, since it is unlikely that new stock had arrived. In most cases, of course, the change in probability will be small, and the difference between the answers will be unimportant. The refinement of the working depends on the use which will be made of the answer. By now students should be able to distinguish between criticizing the mathematics, and criticizing the assumptions on which the mathematics is based.

6. SIGNIFICANCE

While most people nowadays are fairly happy with descriptive statistics many will shy clear of analytic work. But it cannot be too strongly emphasized that it is the analytic side, of which significance is a key concept, that is the real justification for the subject. If two or three students can tackle together books like Moroney's *Facts from Figures* or a good A-level text and do experiments themselves they will find the experience very rewarding. The ideas do not come in one jump; they are gradually acquired as they are seen applied to many different situations.

Significance is an extremely broad subject, and only one aspect of it has been dealt with here. Other ways from which the subject may be approached include:

1. Long runs of heads in a coin tossing experiment. This leads directly to the notion of probability, and makes it very easy to see that one can never totally discount the possibility that the coin is quite fair and that a very rare event has occurred.

2. Changes in accident figures are regularly quoted in the papers, and can provide a fruitful source of discussion. If the pupils have gained the idea that samples from the same population will not all be the same, they should have no difficulty in seeing most accident figures for what they are—inadequate half-truths, which, with a little work, could be turned into powerful arguments.

3. In the first few pages of R. A. Fisher's *Design of Experiments* he deals with great lucidity about the problem of telling whether one can distinguish between tea with the milk added before, and tea with the milk added after. He shows how to design the cheapest experiment which will yield sufficiently significant results.

4. Industrial processes are another important source of ideas. Machine-made goods are subject to variability. What is important is the proportion which lie outside the advertised specifications of the goods. To this may be added (or rather multiplied) the probability of a poor quality item being detected, and the cost to the firm of making good the deficiency.

The idea of significance, while simple, takes some time to understand fully, and the more different ways it can be tackled the better.

In the chapter, the problem set by $1K$ and $1T$ is about the significance of the difference between the means, while the class experiment is an approach to understanding the standard error of the mean. Provided that the argument is not taken too far at this stage, the distinction between the two will not be of importance.

If necessary, Table 4 may be extended or altered to fit the figures produced in the experiment. The teacher will need to suggest suitable class intervals for the grouped frequency function. The point about taking the same number of samples as there are members of the class is to keep the areas of the bar charts the same, to enable instant comparison between them. If the approximation for the standard deviation suggested above is used it will be even easier to see that the spread is inversely proportional to the square root of the size of the sample.

Exercise A (p. 232)

1. (a) 4·0 (calculate to one more significant figure than original data);
(b) 6·5;
(c) 7·00;
(d) 112·7;
(e) 5·04;
(f) 3145·6;
(g) 5·26 (averages, being approximations, should not be given as fractions);
(h) 2·0;
(i) 1·0;
(j) 1·50.

2. For example:
(a) {8, 8 1, 9 7, 10, 12};
(b) {−3, 0, 0, 0, 1};
(c) {−3, 0, 0, 0, 1};
(d) {−0·5, 1, 1·5, 2, 3·5};
(e) {−6, −4, −4, −4, −2}.

3.

	Mean	Mode	Median
(a)	3·1	3	3
(b)	6·7	6	6
(c)	60·0	59	59
(d)	86	80	80

4.

x	f	x	f
3–7	7	28–32	8
8–12	8	33–37	5
13–17	6	38–42	12
18–22	5	43–47	2
23–27	7		

5.

	Mean	Mode	Median
(a)	10·7	10·0	10·5
(b)	27·7	25·5	28·6
(c)	27·2	25·0	28·1
(d)	38·0	38·0	39·0

The distinction between the two class intervals in parts (b) and (c) is very important, and should be emphasized. Medians were worked out by linear interpolation, but this is not very important.

6. For example:

(a) {1, 2, 3, 4, 5};   (b) {-3, 3, 4, 5, 6};
(c) {0, 1, 2, 3, 3};   (d) {5, 5, 6, 7, 12};
(e) {3, 5, 7, 9};   (f) {1, 2, 2·5, 5, 5·5, 6, 6};
(g) {3·4, 4·3, 4·7, 5·5, 6·0, 7·3};
(h) {2·2, 2·4, 2·6, 3·9, 7·4}.

7.

	Range	Median	1st quartile	3rd quartile	Inter-quartile range
(a)	6	4	2	6	4
(b)	9	8	5	10	5
(c)	15	13	11	17	6
(d)	4	3	1·5	4·5	3·0
(e)	20	159	155·5	167	11·5
(f)	9	8	6·5	10	3·5
(g)	3	2·5	1·25	3·75	2·5
(h)	3	-4·5	-5·75	-3·25	2·5
(i)	16	559·5	557·25	570	12·75
(j)	13	9 5	5·5	12·5	7·0
(k)	7	6	4	9	5
(l)	6·9	6·7	2·3	7·4	5·1
(m)	2·8	3·4	2·8	3·95	1·15
(n)	3·0	4·95	3·975	6·6	2·625
(o)	7	4·5	3	6·25	3·25
(p)	9	7	6	10·5	4·5

8. For example:

(a) {0, 5, 6, 7, 8, 10, 20};   (b) {0, 5, 6, 7, 8, 10, 15};
(c) {0, 5, 6, 7, 8, 10, 10};   (d) {5, 5, 6, 7, 8, 10, 10};
(e) impossible.

Exercise B (p. 233)

Special attention should be paid here to presentation. This will usually involve planning the form of the answer before putting pen to paper.

1. (a) The angles of the pie chart will be:

Printing costs	90°
Wages and salaries	180°
Maintenance of capital	54°
Miscellaneous	36°

(b) The money involved will be the same, as the area involved will be the same.

(c) Wages and salaries will have 198° of the pie chart.

2. (a)

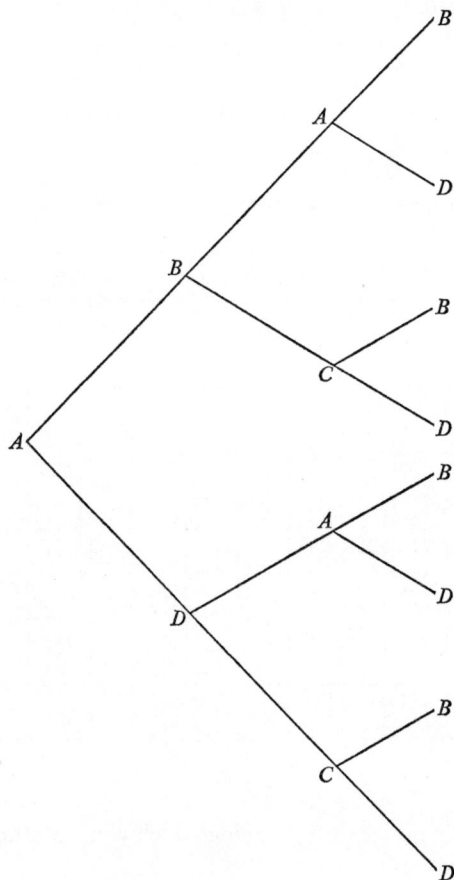

Fig. A

137

(*b*) There are 8 equally likely routes he could take. Three of them exclude *AB*. Probability of not visiting *AB* is therefore 3/8.

Probability of not visiting *BC* is 5/8.
Probability of not visiting *CD* is 5/8.
Probability of not visiting *AD* is 3/8.

(*c*) There are 24 twenty-minute periods. Four of them are spent in *BC*. Therefore probability of getting caught in *BC* is 1/6.

This question is of course highly simplified, but the idea is sound. The major problem would be to persuade the men on the beat to randomize their movements properly.

3. (*a*) 1/20; (*b*) 2·86p; (*c*) 1/25.

4. (*a*) 6·6 hours; (*b*) 9 hours; (*c*) approximately 14 days;
(*d*) approximately 3 days.

5. Trading in new pence is more profitable by 24·5p or 3530 lire.

6. (*a*)

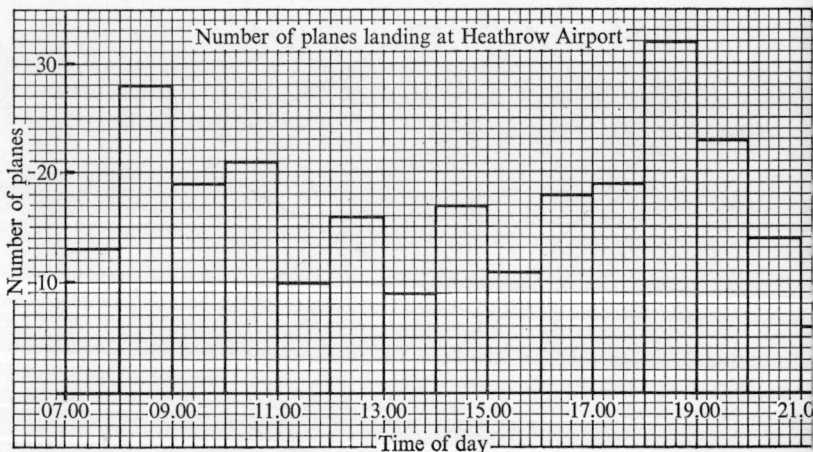

Fig. B

(*b*) There is no sensible meaning which can be attached to the mode here.

(*c*) 17·1 planes per hour.

(*d*) About 32 officers. It is only necessary to consider the period beginning 1800. Assuming that the planes come in regularly, there is a plane arriving about every two minutes. If it takes four men 15 minutes to clear a plane load, 8 planes will have arrived before the first group are free to attend to another plane. Of course, in practice, keeping this staff on all day would be far too expensive, and no account has been taken of unexpected events. The question might provide a lead-in to queueing theory.

7.   (*a*) See Figure C overleaf.

     (*b*) about 580;   (*c*) about 49;   (*d*) exactly 80.

8.   7/81.

Exercise C. Experiments (p. 235)

It is not as easy to think of examples of practical statistical work as textbooks sometimes suggest. This exercise is provided mainly as a source of inspiration, and with no intention that it should be systematically worked through. The aim is to encourage students not only to delve into books, but also to look mathematically at common objects around them. In many cases more details of the work than are given in the questions will need to be thought of before the students tackle the problem. Project cards will be useful here.

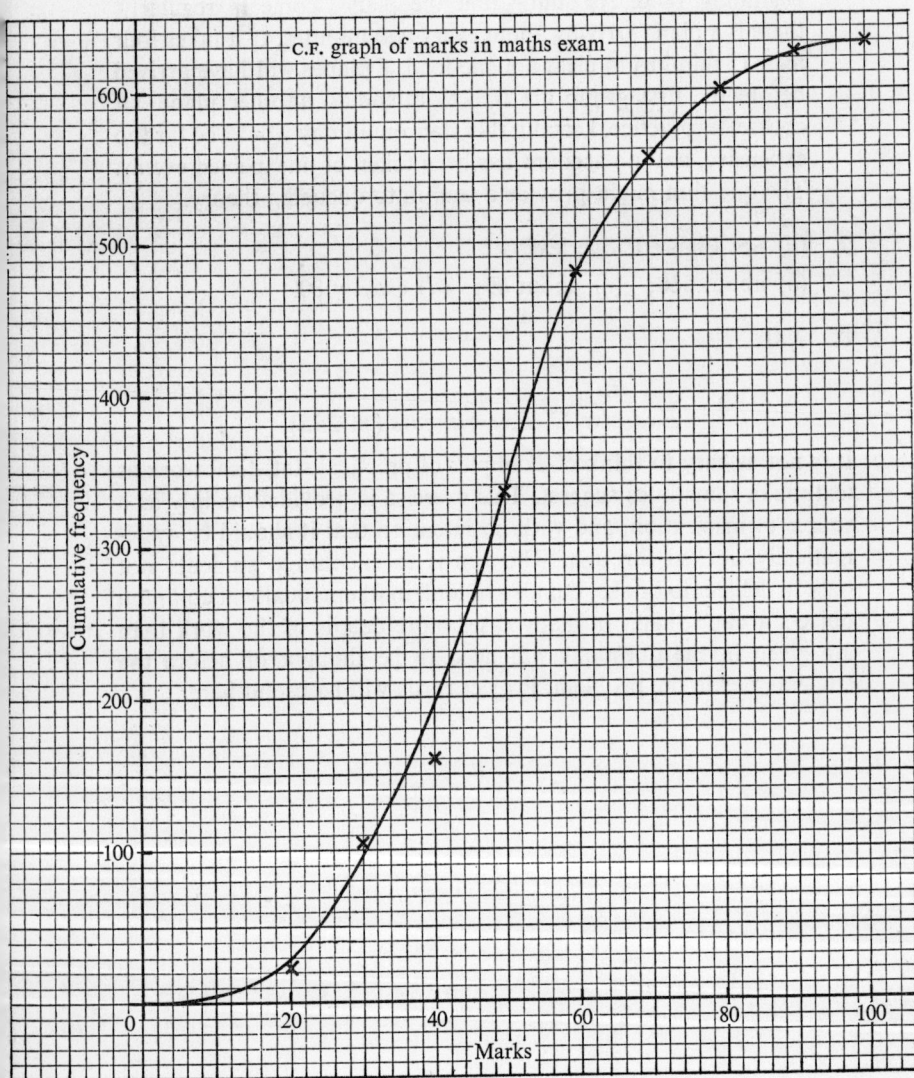

Fig. C

13

GEOMETRY

Though the chapter has ten sections, it may be considered to have three main parts. The first contains an examination of angles, polygons and polyhedra together with symmetry and loci. The second part starts with Section 4 and is a review of transformation geometry. The transformations are taken in the order suggested by the number of properties which remain invariant under each transformation, starting with those that retain the greatest number of constraints and reducing them until topology is reached. (Projective geometry has been omitted from the list, as in Chapter 6, as it seemed to be too difficult at this level.) The third part, Section 10, deals with some of the geometrical facts that can most easily be discussed in terms of vectors.

2. ANGLES, POLYGONS
AND POLYHEDRA

So far, in this course, an intuitive understanding of symmetry has been assumed. In Section 2.4, definitions of some symmetries have been introduced and we can say that a figure is symmetrical if, under some non-identity transformation, it can be mapped onto itself.

While Cartesian coordinates have been used to define some symmetries, rotational symmetry can be expressed generally and concisely using polar coordinates. A figure has rotational symmetry of order n about a point or line, if n rotations through equal angles $(360°/n)$ are equivalent to the identity transformation. (If the rotation is $\mathbf{R}$, then $\mathbf{R}^n = \mathbf{I}$.)

In two dimensions, a figure K has rotational symmetry of order n about the origin $(0, 0)$ if

$$(r, \theta°) \in K \Leftrightarrow \left(r, \left(\theta + \frac{360}{n}\right)^°\right) \in K.$$

141

In three dimensions, a figure has rotational symmetry of order n about the z axis if

$$(r, \theta°, \phi°) \in K \Leftrightarrow \left(r, \left(\theta + \frac{360}{n} \right)°, \phi° \right) \in K,$$

where $\theta°$ is measured in the x, y plane and $\phi°$ is measured perpendicular to that plane.

Exercise A (p. 243)

1. $x = 115°$.

2. (a) The angle is 135°.   (b) It has 9 sides.
   (c) Yes. The exterior angle is 8°, and 8 is a factor of 360. The polygon will have 45 sides.

3. (i) The radius is 2·55 cm;
   (ii) The area is 15·5 cm². Both answers from using 3-figure tables.

4. (a)

Isosceles triangle

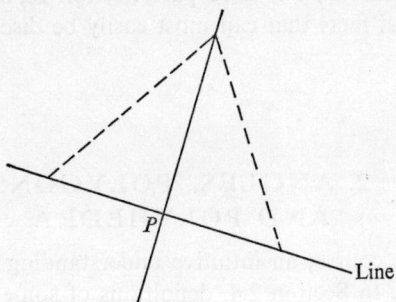

Fig. A

(b)

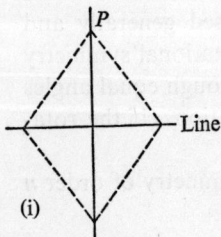

(i)

Rhombus

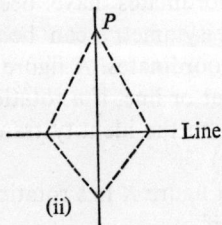

(ii)

Kite

Fig. B

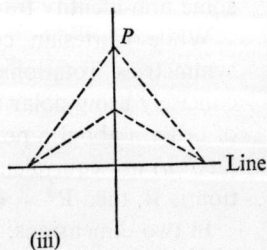

(iii)

Arrowhead

142

5. (i) Lines of symmetry—6.

(ii) Order of rotational symmetry—6.

6. (i) Planes of symmetry—5. 4 of these contain the line PQ, $XYZT$ is the other.

Rotational symmetry about PQ, order 4. Rotational symmetry, order 2, about each of 4 axes in the plane $XYZT$.

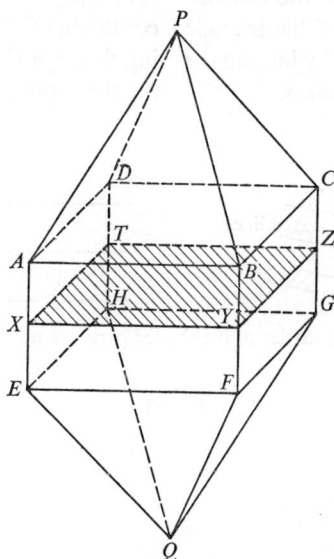

Fig. C

Point symmetry about the intersection of TY and XZ.

(ii) Planes of symmetry—3. 2 of these contain PQ and $XYZT$ is the other.

Rotational symmetry, order 2, about PQ.

Rotational symmetry, order 2, about 2 axes in the plane $XYZT$. Point symmetry as in (i).

3. LOCUS

Exercise B (p. 246)

1. (*a*) 2 dimensions   (*b*) 3 dimensions.

    (i) A circle, fixed point as centre, constant distance as radius.   A sphere fixed point as centre, constant distance as radius.

    (ii) A point, the circumcentre of the triangle formed by joining the three points.   A line, perpendicular to the plane containing the three points, passing through the circumcentre of the three points.

    (iii)

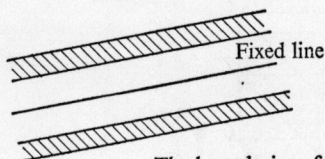 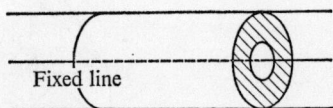

Fixed line   Fixed line

The boundaries of the shaded parts are not in the locus

(*a*)   (*b*)

Fig. D

    (iv)

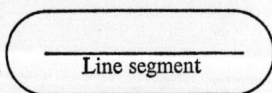 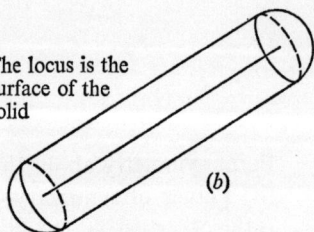

Line segment   The locus is the surface of the solid

(*a*)   (*b*)

Fig. E

2. (*a*) The locus is a single point, the origin.

(*b*) The boundary of the common shading is not part of the locus.

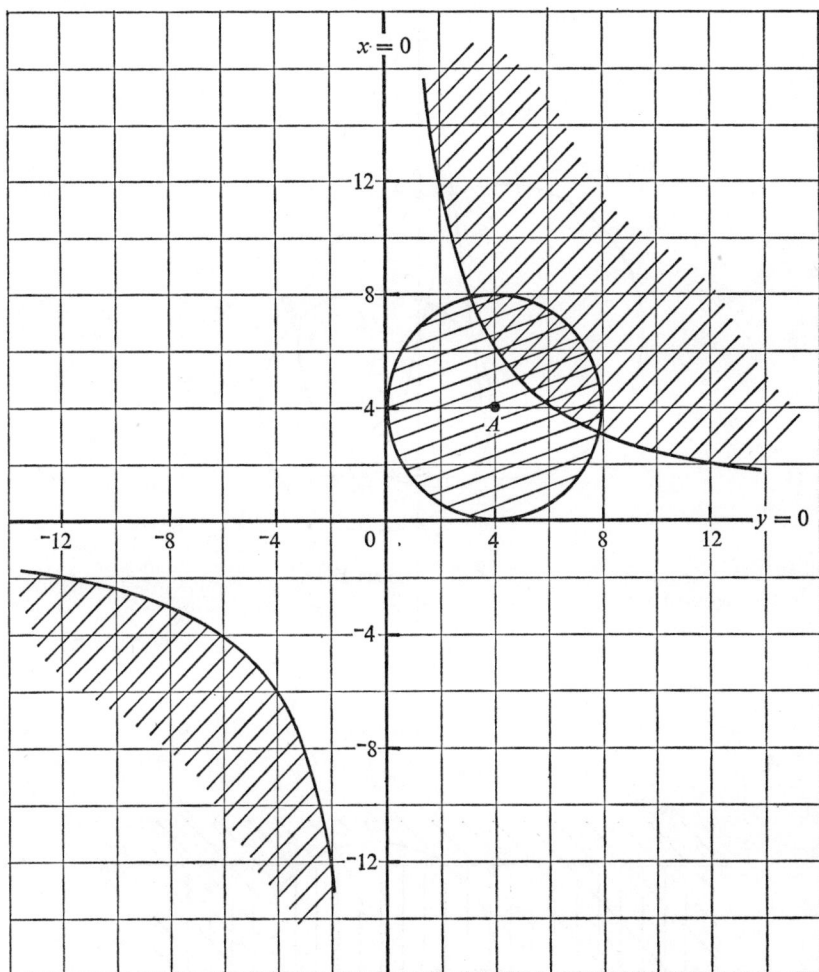

Fig. F

3. See Figure G overleaf.

$$X \cap Y = \{L, M\};$$
$$Y \cap Z = \{N, R\};$$
$$X \cap Z = \{S, T\};$$
$$X \cap Y \cap Z = \varnothing.$$

Note. This figure is *not* accurately drawn.

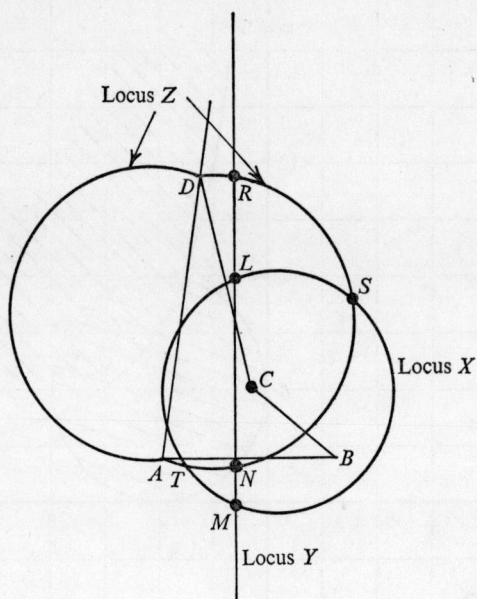

Fig. G

4.

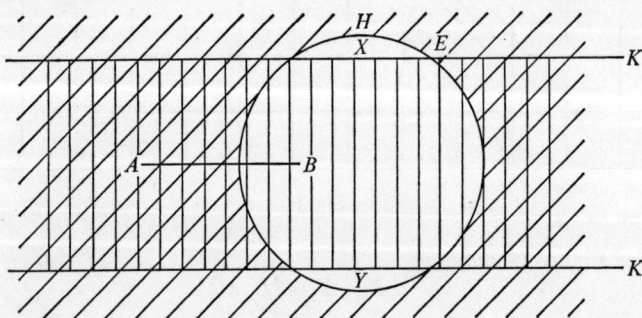

Regions X and Y satisfy both conditions

Fig. H

5.

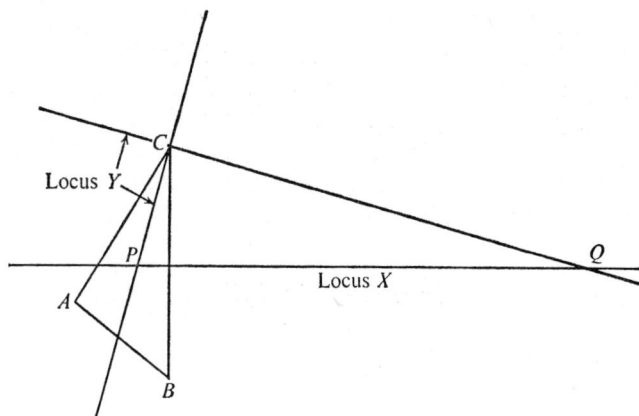

Fig. I

$$X \cap Y = \{P, Q\}.$$
$$PA = 4\cdot2 \text{ cm}, \quad QA = 12\cdot7 \text{ cm}.$$

4. ISOMETRIES

Unless it is clear that a general answer is required (as in answering the question, 'To what single transformation is the combination of two translations equivalent?', when the words, 'A translation' are sufficient), we must be specific in describing any transformation. We might give, for example:

   for a translation, the magnitude and direction;
   for a rotation, the invariant point and the angle of rotation;
   for a reflection, the position of the invariant mirror line;
   for a glide-reflection, the mirror line and the translation;
   for a shear, the invariant line and the image of a given point;
   for a one-way stretch, the invariant line and the scale factor;
   for a two-way stretch, the two invariant lines and the two scale factors.

In the list of properties that are ticked as being invariant in the sections on transformations, one or two need a word of explanation to remove possible ambiguities.

The word 'ratio' is taken to apply to *any* two segments in the plane (and not just to segments along a line). If the latter meaning was taken, then ratio would be invariant under shears and stretches.

147

The word 'parallelism' refers to the fact that if lines are parallel to each other then their images will also be parallel to each other (and not to the idea that a line might be parallel to its image).

In the phrase, 'order of points', the word 'order' indicates the sequence of points along the line and this is unaltered even under a topological transformation. But in the phrase, 'node order', the word refers to the number of arcs associated with any node, again unaltered under topological transformations.

Exercise C (p. 252)

1.

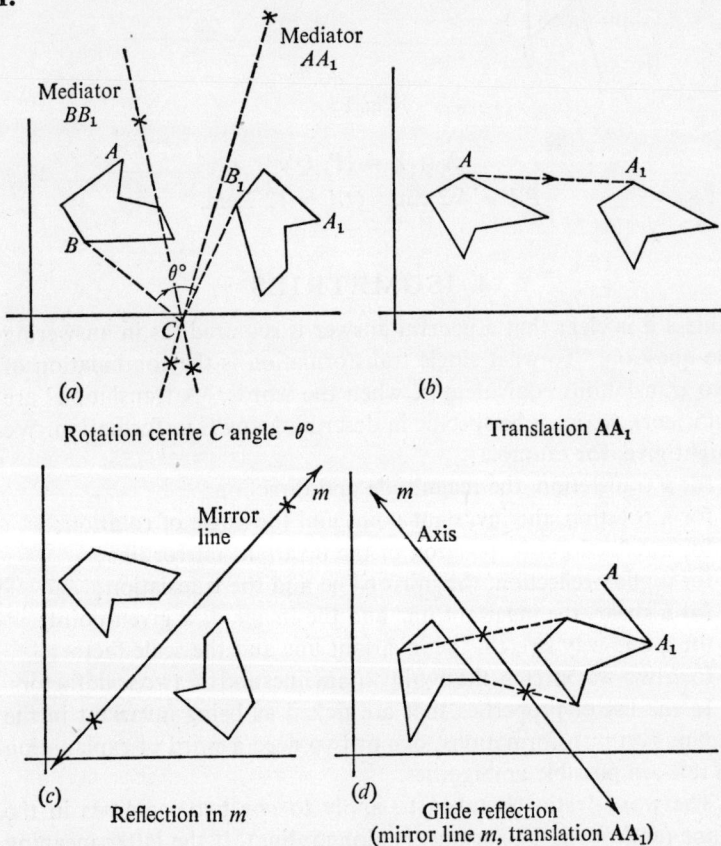

Mediator BB_1

Mediator AA_1

(a)

Rotation centre C angle $^-\theta°$

(b)

Translation AA_1

(c)

Reflection in m

Mirror line

m

(d)

Axis

m

Glide reflection (mirror line m, translation AA_1)

Fig. J

148

2. (*a*) Rotation, about (0, 0), through 180°.
(*b*) Rotation, about (⁻5, ⁻3), through 180°.
(*c*) Reflection in $x = 0$.
(*d*) Glide-reflection, mirror line $y = -3$, translation $\begin{pmatrix} 10 \\ 0 \end{pmatrix}$.
(*e*) Translation $\begin{pmatrix} 10 \\ -6 \end{pmatrix}$.

3. (*a*) Rotation about (4, ⁻2) through 180°.
(*b*) Glide-reflection, mirror line $y = 1$, translation $\begin{pmatrix} 2 \\ 0 \end{pmatrix}$.

4. Glide-reflection, mirror line $y = -x - 8$, translation $\begin{pmatrix} 2 \\ -2 \end{pmatrix}$.
Rotation, centre (2, ⁻8), angle ⁻90°.

5. Vertices of the image triangle
$A_1(-0·75, 1·82)$; $B_1(0·14, 3·87)$; $C_1(-1·92, 4·76)$.

6. Vertices of the image triangle;
(i) $A_1(4, -2)$, $B_1(3, -4)$, $C_1(1, -3)$;
(ii) $A_2(-2, 4)$, $B_2(-3, 2)$, $C_2(-5, 3)$.

5. ENLARGEMENT

If two similar plane figures are such that one is not a direct enlargement of the other, there are many methods of transforming the object to the image figure by a combination of an enlargement, any centre, appropriate scale factor, with one or more isometries.

An elegant method is shown in Figure K, for the case when both object and image have the same sense. The centre of rotation and the centre of enlargement coincide.

If the senses are different, again there is a method worthy of special mention (see Figure L). Here the two possible mirror lines pass through the centre of enlargement.

If the senses of the similar figures are alike, the centre of the spiral similarity may be found by producing corresponding line segments AB, $A'B'$ to meet at C. The second point of intersection of the circles $AA'C$, $BB'C$ is the required centre (see Figure M).

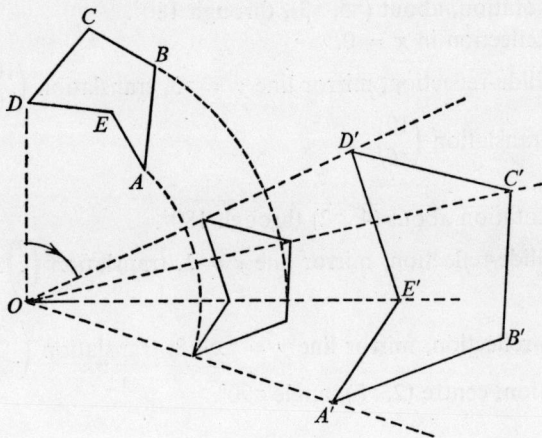

Fig. K

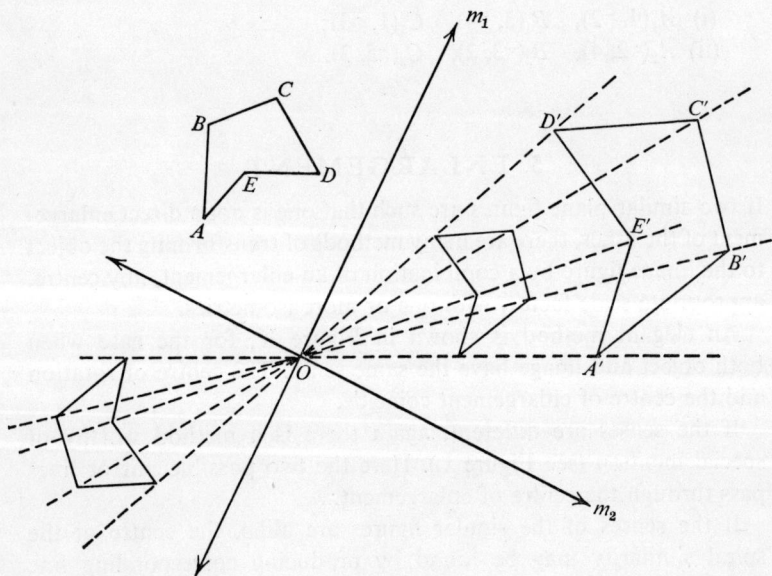

Fig. L

When the senses are different, if AB, $A'B'$ are corresponding line segments (ratio k), points P and Q dividing AA' internally and externally in the ratio k, and points L, M dividing BB' internally and externally in the ratio k, are found. The lines PL, QM are the mirror lines (see Figure N).

It is left to the reader to show the validity of these constructions.

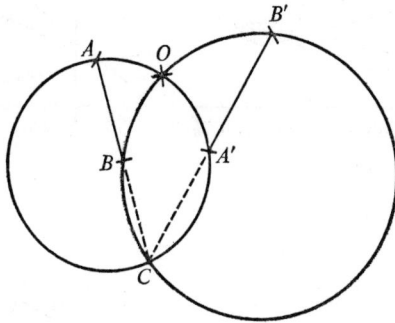

Fig. M

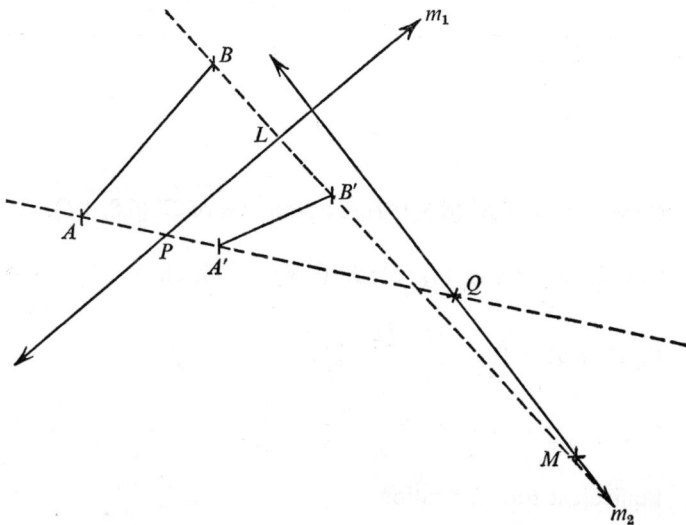

Fig. N

151

6. SHEARING

Exercise D (p. 256)

1.

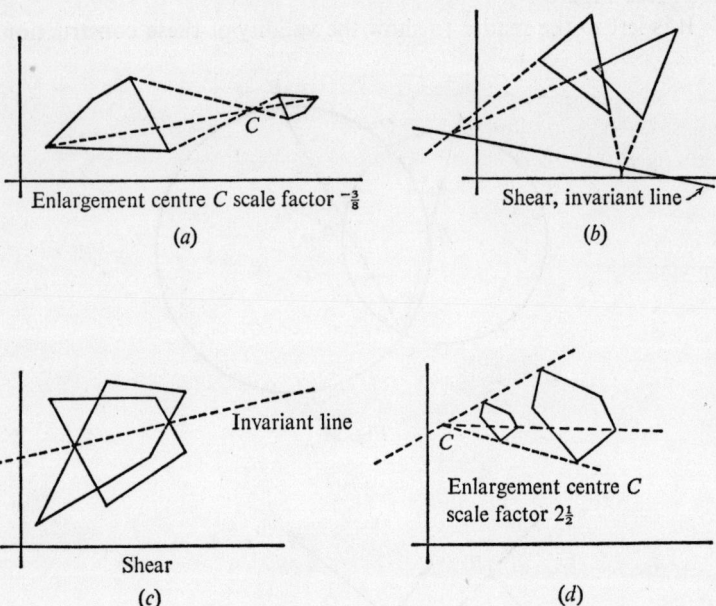

Enlargement centre C scale factor $-\frac{3}{8}$

(a)

Shear, invariant line

(b)

Invariant line

Shear

(c)

Enlargement centre C
scale factor $2\frac{1}{2}$

(d)

Fig. O

2. Coordinates of B' (6·6, 0·2). Coordinates of C' (6·8, 1·6).

3. Coordinates are A' (1, $^-$3); B' (7, 0); C' (4, 6).

4. $E_A(PQRS) = \begin{pmatrix} 5 & 11 & 11 & 3 \\ 11 & 11 & -1 & 5 \end{pmatrix}$.

$E_B E_A(PQRS) = \begin{pmatrix} 3·5 & 0·5 & 0·5 & 4·5 \\ -7 & -7 & -1 & -4 \end{pmatrix}$.

Equivalent transformation

$$\begin{pmatrix} x \\ y \end{pmatrix} \rightarrow \begin{pmatrix} -1·5 & 0 \\ 0 & -1·5 \end{pmatrix} \begin{pmatrix} x \\ y \end{pmatrix} + \begin{pmatrix} 5 \\ 0·5 \end{pmatrix},$$

i.e. enlargement scale factor -1.5, centre $(2, 0.2)$.

$$E_A = \begin{pmatrix} 3 & 0 & 2 \\ 0 & 3 & -4 \\ 0 & 0 & 1 \end{pmatrix} \begin{pmatrix} x \\ y \\ 1 \end{pmatrix}, \quad E_B = \begin{pmatrix} -0.5 & 0 & 6 \\ 0 & -0.5 & -1.5 \\ 0 & 0 & 1 \end{pmatrix} \begin{pmatrix} x \\ y \\ 1 \end{pmatrix}.$$

Sides are parallel and proportional $1:1.5$.

Areas are in the ratio $1:2.25$.

5. First shear
$$\begin{pmatrix} x \\ y \end{pmatrix} \rightarrow \begin{pmatrix} 3 & -2 \\ 2 & -1 \end{pmatrix} \begin{pmatrix} x \\ y \end{pmatrix}$$

giving B' $(-3, -1)$; C' $(12, 8)$.

Second shear
$$\begin{pmatrix} x \\ y \end{pmatrix} \rightarrow \begin{pmatrix} 1 & 3 \\ 0 & 1 \end{pmatrix} \begin{pmatrix} x \\ y \end{pmatrix} + \begin{pmatrix} -6 \\ 0 \end{pmatrix}$$

giving $B''(-6, -1)$; $C''(30, 8)$.

No single shear. Two shears are equivalent to a single shear if the invariant lines are parallel.

8. TOPOLOGY

Exercise E (p. 261)

1. *a, e* are topologically equivalent.
  c, d, f are topologically equivalent.

2. *a, c* are topologically equivalent.
  b, d, e are topologically equivalent.

3.

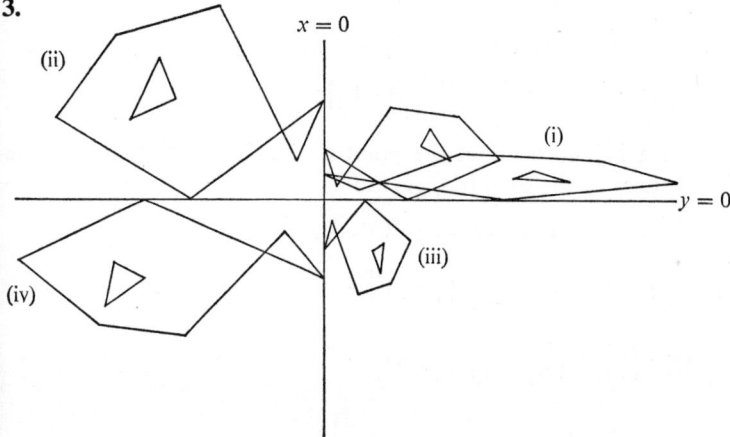

Fig. P

9. COMBINATION OF TRANSFORMATIONS

'What is equivalent to the combination of two isometries?' This is not such a hard question as it might appear. If one thinks of the isometries as two sets, {Translations, Rotations} and {Reflections, Glide-Reflections}, the number of possible answers is immediately halved. For example, a reflection followed by a rotation, is an opposite isometry followed by a direct isometry, and so is equivalent to an opposite isometry, either a reflection or a glide-reflection. Replacing each isometry by its equivalent reflections will decide which it is, in a particular case.

Exercise F (p. 266)

1. (a) **I**; (b) **H**; (c) **Y**; (d) **H**; (e) **H**.

2. (a) $\mathbf{A} = \begin{pmatrix} 2 \\ -5 \end{pmatrix}$; (b) $\mathbf{B} = \begin{pmatrix} 4 \\ 1 \end{pmatrix}$; (c) $\mathbf{C} = \begin{pmatrix} -2 \\ 5 \end{pmatrix}$;

   (d) **D, E** are not unique; there are an infinite number of solutions.
   $$\mathbf{M}^{-1}\mathbf{L}^{-1} = (\mathbf{LM})^{-1} = \begin{pmatrix} -2 \\ 5 \end{pmatrix}.$$

3. $\mathbf{R}_A: \begin{pmatrix} x \\ y \end{pmatrix} \to \begin{pmatrix} 0 & -1 \\ 1 & 0 \end{pmatrix} \begin{pmatrix} x \\ y \end{pmatrix} + \begin{pmatrix} 5 \\ 1 \end{pmatrix}$;

   $\mathbf{R}_B: \begin{pmatrix} x \\ y \end{pmatrix} \to \begin{pmatrix} 0 & -1 \\ 1 & 0 \end{pmatrix} \begin{pmatrix} x \\ y \end{pmatrix} + \begin{pmatrix} 3 \\ 1 \end{pmatrix}$;

   $\mathbf{R}_B\mathbf{R}_A: \begin{pmatrix} x \\ y \end{pmatrix} \to \begin{pmatrix} -1 & 0 \\ 0 & -1 \end{pmatrix} \begin{pmatrix} x \\ y \end{pmatrix} + \begin{pmatrix} 2 \\ 6 \end{pmatrix}$;

   i.e. a half-turn about the point (1, 3). The coordinates of the vertices of the final triangle are
   $$P^*(-1, 5); \quad Q^*(-1, 4); \quad R^*(-3, 4).$$

4. $\mathbf{H}_A: \begin{pmatrix} x \\ y \end{pmatrix} \to \begin{pmatrix} -1 & 0 \\ 0 & -1 \end{pmatrix} \begin{pmatrix} x \\ y \end{pmatrix} + \begin{pmatrix} 4 \\ 6 \end{pmatrix}$;

   $\mathbf{H}_B: \begin{pmatrix} x \\ y \end{pmatrix} \to \begin{pmatrix} -1 & 0 \\ 0 & -1 \end{pmatrix} \begin{pmatrix} x \\ y \end{pmatrix} + \begin{pmatrix} 2 \\ 4 \end{pmatrix}$;

   $\mathbf{H}_B\mathbf{H}_A: \begin{pmatrix} x \\ y \end{pmatrix} \to \begin{pmatrix} 1 & 0 \\ 0 & 1 \end{pmatrix} \begin{pmatrix} x \\ y \end{pmatrix} + \begin{pmatrix} -2 \\ -2 \end{pmatrix}$;

154

i.e. a translation $\begin{pmatrix} -2 \\ -2 \end{pmatrix}$.

Coordinates of the vertices of the final triangle are

$$P^*(1, {}^-1), \quad Q^*(1, 0), \quad R^*(3, 0).$$

Note $\mathbf{AB} = \begin{pmatrix} -1 \\ -1 \end{pmatrix}$, i.e. the translation is twice the distance between the centres of the half-turns and is parallel to this direction.

5. There are many answers to the following questions:

(a) two shears
   (i) $BGLF \rightarrow BLRF$ with FB invariant line,
   (ii) $BLRF \rightarrow KFLR$ with LR invariant line;

(b) three shears
   (i) $BGLF \rightarrow FGML$ with FL invariant line,
   (ii) $FGML \rightarrow FGLK$ with FG invariant line,
   (iii) $FGLK \rightarrow FLRK$ with FK invariant line;

(c) four shears
   (i) $BGLF \rightarrow BCGF$ with BF invariant line,
   (ii) $BCGF \rightarrow KCGQ$ with GC invariant line,
   (iii) $KCGQ \rightarrow KLRQ$ with KQ invariant line,
   (iv) $KLRQ \rightarrow FLRK$ with LR invariant line.

6. (a) $BGLF \rightarrow ABGF$ with BG invariant line,
      $ABGF \rightarrow LMTS$ translation $\mathbf{AL}$;

   (b) $BGLF \rightarrow FGML$ with FL invariant line,
      $FGML \rightarrow LMTS$ half-turn about the mid-point of LM;

   (c) $BGLF \rightarrow BCGF$ with BF invariant line,
      $BCGF \rightarrow LMTS$ axis GS, Translation $\mathbf{CM}$.

7. (a) (i) enlargement centre Q scale factor 2,
      (ii) translation $\mathbf{QN}$;

   (b) (i) enlargement centre W scale factor 2,
      (ii) half-turn about M;

   (c) (i) enlargement centre W scale factor 2,
      (ii) reflection in CMY;

(d) (i) enlargement centre H scale factor 2,

    (ii) glide reflection, axis line midway between $IJKLMN$ and $UOQRST$, translation U to the mid-point of RS.

8. Coordinates are given by

$$B'(0, 5); \quad C'(0, 8); \quad B''(6, 5); \quad C''(6, 2).$$

A rotation about the point $(6, 0)$ through $^-90°$. No, they are equivalent to a translation if the axes of the glide-reflections are parallel.

9. $\mathbf{RT} = (\mathbf{M_3 M_2})\,(\mathbf{M_2 M_1}) = \mathbf{M_3 M_1}$ (See Figure Q.)

    $=$ rotation about $A(^-2{\cdot}1,\ ^-4{\cdot}6)$ through $60°$.

$\mathbf{TR} = (\mathbf{M_3' M_2'})\,(\mathbf{M_2' M_1'}) = \mathbf{M_3' M_1'}$

    $=$ rotation about $B(^-4{\cdot}9,\ ^-0{\cdot}5)$ through $^-60°$.

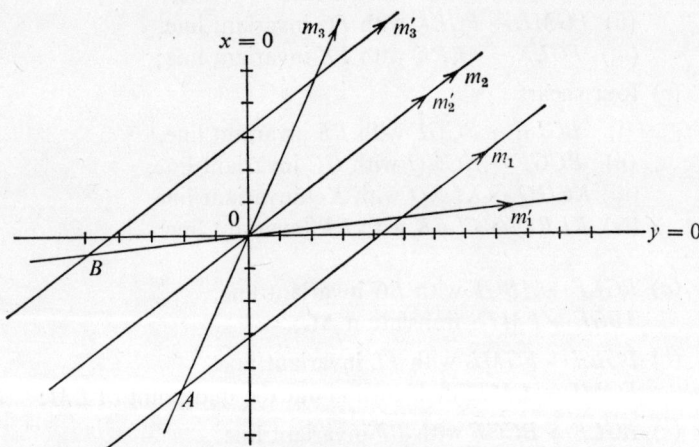

Fig. Q

10. $\mathbf{R_B R_A} = (\mathbf{M_3 M_2})\,(\mathbf{M_2 M_1}) = \mathbf{M_3 M_1}$ (See Figure R.)

    $=$ rotation about $C(6{\cdot}7,\ ^-1{\cdot}4)$ through $20°$.

When $\mathbf{R_B}$ is a rotation through $^-40°$, the mirrors m_1, m_3 would be parallel and so the equivalent transformation would be a translation through twice the distance between parallel mirrors.

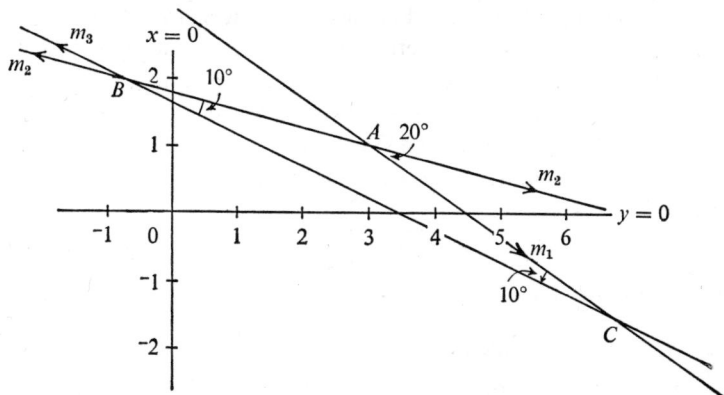

Fig. R

10. VECTOR GEOMETRY

We have attempted to produce an intuitive approach to vectors in the O-level course which is sound in principle so that no change will be necessary in the Sixth Form. The following have been the guiding ideas:

(i) A vector is an element of a group which, when combined with a number field, forms a vector space. (The principal defining characteristics of a vector space are:

$$\lambda(\mathbf{a}+\mathbf{b}) = \lambda\mathbf{a}+\lambda\mathbf{b};$$
$$(\lambda+\mu)\,\mathbf{a} = \lambda\mathbf{a}+\mu\mathbf{a};$$
$$(\lambda\mu)\,\mathbf{a} = \lambda(\mu\mathbf{a});$$
$$1\mathbf{a} = \mathbf{a};$$

where **a** and **b** are vectors and λ, μ and 1 are elements of the number field.)

(ii) Quantities that can be expressed as vectors are called 'vector quantities'. It is noted that such quantities may not always be expressed in vector form (e.g. the magnitude and direction expression of a velocity). We use terms such as 'force vector', 'displacement vector'.

(iii) An expression such as

$$\begin{pmatrix} a \\ b \\ c \end{pmatrix}$$

is called a 'column matrix'. Column matrices are only vectors if they can be combined according to the laws of a vector space.

157

(iv) In context, the word 'vector' is used sometimes to denote a displacement vector (as in Vector Geometry) and sometimes to denote a column matrix representing a vector quantity.

(v) We have made no attempt to distinguish between bound and free vectors, nor have we defined a vector as an equivalence class. These ideas seem more suitable to the Sixth Form than to the O-level course.

Exercise G (p. 272)

1. D is the point (8, 2).

2. A, B, C are collinear.

3. The point is (1, 0).

4. Equivalent vector is
$$\begin{pmatrix} -6 \\ -12 \\ 24 \end{pmatrix},$$
its length is 27·5 units.

Zero vector
$$\begin{pmatrix} 0 \\ 0 \\ 0 \end{pmatrix}$$
this indicates that the points A, B, C are coplanar.

5. $\mathbf{AB} = \begin{pmatrix} 103 \cdot 9 \\ 60 \end{pmatrix}, \quad \mathbf{BC} = \begin{pmatrix} -100 \\ -173 \cdot 2 \end{pmatrix},$

   $\mathbf{CD} = \begin{pmatrix} -76 \cdot 6 \\ 64 \cdot 3 \end{pmatrix}, \quad \mathbf{AD} = \begin{pmatrix} -72 \cdot 7 \\ -48 \cdot 9 \end{pmatrix}.$

   The course is 050·4°.

   The whole flight is 507·6 n.m., and takes 1 hour 41·5 min.

6. $AB = \sqrt{18} = 4 \cdot 24$;
   $BC = \sqrt{8} = 2 \cdot 83$;
   $AC = \sqrt{14} = 3 \cdot 74$;

   D is the mid-point of BC, (2, 0, 1),

   E is the mid-point of CA, ($\frac{1}{2}$, 0, $^-\frac{1}{2}$),

   F is the mid-point of AB, ($\frac{1}{2}$, $^-$1, $\frac{1}{2}$),

   G is the centroid of triangle ABC, (1, $^-\frac{1}{3}$, $\frac{1}{3}$).

7. Coordinates E (mid-point of AC) (2, 2).

    Coordinates F (4, $^-2$).

    Coordinates L (^-2+6k, $1-3k$).

    $$\mathbf{BL} = \begin{pmatrix} -7+6k \\ 5-3k \end{pmatrix}; \quad \mathbf{BC} = \begin{pmatrix} 1 \\ 7 \end{pmatrix},$$

    $$k = \tfrac{6}{5}.$$

    Coordinates $\qquad L\left(\dfrac{26}{5}, \dfrac{-13}{5}\right).$

14

MATRICES

In this chapter, there are references to information matrices in Section 1, to the algebra of matrices in Sections 2 and 4, and to some applications of matrices to equations and geometry in Sections 3, 5 and 6.

The text is rightly confined to those aspects of matrix work that are fairly close to the examination syllabus, but perhaps it would be sensible to state the more general reasons for including matrices in the course, reasons which include reference to the examination work.

(i) To provide opportunities to discuss in mathematical terms a wide variety of experiences, e.g. routes, dominance, polyhedra as networks, circuits, traffic flow, critical paths. Several of these are ideas that would be taken up in later work if the pupils continue with mathematics, for example, in electrical circuits and problems of organization.

(ii) To provide an algebra for transformation geometry (just as coordinate geometry provided an algebra for the traditional geometry course). The first steps of this development are mentioned in Sections 3 and 6, but it is taken much further in Chapter 6, 'Invariants in Geometry' and could almost be generalized from that stage to provide a method of 'proving' theorems.

(iii) To provide a basis for later work that some pupils might need by showing the possible application of matrices to simultaneous linear equations.

2. COMBINATION OF MATRICES
Exercise A (p. 279)

1. (a)

$$G = \begin{pmatrix} 230 & 28 & 28 \\ 392 & 46 & 52 \\ 275 & 40 & 0 \\ 0 & 31 & 27 \end{pmatrix}, \quad H = \begin{pmatrix} 286 \\ 490 \\ 315 \\ 58 \end{pmatrix},$$

$$K = (7919 \quad 1596 \quad 1388).$$

(b) $\mathbf{KJ} = \mathbf{VH} = (10903)$.

Both equal $\mathbf{VGJ}$. Multiplication of matrices is associative.

(c) $\mathbf{V}$ gives cost of individual meals.

$\mathbf{H}$ gives weekly cost of all breakfasts, lunches, teas and suppers.

$\mathbf{K}$ gives weekly cost for meals of boys, staff and domestics.

$\mathbf{VH}$ and $\mathbf{KJ}$ both give the total weekly cost of meals. (All in new pence.)

2. (a)
$$\mathbf{RS} = \begin{pmatrix} 202 \\ 222 \\ 222 \end{pmatrix} = 2\mathbf{T}.$$

(b)
$$\mathbf{RR'} = \begin{pmatrix} 211 \\ 132 \\ 123 \end{pmatrix}. \quad \mathbf{W} = \begin{pmatrix} 200 \\ 030 \\ 003 \end{pmatrix}.$$

$\mathbf{W}$ gives the nodal value (no. of arcs) at each node A, B and C.

3.
$$\mathbf{M} = \begin{pmatrix} 2120 \\ 1010 \\ 2101 \\ 0010 \end{pmatrix}, \quad \mathbf{R} = \begin{pmatrix} 211100 \\ 000110 \\ 011011 \\ 000001 \end{pmatrix}, \quad \mathbf{W} = \begin{pmatrix} 5000 \\ 0200 \\ 0040 \\ 0001 \end{pmatrix};$$

$$\mathbf{R'} = \begin{pmatrix} 2000 \\ 1010 \\ 1010 \\ 1100 \\ 0110 \\ 0011 \end{pmatrix}, \quad \mathbf{S} = \begin{pmatrix} 1010 \\ 0011 \\ 0101 \\ 0110 \\ 0110 \\ 0020 \end{pmatrix}, \quad \mathbf{T} = \begin{pmatrix} 1121 \\ 0110 \\ 0121 \\ 0010 \end{pmatrix}.$$

$$\mathbf{RS} = 2\mathbf{T}. \quad \mathbf{RR'} = \mathbf{M} + \mathbf{W}.$$

4. (a)
$$\mathbf{N^2} = \begin{pmatrix} 31301 \\ 04431 \\ 32721 \\ 03232 \\ 10201 \end{pmatrix}.$$

This gives the number of two-stage routes.

(b)
$$\mathbf{U^2} = \begin{pmatrix} 00201 \\ 00001 \\ 11000 \\ 11001 \\ 01110 \end{pmatrix}, \quad \mathbf{U^3} = \begin{pmatrix} 11002 \\ 11000 \\ 01110 \\ 12110 \\ 00202 \end{pmatrix}, \quad \mathbf{U^4} = \begin{pmatrix} 23110 \\ 01110 \\ 00202 \\ 01312 \\ 22002 \end{pmatrix}.$$

The 'Final order' is D, A, E, C, B.

(c) $\qquad P^2 = \begin{pmatrix} 0.44 & 0.56 \\ 0.28 & 0.72 \end{pmatrix}$, $\quad P^3 = \begin{pmatrix} 0.38 & 0.62 \\ 0.31 & 0.69 \end{pmatrix}$

$$P^4 = \begin{pmatrix} 0.35 & 0.65 \\ 0.32 & 0.68 \end{pmatrix}, \quad P^5 = \begin{pmatrix} 0.34 & 0.66 \\ 0.33 & 0.67 \end{pmatrix}.$$

The limiting value is $\begin{pmatrix} \frac{1}{3} & \frac{2}{3} \\ \frac{1}{3} & \frac{2}{3} \end{pmatrix}$.

5. $\mathbf{Z} = \begin{pmatrix} 15 & 18 \\ 11 & 13 \\ 16 & 17 \\ 14 & 16 \end{pmatrix}$. Under scheme (a) the order would be $R, A, S, M.$ Under scheme (b) the order would be $A, R, S, M.$

6. (a) $\mathbf{AC} = \begin{pmatrix} 9 & 5 & 3 \\ 5 & -3 & 6 \end{pmatrix}$, $\mathbf{BC} = \begin{pmatrix} 4 & -4 & 6 \\ 4 & 0 & 3 \end{pmatrix}$, $\mathbf{CA}$ is not possible.

$\mathbf{ABC} = \begin{pmatrix} 24 & -4 & 21 \\ -4 & -8 & 3 \end{pmatrix}$, $\mathbf{ACB}$ is not possible.

(b) $\mathbf{AA'} = \begin{pmatrix} 26 & -13 \\ -13 & 13 \end{pmatrix}$, $\mathbf{A'A} = \begin{pmatrix} 5 & -1 \\ -1 & 34 \end{pmatrix}$, $\mathbf{CC'} = \begin{pmatrix} 25 & 4 \\ 4 & 2 \end{pmatrix}$,

$\mathbf{C'C} = \begin{pmatrix} 17 & 1 & 12 \\ 1 & 1 & 0 \\ 12 & 0 & 9 \end{pmatrix}$, $\mathbf{C'AC} = \begin{pmatrix} 41 & 17 & 18 \\ 5 & -3 & 6 \\ 27 & 15 & 9 \end{pmatrix}$.

5. SIMULTANEOUS LINEAR EQUATIONS

Exercise B (p. 286)

1. (a) Enlargement, centre O, scale factor -3 (see Figure A).

(b) One-way stretch, scale factor 3, across the page, combined with reflection in $y = 0$ (in either order).

(c) Enlargement, centre O, scale factor $\sqrt{2}$; combined with rotation of $45°$ (in either order).

(d) Two-way stretch, scale factor 2 across the page and -3 up the page; followed by a shear of scale factor $\frac{1}{2}$, up the page; etc. (several possible combinations of stretches and shears).

(e) Enlargement, centre O, scale factor 5, combined with a rotation of $-53°$, (either order) (see Figure B).

(f) Collapses the plane onto the line $y = 3x$.

(g) A shear, a two-way stretch, and a rotation. The area is unaltered.

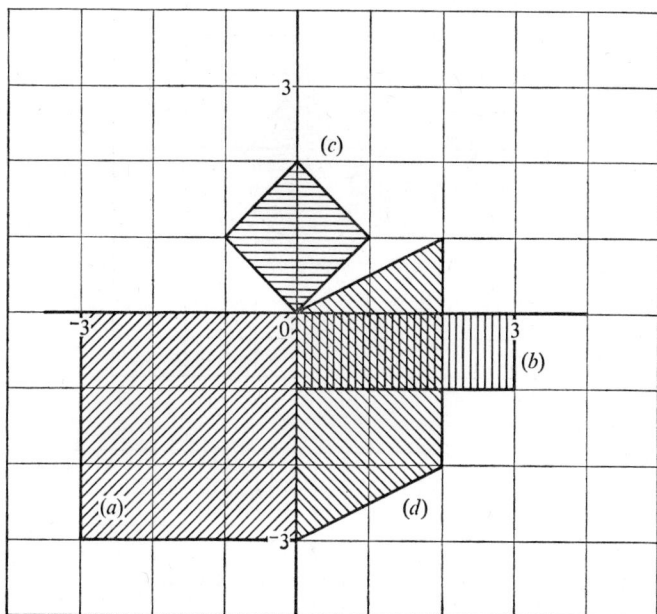

Fig. A

(h) A two-way stretch and a rotation; or an enlargement, scale factor $\sqrt{5}$; a one-way stretch, scale factor -2 up the page; and a rotation of $27°$.

(i) Reflection in $y = 2x$ (or a combination of a reflection and a rotation) (see Figure C).

(j) Rotation through $-53°$ about the origin.

2. (a) $\begin{pmatrix} 0 & -1 \\ 1 & 0 \end{pmatrix}$; (b) $\begin{pmatrix} 1 & -1 \\ 0 & 1 \end{pmatrix}$; (c) $\begin{pmatrix} 1\frac{1}{2} & -1 \\ 1 & 1\frac{1}{2} \end{pmatrix}$;

(d) $\begin{pmatrix} 1 & -\frac{1}{2} \\ 1 & 1\frac{1}{2} \end{pmatrix}$; (e) $\begin{pmatrix} -\frac{1}{2} & 1 \\ 1\frac{1}{2} & 1 \end{pmatrix}$; (f) $\begin{pmatrix} -\frac{1}{2} & 1 \\ -1 & 2 \end{pmatrix}$.

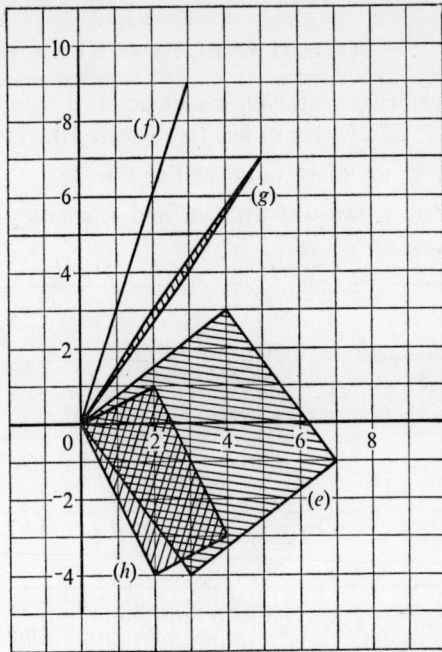

Fig. B

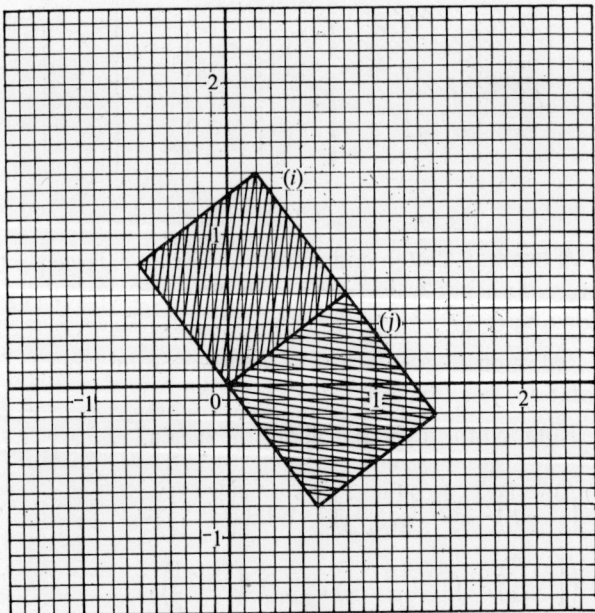

Fig. C

164

3. $\mathbf{U} = \begin{pmatrix} 2 & -1 \\ 1 & 0 \end{pmatrix}$ is a rotation, followed by a shear.

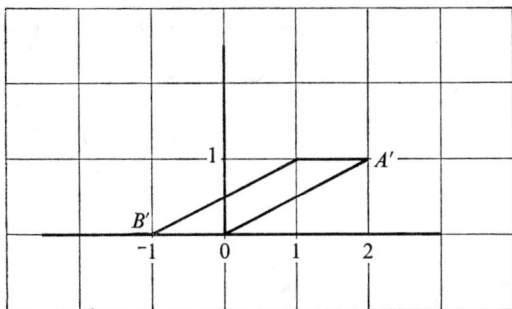

Fig. D

4. (a) $\begin{pmatrix} 1 & -2 \\ 0 & 3 \end{pmatrix}.$

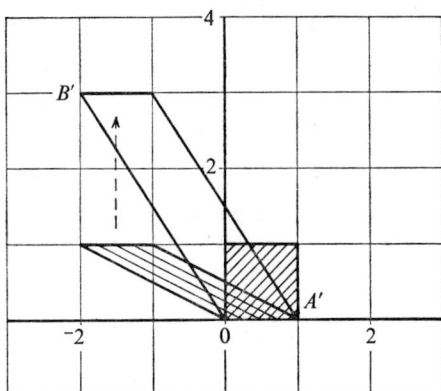

Fig. E

(b) $\begin{pmatrix} 1 & -6 \\ 0 & 3 \end{pmatrix}.$

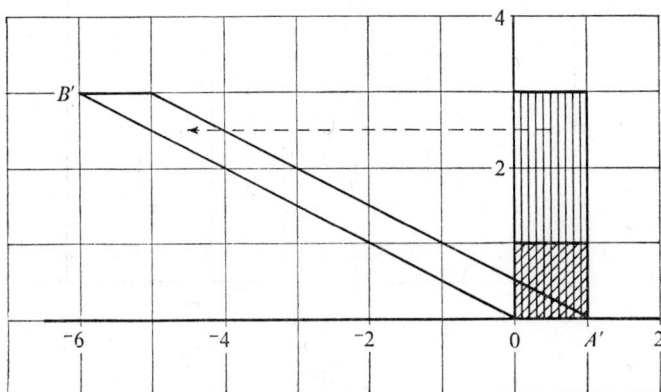

Fig. F

165

(c)
$$\begin{pmatrix} 3 & -4 \\ 4 & 3 \end{pmatrix}.$$

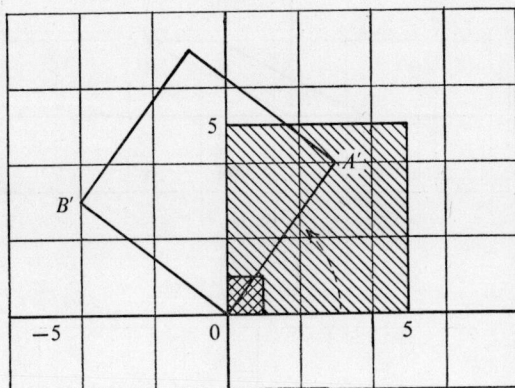

Fig. G

(d)
$$\begin{pmatrix} 0 & 1 \\ -1 & 0 \end{pmatrix}.$$

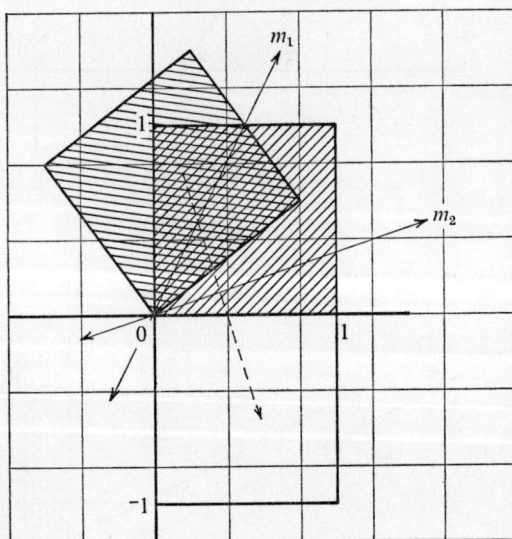

Fig. H

166

(e) $\begin{pmatrix} -1 & -6 \\ 1 & 0 \end{pmatrix}.$

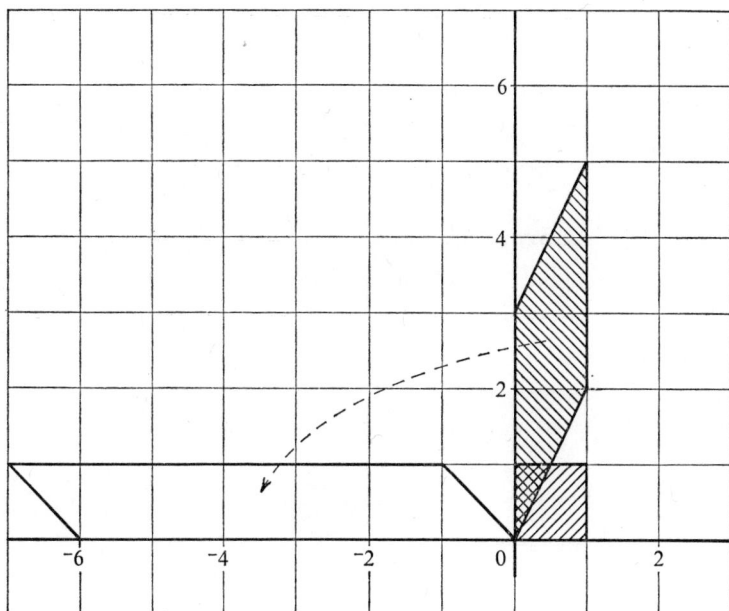

Fig. I

(f) $\qquad\qquad\qquad\begin{pmatrix} 0 & 0 \\ 0 & 0 \end{pmatrix}.$

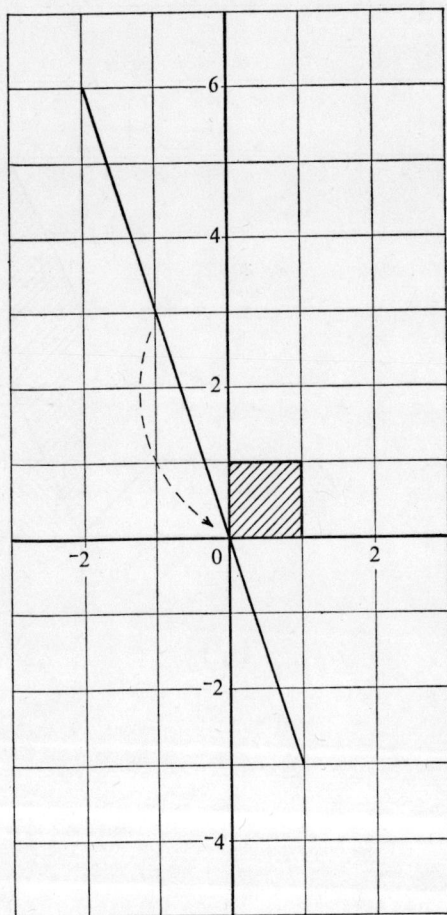

Fig. J

The first transformation collapses the plane onto the line $3x + y = 0$.

The second collapses all points on this line onto the origin.

5.   (a) $\begin{pmatrix} 5 & ^-4 \\ ^-6 & 5 \end{pmatrix}$;   (b) $\begin{pmatrix} 2 & ^-1 \\ ^-6\frac{1}{2} & 3\frac{1}{2} \end{pmatrix}$;   (c) $\begin{pmatrix} ^-3 & ^-8 \\ 2 & 5 \end{pmatrix}$;

    (d) $\begin{pmatrix} ^-16 & 7 \\ 7 & ^-3 \end{pmatrix}$;   (e) $\begin{pmatrix} 1 & 0 \\ 1 & ^-1 \end{pmatrix}$;   (f) $\begin{pmatrix} 0\cdot6 & 0\cdot8 \\ ^-0\cdot8 & 0\cdot6 \end{pmatrix}$;

    (g) $\begin{pmatrix} 0 & ^-\frac{1}{2} \\ \frac{1}{3} & \frac{1}{6} \end{pmatrix}$;   (h) $\begin{pmatrix} \frac{7}{19} & \frac{5}{19} \\ \frac{1}{19} & \frac{-2}{19} \end{pmatrix}$;   (i) $\begin{pmatrix} \frac{4}{3} & 1 \\ \frac{-4}{3} & 2 \end{pmatrix}$;

    (j) No inverse.

6.   (a) $(^-13, \ ^-11)$;   (b) $(0\cdot29, \ 0\cdot30)$;   (c) $(5, \ ^-1)$;
    (d) $(^-0\cdot4, \ 1\cdot6)$;   (e) $(^-102, \ 223)$;   (f) no solutions;
    (g) $(^-5, \ 11)$;   (h) $(6, 13)$;

    (i) all members of the form $(5k-3, \ 3k)$; i.e. all points on the line $5y = 3x+9$;

    (j) $(14, \ 19)$.

6. THE MATRICES FOR SOME COMMON TRANSFORMATIONS

Exercise C (p. 289)

1.   (a)   (i) $\begin{pmatrix} 1 & ^-1 \\ ^-2 & ^-6 \end{pmatrix}$, $\begin{pmatrix} 7 & 0 \\ 0 & 7 \end{pmatrix}$, $\begin{pmatrix} 0 & 0 \\ ^-2 & ^-10 \end{pmatrix}$;

    (ii) $\begin{pmatrix} 0 & 0 \\ 6 & ^-18 \end{pmatrix}$, $\begin{pmatrix} 2 & 10 \\ ^-4 & ^-20 \end{pmatrix}$, $\begin{pmatrix} 0 & 0 \\ 0 & 0 \end{pmatrix}$, $\begin{pmatrix} 5 & 8 \\ 8 & 13 \end{pmatrix}$;

    (b)   (i) $\begin{pmatrix} ^-2 & ^-1 \\ 0 & 3 \end{pmatrix}$, $\begin{pmatrix} 3 & ^-2 \\ ^-2 & 3 \end{pmatrix}$, $\begin{pmatrix} \frac{1}{2} & ^-\frac{3}{2} \\ ^-1 & 3 \end{pmatrix}$, $\begin{pmatrix} 0 & ^-2 \\ ^-2 & ^-2 \end{pmatrix}$;

    (ii) $\begin{pmatrix} ^-3 & 2 \\ 2 & ^-1 \end{pmatrix}$,   no solution, $\begin{pmatrix} 4 & 7 \\ ^-6 & ^-9 \end{pmatrix}$,

       $\begin{pmatrix} ^-6 & ^-9 \\ 4 & 5 \end{pmatrix}$, $\begin{pmatrix} 0 & 0 \\ 0 & 0 \end{pmatrix}$, $\begin{pmatrix} 3a & 3b \\ a & b \end{pmatrix}$ for any a, b.

2.   (a)   (i) $\begin{pmatrix} ^-2 & ^-2 & 4 \\ ^-12 & 9 & 3 \\ 1 & 2 & 3 \end{pmatrix}$;   (ii) not possible—different shapes;

(iii) not possible—different shapes;

(iv) $\begin{pmatrix} 3 & -2 & 6 \\ 6 & -1 & 3 \end{pmatrix}$.

(b) (i) $\begin{pmatrix} 1 & 0 & 2 \\ -9 & 20 & 0 \\ 0 & 12 & 1 \end{pmatrix}$; (ii) $\begin{pmatrix} 1 & -2 & -0 \\ -33 & 17 & -9 \\ -1 & 2 & 4 \end{pmatrix}$;

(iii) $\begin{pmatrix} 4 & 0 & 0 \\ 0 & 4 & 0 \\ 0 & 0 & 4 \end{pmatrix}$; (iv) $\begin{pmatrix} 4 & 0 & 0 \\ 0 & 4 & 0 \\ 0 & 0 & 4 \end{pmatrix}$; (v) $\begin{pmatrix} 21 & -13 & -4 \\ -20 & -13 & 12 \end{pmatrix}$;

(vi) not compatible; (vii) $\begin{pmatrix} 0 & -10 \\ 0 & -17 \\ 4 & 5 \end{pmatrix}$;

(viii) not compatible; (ix) $\begin{pmatrix} 11 & 8 \\ 9 & -2 \end{pmatrix}$; (x) $\begin{pmatrix} 2 & -4 & 6 \\ -6 & 0 & 1 \\ 15 & -6 & 7 \end{pmatrix}$.

(c) (i) $\begin{pmatrix} 4 & 0 & 0 \\ 126 & 82 & -84 \\ 107 & 59 & -70 \end{pmatrix}$; (ii) $\begin{pmatrix} -1 & 2 & 8 \\ -9 & 4 & -6 \\ -7 & 5 & 7 \end{pmatrix}$;

(iii) not compatible; (iv) not compatible;

(v) $\begin{pmatrix} 193 & 72 \\ 81 & 76 \end{pmatrix}$; (vi) $\begin{pmatrix} 41 & 23 \\ 41 & 19 \end{pmatrix}$.

3. (a) $\begin{pmatrix} 4 & -5 \\ -7 & 9 \end{pmatrix}$; (b) $\begin{pmatrix} -7 & -9 \\ -4 & -5 \end{pmatrix}$; (c) $\begin{pmatrix} -5 & 9 \\ -4 & 7 \end{pmatrix}$;

(d) $\begin{pmatrix} 1 & 1\frac{1}{2} \\ -2\frac{1}{2} & 4 \end{pmatrix}$; (e) no inverse; (f) $\begin{pmatrix} 1 & 0 \\ \frac{1}{2} & \frac{1}{2} \end{pmatrix}$;

(g) $\begin{pmatrix} \frac{5}{3} & \frac{1}{3} \\ 1 & 0 \end{pmatrix}$; (h) no inverse; (i) $\begin{pmatrix} \frac{1}{4} & 0 \\ 0 & -\frac{1}{3} \end{pmatrix}$; (j) $\begin{pmatrix} -7 & -4 \\ 5 & 3 \end{pmatrix}$.

4. Rewrite the third equation as $-x + -y + 2z = -9$, put the equations into matrix form, and pre-multiply each side by the matrix **P** of Question 2. This gives

$$4\begin{pmatrix} x \\ y \\ y \end{pmatrix} = \begin{pmatrix} -16 \\ 0 \\ -26 \end{pmatrix}.$$

Hence

$$\begin{pmatrix} x \\ y \\ z \end{pmatrix} = \begin{pmatrix} -4 \\ 0 \\ -6\frac{1}{2} \end{pmatrix}.$$

5.

$$\text{from} \begin{array}{c} \\ H \\ J \\ K \\ L \end{array} \begin{array}{cccc} \overset{\text{to}}{} & & & \\ H & J & K & L \\ \begin{pmatrix} 1 & 1 & 1 & 1 \\ 0 & 2 & 1 & 0 \\ 1 & 0 & 0 & 3 \\ 1 & 0 & 2 & 0 \end{pmatrix} \end{array}; \quad \text{from} \begin{array}{c} \\ H \\ J \\ K \\ L \end{array} \begin{array}{cccc} \overset{\text{to}}{} & & & \\ H & J & K & L \\ \begin{pmatrix} 3 & 3 & 4 & 4 \\ 1 & 4 & 2 & 3 \\ 4 & 1 & 7 & 1 \\ 3 & 1 & 1 & 7 \end{pmatrix} \end{array};$$

$$\left\{ \begin{array}{l} H \longrightarrow J \xrightarrow{\text{clockwise}} J, \\ H \longrightarrow J \xrightarrow[\text{clockwise}]{\text{anti-}} J, \\ H \xrightarrow[\text{clockwise}]{\text{anti-}} H \longrightarrow J, \end{array} \right\};$$

$$\left\{ \begin{array}{l} H \xrightarrow[\text{clockwise}]{\text{anti-}} H \longrightarrow K, \\ H \longrightarrow J \longrightarrow K, \\ H \longrightarrow L \longrightarrow K, \\ H \longrightarrow L \longrightarrow K \end{array} \right\}.$$

6. Possible networks are:

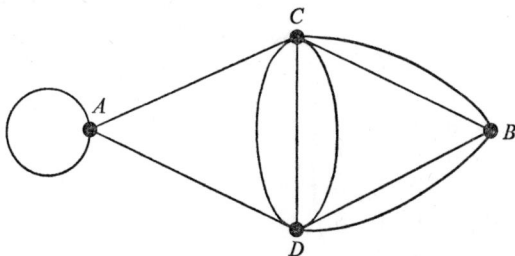

Fig. K

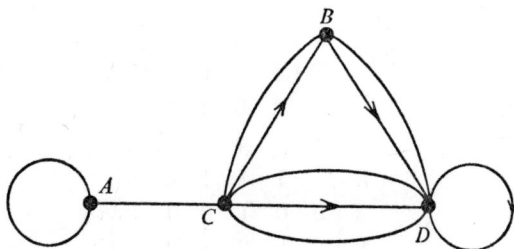

Fig. L

7. 1-stage

$$
\begin{array}{c c}
 & \begin{array}{c c c c c c} A & B & C & D & E & F \end{array} \\
\begin{array}{c} A \\ B \\ C \\ D \\ E \\ F \end{array} &
\begin{pmatrix}
0 & 1 & 0 & 1 & 0 & 0 \\
0 & 0 & 0 & 0 & 1 & 1 \\
1 & 0 & 0 & 1 & 0 & 0 \\
0 & 0 & 0 & 0 & 1 & 0 \\
0 & 0 & 0 & 0 & 0 & 0 \\
0 & 0 & 1 & 0 & 1 & 0
\end{pmatrix},
\end{array}
$$

2-stage							No. of 2-stage dominance	Position
	A	B	C	D	E	F		
A	0	0	0	0	2	1	3	1st =
B	0	0	1	0	1	0	2	3rd =
C	0	1	0	1	1	0	3	1st =
D	0	0	0	0	0	0	0	5th
E	0	0	0	0	0	0	0	6th
F	1	0	0	1	0	0	2	3rd =

3-stage							No. of 3-stage dominance	Final position
	A	B	C	D	E	F		
A	0	0	1	0	1	0	2	2
B	1	0	0	1	0	0	2	4
C	0	0	0	0	2	1	3	1
D	0	0	0	0	0	0	0	5
E	0	0	0	0	0	0	0	6
F	0	1	0	1	1	0	3	3

8. (a)

$$
\mathbf{M} =
\begin{array}{c c}
 & \begin{array}{c c c c} W & X & Y & Z \end{array} \\
\begin{array}{c} W \\ X \\ Y \\ Z \end{array} &
\begin{pmatrix}
0 & 1 & 1 & 2 \\
1 & 0 & 1 & 0 \\
1 & 1 & 0 & 1 \\
2 & 0 & 1 & 0
\end{pmatrix},
\end{array}
$$

$$
\mathbf{R} =
\begin{array}{c c}
 & \begin{array}{c c c c c c} 1 & 2 & 3 & 4 & 5 & 6 \end{array} \\
\begin{array}{c} W \\ X \\ Y \\ Z \end{array} &
\begin{pmatrix}
1 & 1 & 1 & 1 & 0 & 0 \\
0 & 0 & 1 & 0 & 1 & 0 \\
0 & 0 & 0 & 1 & 1 & 1 \\
1 & 1 & 0 & 0 & 0 & 1
\end{pmatrix},
\end{array}
$$

172

$$S = \begin{array}{c} \\ 1 \\ 2 \\ 3 \\ 4 \\ 5 \\ 6 \end{array} \begin{array}{cccc} a & b & c & d \\ \left(1 \right. & 1 & 1 & 0 \\ 0 & 1 & 1 & 0 \\ 1 & 0 & 0 & 1 \\ 0 & 0 & 1 & 1 \\ 1 & 0 & 0 & 1 \\ \left. 1 \right. & 0 & 1 & 0 \end{array} \Big), \quad T = \begin{array}{c} W \\ X \\ Y \\ Z \end{array} \begin{array}{cccc} a & b & c & d \\ \left(1 \right. & 1 & 1 & 1 \\ 1 & 0 & 0 & 1 \\ 1 & 0 & 1 & 1 \\ \left. 1 \right. & 1 & 1 & 0 \end{array} \Big);$$

$$RR' = \begin{array}{c} W \\ X \\ Y \\ Z \end{array} \begin{array}{cccc} W & X & Y & Z \\ \left(4 \right. & 1 & 1 & 2 \\ 1 & 2 & 1 & 0 \\ 1 & 1 & 3 & 1 \\ \left. 2 \right. & 0 & 1 & 3 \end{array} \Big)$$

which differs from **M** in the elements on the leading diagonal; in **RR'** these give the node-sum at the nodes.

$$RS = \begin{pmatrix} 2 & 2 & 2 & 2 \\ 2 & 0 & 0 & 2 \\ 2 & 0 & 2 & 2 \\ 2 & 2 & 2 & 0 \end{pmatrix} = 2T.$$

(b)

$$M = \begin{array}{c} A \\ B \\ C \\ D \\ E \\ F \end{array} \begin{array}{cccccc} A & B & C & D & E & F \\ \left(0 \right. & 1 & 0 & 2 & 0 & 0 \\ 1 & 0 & 1 & 0 & 3 & 0 \\ 0 & 1 & 0 & 0 & 0 & 1 \\ 2 & 0 & 0 & 0 & 1 & 1 \\ 0 & 3 & 0 & 1 & 0 & 1 \\ \left. 0 \right. & 0 & 1 & 1 & 1 & 0 \end{array} \Big),$$

$$T = \begin{array}{c} A \\ B \\ C \\ D \\ E \\ F \end{array} \begin{array}{ccccccc} p & q & r & s & t & u & v \\ \left(1 \right. & 1 & 1 & 0 & 0 & 0 & 0 \\ 1 & 0 & 1 & 1 & 1 & 1 & 0 \\ 1 & 0 & 0 & 0 & 0 & 1 & 0 \\ 1 & 1 & 1 & 0 & 0 & 0 & 1 \\ 0 & 0 & 1 & 0 & 1 & 1 & 1 \\ \left. 1 \right. & 0 & 0 & 0 & 0 & 1 & 1 \end{array} \Big),$$

$$TT' = \begin{array}{c} A \\ B \\ C \\ D \\ E \\ F \end{array} \begin{array}{cccccc} A & B & C & D & E & F \\ \left(3 \right. & 2 & 1 & 3 & 1 & 1 \\ 2 & 5 & 2 & 2 & 4 & 2 \\ 1 & 2 & 2 & 1 & 1 & 2 \\ 3 & 2 & 1 & 4 & 2 & 2 \\ 1 & 4 & 1 & 2 & 5 & 2 \\ \left. 1 \right. & 2 & 2 & 2 & 2 & 3 \end{array} \Big).$$

173

M gives direct routes between nodes along arcs. **TT'** gives direct routes between nodes through regions. (**RR'** involves 'setting-out' from a *node* along an *arc* until another *node* reached—including return to the original node. **TT'** involves 'setting-out' from a *node* into a *region* and then returning to a *node*—including the original one—on the boundary of that region.)

9. (*a*) (72 9 24): yearly sales of the different models.

(*b*) $\begin{pmatrix} 19 \\ 32 \\ 31 \\ 23 \end{pmatrix}$: total number of cars sold in each quarter.

(*c*) $\begin{pmatrix} 11 & 750 \\ 19 & 050 \\ 19 & 200 \\ 14 & 650 \end{pmatrix}$: total receipts (in £s) for each quarter.

(*d*) (64 650): total value of cars sold during the year.

10.

(*a*)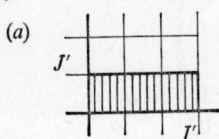

(*b*)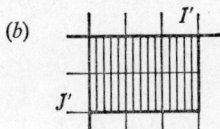

(*c*)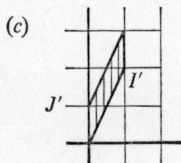

(*e*)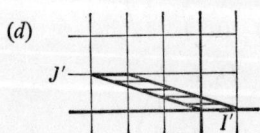

$J'(1, {}^-2)$

$I'(4, {}^-9)$

(*d*)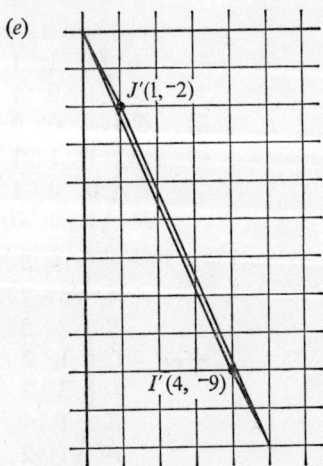

174

(f)

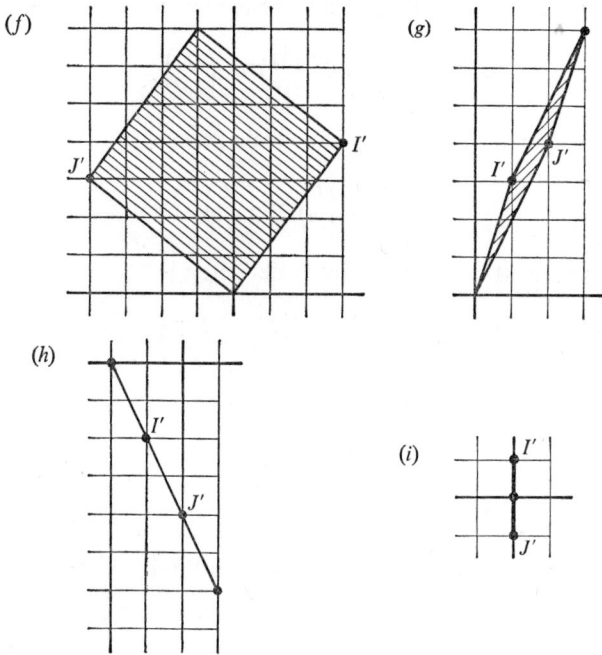

(g)

(h)

(i)

Fig. M

11. $\begin{pmatrix} 1 & -1 \\ 1 & 1 \end{pmatrix}$; $\begin{pmatrix} 0 & -3 \\ -2 & 0 \end{pmatrix}$; $\begin{pmatrix} -3 & 2 \\ 3 & 1 \end{pmatrix}$; $\begin{pmatrix} 1 & -2 \\ -2 & 4 \end{pmatrix}$.

12.

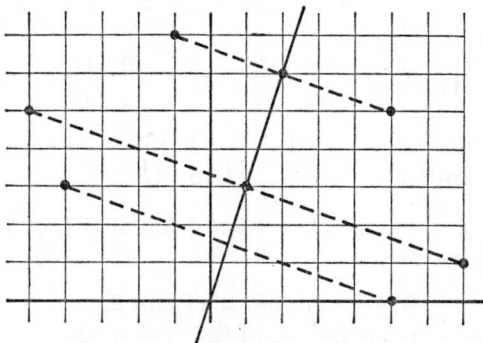

$(7, 1) \rightarrow (-5, 5)$;
$(-7, 7) \rightarrow (5, 5)$;
$(5, 0) \rightarrow (-4, 3)$;
$(x, y) \rightarrow (-\tfrac{4}{5}x + \tfrac{3}{5}y, \tfrac{3}{5}x + \tfrac{4}{5}y)$.

Fig. N

Matrix is $\begin{pmatrix} -\tfrac{4}{5} & \tfrac{3}{5} \\ \tfrac{3}{5} & \tfrac{4}{5} \end{pmatrix}$.

13. 1-way stretch, $x = 0$ invariant, scale factor $\frac{1}{2}$

$$\begin{pmatrix} \frac{1}{2} & 0 \\ 0 & 1 \end{pmatrix} \begin{pmatrix} t \\ t^2 \end{pmatrix} = \begin{pmatrix} \frac{1}{2}t \\ t^2 \end{pmatrix} = \begin{pmatrix} u \\ 4u^2 \end{pmatrix}.$$

1-way stretch, $y = 0$ invariant, scale factor 4

$$\begin{pmatrix} 1 & 0 \\ 0 & 4 \end{pmatrix} \begin{pmatrix} t \\ t^2 \end{pmatrix} = \begin{pmatrix} t \\ 4t^2 \end{pmatrix}.$$

Enlargement centre at origin, scale factor $\frac{1}{4}$

$$\begin{pmatrix} \frac{1}{4} & 0 \\ 0 & \frac{1}{4} \end{pmatrix} \begin{pmatrix} t \\ t^2 \end{pmatrix} = \begin{pmatrix} \frac{1}{4}t \\ \frac{1}{4}t^2 \end{pmatrix} = \begin{pmatrix} v \\ 4v^2 \end{pmatrix}.$$

In general, the set of 2-way stretches

$$\begin{pmatrix} a & 0 \\ 0 & 4a^2 \end{pmatrix}.$$

Yes. By a 2-way stretch $\begin{pmatrix} a & 0 \\ 0 & a^2 \end{pmatrix}$ for any value of 1.

(This will include reflection in $x = 0$, which is given by $a = {}^-1$.)

14. (*a*) $\mathbf{HJ} = \begin{pmatrix} 2 & {}^-1 \\ 1 & 0 \end{pmatrix}$. Shear, invariant line $y = x$, of factor 2.

$\mathbf{JH} = \begin{pmatrix} 0 & {}^-1 \\ 1 & 2 \end{pmatrix}$. Shear, invariant line $y = x$, of factor 2.

$\mathbf{HK} = \begin{pmatrix} 2 & {}^-2 \\ 0 & {}^-1 \end{pmatrix}$. $\mathbf{KH} = \begin{pmatrix} 2 & 4 \\ 0 & {}^-1 \end{pmatrix}$. $\mathbf{JK} = \begin{pmatrix} 0 & 1 \\ 2 & 0 \end{pmatrix}$.

(*b*) $\mathbf{K} = \begin{pmatrix} 2 & 0 \\ 0 & 1 \end{pmatrix} \begin{pmatrix} 1 & 0 \\ 0 & {}^-1 \end{pmatrix}$ or $\begin{pmatrix} 1 & 0 \\ 0 & {}^-1 \end{pmatrix} \begin{pmatrix} 2 & 0 \\ 0 & 1 \end{pmatrix}$;

i.e. a combination of stretch in $y = 0$ and 1-way stretch of scale factor 2, $y = 0$ invariant.

(*c*) $\mathbf{H}$ is a shear, $y = 0$ invariant, of scale factor 2.
$\mathbf{H}^{-1}$ is a shear, $y = 0$ invariant, of scale factor $^-2$.

$$\mathbf{H}^{-1} = \begin{pmatrix} 1 & {}^-2 \\ 0 & 1 \end{pmatrix}.$$

15. (*a*)

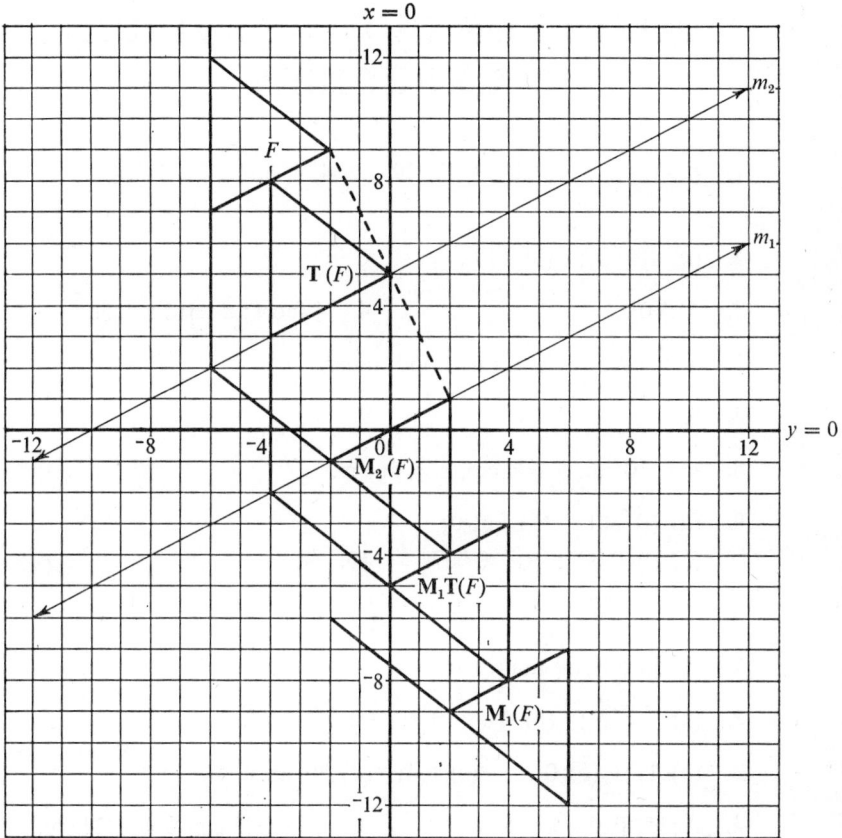

Fig. O

(*b*) $\mathbf{T}(m_2) = m_1$.   (*c*) $\mathbf{U}$ is the translation $\begin{pmatrix} -4 \\ 8 \end{pmatrix}$.

(*d*) $\mathbf{V}$ is the translation $\begin{pmatrix} -2 \\ 4 \end{pmatrix}$, i.e. $\mathbf{T}^{-1}$.

(*e*) From (*c*) $\mathbf{M}_2$ is $\mathbf{M}_1$ followed by $\mathbf{U}$, i.e. reflection in $y = 2x$
followed by the translation $\begin{pmatrix} -4 \\ 8 \end{pmatrix}$.

$$\mathbf{M}_2 : \begin{pmatrix} x \\ y \end{pmatrix} \rightarrow \begin{pmatrix} \frac{3}{5} & \frac{4}{5} \\ \frac{4}{5} & -\frac{3}{5} \end{pmatrix} \begin{pmatrix} x \\ y \end{pmatrix} + \begin{pmatrix} -4 \\ 8 \end{pmatrix}.$$

MISCELLANEOUS REVISION EXERCISES

1

1. (a) {2, 3, 5, 7, 11, 13, 17, 19}, {2, 4, 6, 8, 10, 12, 14}, {2}.
(b) 7, 1.

2. (a) 10100_2; (b) 110_2.

3. 4×10^9.   **4.** 4 faces; a tetrahedron.

5. Yes, because it has two odd nodes.

6. 9.   **7.** Yes.

8. $a = 10$ cm, $b = 4$ cm, $c = 6\frac{2}{3}$ cm.

9. (a) (i) 361; (ii) 361·0;
(b) (i) 0·007; (ii) 0·007.   **10.** $\frac{3}{13}$.

2

1. Addition and multiplication.

2. (a) 7×10^6; (b) $4\cdot8 \times 10^{-4}$; (c) $7\cdot1 \times 10^8$.

3. (a) 11; (b) 0·73; (c) 8·4; (d) 20 cm.

4. A:15, B:30, C:15.   **5.** $a = 6\cdot58$ cm, $b = 9\cdot24$ cm.

6. (a) $x = {}^-3$; (b) $x = 1$; (c) $x > 6$;
(d) $x > {}^-2$; (e) $x = 2\frac{1}{2}$.

7. (a) 4; (b) 10; (c) 16.   **8.** $\frac{1}{12}$.

9. $\begin{pmatrix} 3 & {}^-6 \\ 1 & 10 \end{pmatrix}$.   **10.** 7.

3

1. (a) 0·19 (2 s.f.); (b) ⁻1·2.   **2.** 3000 n.m.

3. $n(A \cap B') = 3$. See Figure A.

4. See Figure B.

5. 1467_8.

6. $x = \sqrt{\left(\dfrac{lt^2 - 4}{3}\right)}$.

7. (a) $x \to \frac{1}{3}(x-2)$; (b) $x \to \frac{1}{5}(4x+2)$; (c) $x \to 6-x$.

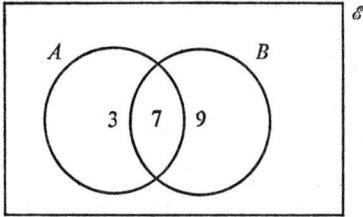

Fig. A

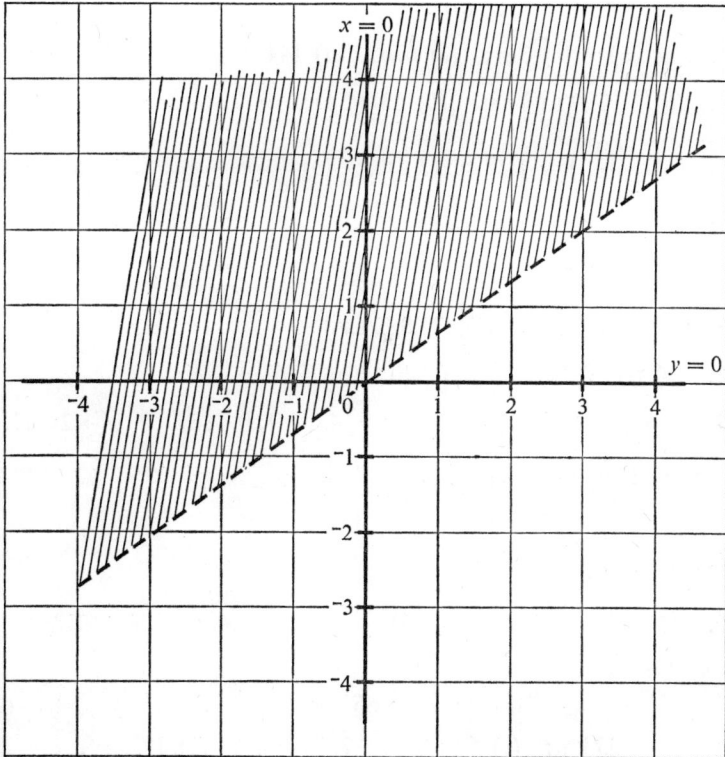

Fig. B

8. $BC = \begin{pmatrix} 3 \\ 2 \end{pmatrix}$; D is (6, 3).

9. (a) x^2+2x+1; (b) $2x^2+9x-18$; (c) $8x^3-42x^2+54x$.

10. 1020 cm³.

4

1. (a) Yes: sides proportional.
    (b) Yes: each has angles 72°, 61°, 47°.
    (c) No: angles not necessarily equal.

2. (a) 0·9; (b) $\frac{4}{11}$. 　　　　3. $p = 1, q = {}^-5$.

4. (a) 12; (b) {12, 20}.

5. (a) 0·963 (3 s.f.); (b) 300. 　　6. Two.

7. (a) 361; (b) 361; (c) 676; (d) 144.

8. (a) 1·27 (3 s.f.) cm; (b) 23° (2 s.f.).

9. (a) $\sqrt{\left(\frac{10}{\pi}\right)} = 1·78$ cm (3 s.f.); (b) $147\pi = 462$ cm² (3 s.f.).

10. 30°

5

1. (a) 3·29 (3 s.f.); (b) 74·0 (3 s.f.).

2. (a) (i) $^-0·766$; (ii) $^-0·940$. (b) 40·5°, 139·5°.

3. $x = 2, y = \frac{1}{9}$. 　　　　4. {-1, 0, 1, 2}; $f: x \to 2x-1$.

5. (a) $\begin{pmatrix} -2 & 0 \\ 0 & -2 \end{pmatrix}$. (b) $x = 5, y = 8$.

6. $x = \dfrac{a+bd^2}{2d^2-1}$. 　　　　7. $p = 2, q = 5$.

8. 477_8. 　　9. (2, 3). 　　10. (30° N, 160° W)

6

1. (b) 3·93 km; (c) 5 km. 　　2. (a) 27; (b) 19.

3. $\pm\frac{12}{13}$. 　　4. (a) (0); (b) $x = 2, y = {}^-4$.

5. (a) $\begin{pmatrix} 2 & 3 \\ 1 & 3 \end{pmatrix}$; (b) $\begin{pmatrix} 3 & 0 \\ 0 & 3 \end{pmatrix}$; (c) $\begin{pmatrix} 1 & 2 \\ 0 & 1 \end{pmatrix}$.　　**6.** 6·93 cm.

7. A: mean $27\frac{3}{11}$, interquartile range 4; B: mean $27\frac{1}{11}$, interquartile range 16. Though not obtaining top scores, A has the better mean score, and is the more consistent.

8. (a) (1, 1); (b) (5, 3); (c) (3, 3); (d) (⁻1, 3).

9. Any matrix $\begin{pmatrix} a & b \\ c & d \end{pmatrix}$ for which $ad - bc = 0$. All points are mapped onto a straight line.

10. (a) $x = 0, 5$; (b) $(x-3)(x+4) = 0$.

7

1. (a) 5 m/s; (b) 0·2 £/kg; (c) 0·05 l/kl; (d) 100 M/£; (e) 0·0083 km/s², 60 km; (f) 10^5 l/h², 5×10^6 l.

2. 13, 28.　　　　　**3.** (a) 212_3; (b) 54_{10}; (c) 313_4.

4. (a) 133 (3 s.f.); (b) 0·0768 (3 s.f.); (c) 27·1 (3 s.f.).

5. $BD = 3·8$ cm, $AD = 3·2$ cm, $AC = 6·4$ cm.

6. (a) and (c).　　**7.** (a) 135°; (b) 12 sides.

8.

	A	B	C	D
A	0	0	1	1
B	1	0	0	1
C	0	1	0	1
D	1	0	1	0

9. 5.　　　　　　　　**10.** $\frac{5}{6}$.

8

1. 10 001 111.　　　**2.** 500　　　**3.** $x = 1, y = 2$.

4. (a) $(x+2)(x-2)$; (b) $(x+1)(x-4)$.

5. (a) ⁻2; (b) ⁻8.　　**6.** (2, 1).　　　**7.** 34° N.

8. (a) $\frac{1}{6}$; (b) $\frac{7}{12}$.　　　　**9.** 81.

10. (a) $\subset$; (b) and (c) none appropriate; (d) $\in$; (e) $\supset$.

9

1. 2.   **2.** $y + 2x = 3$.

3. (a) 2·31 cm (3 s.f.); (b) 4·62 cm² (3 s.f.).

4. $\dfrac{6x - 1}{6x}$.   **5.** (a) ⁻0·5; (b) 0·866.

6. (a) 3; (b) 9. (There are 15 routes from A to B altogether.)

7. Triangles ABD, BCD are equilateral, all lengths being equal to the radii.

8. $A \cap B \cap C$ is bounded by the triangle whose vertices are (1, 2), (2, 4) and (4, 2).

9. (a) 5; (b) 720°; (c) 36°.

10. (a) has two odd nodes; (c) has none, so both of these are traversable; (b) has four odd nodes, so is not traversable.

10

1. 123_8.   **2.** $x = 7$.   **3.** $y = 2$.

4. 0·42.   **5.** $1\cdot2 \times 10^5$.   **6.** 5 km.

7. (a) See Figure C; (b) (i) not true; (ii) true; (iii) true.

8. $A = 64$.   **9.** 34°.   **10.** $y = 5x^2$.

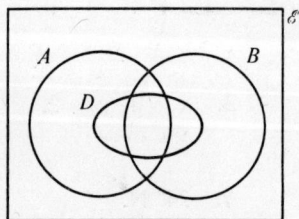

(i)

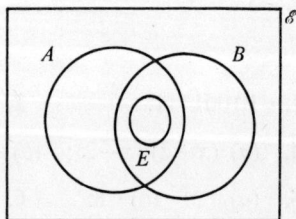

(ii)

Fig. C

11

1. Any points whose coordinates are of the form $(3, y)$.
2. (a) $(^-2, 4)$; (b) $(0, 0)$. **3.** (a) 2; (b) $(0, 2)$.
4. $\omega = \dfrac{a}{h} - b$ or $\dfrac{a - bh}{h}$. **5.** $^-4$.
6. Half-turn about mid-point of CC'.
   Enlargement, centre mid-point of CC', scale factor $^-1$.

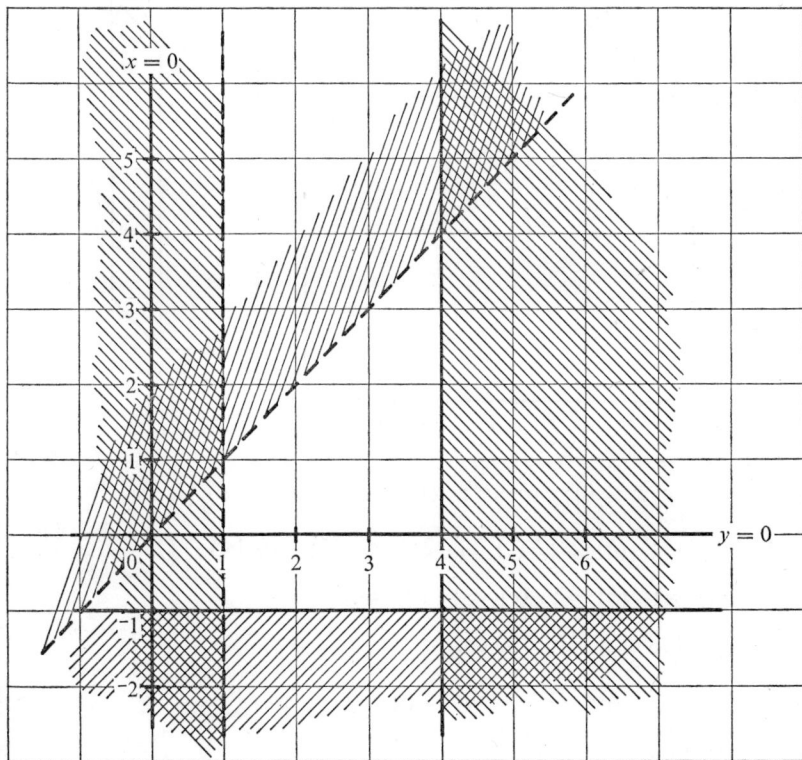

Fig. D

7. See Figure D.
8. (a) $8\frac{3}{4}$ cm; (b) $49 : 121$. **9.** $x = 5\frac{2}{3}, y = \frac{1}{3}$.
10. $\{6, 7\}, \{6, 8\}, \{6, 9\}, \{7, 8\}, \{7, 9\}, \{8, 9\}$; $\frac{5}{6}$.

12

1. (a) $^-5$ cm;   (b) 10 cm;

2. (a) 14;   (b) $11\frac{1}{2}$;   * could denote multiplication, for example.

3. (a) 2 m/s^2;   (b) 125 m.   4. 12 cm, $\frac{27}{8}$.

5. See Figure E.   6. $^-1$; $\begin{pmatrix} 9 & ^-7 \\ 5 & ^-4 \end{pmatrix}$; $x = 8, y = 3$.

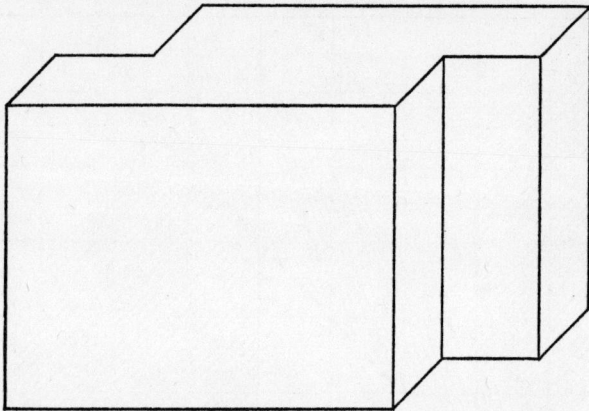

Fig. E

7. (a) $\{x: x \leqslant 0\}$;   (b) $\varnothing$;   (c) $\{x: x > ^-2\}$;   (d) $\{1, 2\}$.

8. (a) 13;   (b) 28;   (c) $3n-2$;   (d) 35;   (e) 145;   (f) $\dfrac{n(3n-1)}{2}$.

9. (a) $\Leftarrow$;   (b) $\Rightarrow$;   (c) $\Leftrightarrow$;   (d) $\Leftrightarrow$.

10. (a) 178 cm;   (b) 180 cm.

13

1. 1·8 cm.

2. Bus 101°, car and motor cycle 32°, bicycle 140°, train 22°, foot 65°.   3. $2(x-3)(x+11)$.   4. 146_7, 83_{10}.

5. (10, 2).

6. See Figure F; required region is unshaded.

184

7. 2·6 m.   **8.** (a) 16·3°;   (b) $\frac{24}{25}$;   (c) $-\frac{7}{24}$.

9. $x = 4$.   **10.** $p = -3, q = 2$.

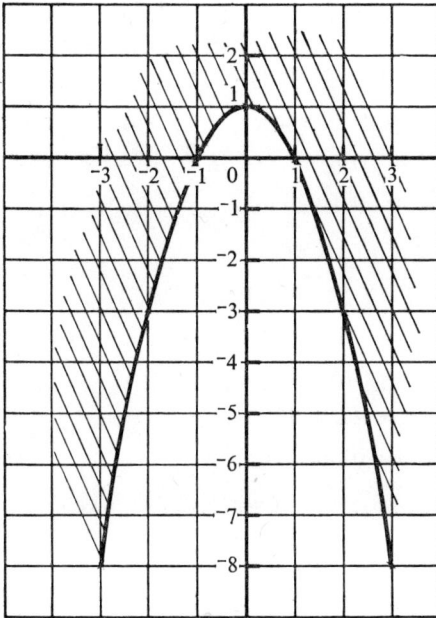

Fig. F

14

1. $\{-1, 4\}$.   **2.** (a) 10;   (b) 5.

3. 3:1.

4. (a) Base 8; $48 \times 27 = 1296$.   (b) Base 5; $24 \times 15 = 360$.

5. (a) 150°;   (b) 105°.

6. $h = \dfrac{v^4 - g^2 c^2}{2v^2 g}$.

7. (a) 1·70;   (b) 78·5;   (c) 0·850;   (d) 0·14.

8. $m = 3, n = -1$.   **9.** $B(5, 3)$, $E(0, 2)$, 14 unit².

10. (a) £32;   (b) 45%.

15

1. $4\frac{1}{2}$.

2. (*a*) 20 cm; (*b*) 17 cm; (*c*) 61·9°;
(*d*) no, since $17^2 + 25^2 \neq 28^2$.

3. (*a*) The lines $y = 2, y = x$; (*b*) the lines $y = x, x = 0$;
(*c*) the lines $y = x, y = 2, x = 0$. (*d*) the line $y = x$.

4. 0·4 m, 0·192 m², 0·02048 m³.

5. From 90·3 cm² to 110 cm².

6. (*a*) $AB + DC = (AP + PB) + (DR + RC)$
$= AS + BQ + SD + QC$
$= (AS + SD) + (BQ + QC)$
$= AD + BC.$

(*b*) Symmetrical about AC.

7. (*a*) $(x+1)(x+3)$; (*b*) $x = {}^{-}1, {}^{-}3$.

8. 60 000 kg.

9. $fg: x \to 3(x+2)$; $gf: x \to 3x+2$; $fhg: x \to 3(x+2)^2$.

10. (*a*) $\frac{1}{20}$; (*b*) $\frac{1}{400}$.

16

1. (*a*) $\frac{1}{36}$; (*b*) $\frac{1}{9}$; (*c*) 0; (*d*) $\frac{5}{36}$.

2. $\binom{3}{2}$. **3.** (*a*) $\{2, \frac{3}{2}\}$; (*b*) $\{{}^{-}1, 2\}$.

4. $0 \leqslant 3 \sin x° \leqslant 1·5$. **5.** 2:9, 3:1.

6. $(2^x)^3 < (3^x)^2 < 3^{x^2} < 2^{x^3}$.

7. (*c*) is never true; (*a*) is true for two values of x; (*b*) is always true; (*d*) is true for one value of x.

8. The lines joining the centres form a 3, 4, 5 triangle.

9. (*a*) $\frac{1}{2}(x+y)$; (*b*) $y-x$; (*c*) $\frac{1}{2}x-y$.

10. £1·56.

17

1. (*a*) See Figure G;   (*b*) See Figure H.

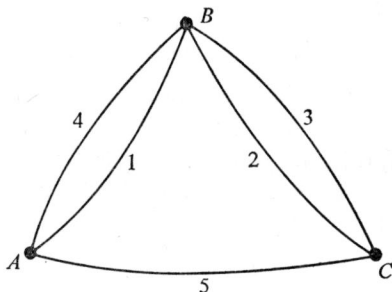

Fig. G

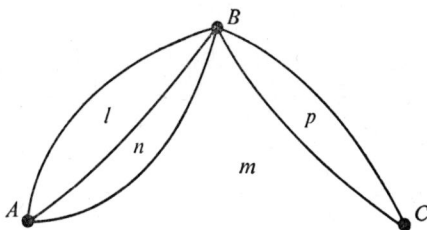

Fig. H

2. (*a*) 99;   (*b*) 50, 148.   **3.** $1\frac{13}{21}$.

4. 30 cm², 24 cm².

5. (*a*) $r = 3$ or 13;   (*b*) $3 < r < 13$;   (*c*) $r < 3$ or $r > 13$.

6. (*a*) $A \cap B = \{3, 5, 7\}$, $A \cup B = \{1, 2, 3, 5, 7, 9\}$,
    $A' = \{1, 4, 6, 8, 9\}$, $B' = \{2, 4, 6, 8\}$;
  (*b*) $(A \cap B)' = \{1, 2, 4, 6, 8, 9\} = A' \cup B'$.

7. (*a*) 7·07 cm;   (*b*) 8·72 cm;   (*c*) $25 + 35 \cdot 7 = 60 \cdot 7$ cm².

8. $a^2 + 6ab + 9b^2$.   **9.** $\sqrt{50}$ cm $= 7 \cdot 07$ cm (3 s.f.).

10. 6.

18

1. $(50° \text{ S}, 160° \text{ W})$. 2. $R < Q < P$. 3. 1001_2.

4. $\frac{64}{169} \rightarrow \frac{8}{13}$, $1·44 \rightarrow 1·2$, $0·09 \rightarrow 0·3$.

5. $x = \frac{10}{11}$. 6. $\text{OC} = \begin{pmatrix} 3 \\ 9\frac{1}{2} \end{pmatrix}$.

7. There are many possibilities: e.g.
   (a) $6 \in \{x: x^2 - 5x - 6 = 0\}$;
   (b) {squares} $\cap$ {rectangles} $\subset$ {parallelograms};
   (c) $x = \pm 3 \Leftrightarrow 4x^2 = 36$ for real values of x.

8. $y < 23$.

9. (a) $(6, 8)$; (b) $(^-6, ^-8)$; (c) $7\sqrt{2} \approx 9·9$; (d) $0·990$ (3 s.f.);
   (e) about $172°$.

10. (a) $x = 60$; (b) $56·8, 123·2$; (c) $0 < g(x) < 1$; (d) 14.

19

1. (a)   2. (d).   3. (d).

4. (b).   5. (a), (c).   6. (c).

7. (i) (d); (ii) (a). 8. (b).   9. (c).

10. (c).

20

1. (d).   2. (i) (c); (ii) (a); (iii) (b).

3. (c).   4. (c)   5. (b).

6. (c).   7. (a). 8. (a).

9. (a); (d).   10. (a); (d).

21

1. (c).   2. (d).

3. (i) (b); (ii) (c); (iii) (b); (iv) (b); (v) (a).

4. (a); (d).   5. (a).   6. (b), (d) are true. 7. (d).

8. (i) (b); (ii) (a). 9. (a).   10. (e).

22

1. (*b*). 2. (*d*). 3. (*a*).

4. (*c*) and (*e*). 5. (*d*). 6. (*e*).

7. (*d*). 8. (*d*). 9. Both (*b*) and (*e*).

10. (*b*).

23

1. (*a*) T; (*b*) F; (*c*) T; (*d*) T.

2. (*a*) F; (*b*) F; (*c*) T. 3. (*a*) T; (*b*) F; (*c*) T; (*d*)T.

4. (*a*) F; (*b*) F; (*c*) F; (*d*) T.

5. (*a*) F; (*b*) F; (*c*) F; (*d*) F; (*e*) F.

6. (*a*) F; (*b*) F; (*c*) T; (*d*) F. 7. (*a*) F; (*b*) T; (*c*) T; (*d*) F.

8. (*a*) F; (*b*) T; (*c*) F; (*d*) F; (*e*) F; (*f*) T.

9. (*a*) $\mathrm{T}\,(\frac{8}{36}, \frac{4}{36})$; (*b*) $\mathrm{T}\,(\frac{2}{4}, \frac{6}{16})$; (*c*) $\mathrm{T}\,(\frac{16}{81})$.

10. (*a*) T; (*b*) F; (*c*) F; (*d*) T; (*e*) F.

24

1. (*a*) 2, 5; (*b*) 1; (*c*) $17 \leqslant x \leqslant 25$.

2. (*a*) (i) $^-3$, (ii) 9; (*b*) about $2\frac{1}{3}$. 3. (*a*) $\begin{pmatrix} 1 & 0 \\ 0 & 1 \end{pmatrix}$;
   (*b*) each transformation is the inverse of the other.

4. (*a*) 12:1; (*b*) this depends upon the particular values of height and radius.

5. (i) (*a*) $^-8$, (*b*) $^-2$, (*c*) 4, (*d*) $^-2$, (*e*) 4;
   (ii) $6-(2+1) = 7-4$.

6. (*a*) 7 m/s; (*b*) 2 m/s²; (*c*) 3 m/s; (*d*) 26 m.

7. (*a*) $AD = DE$, $EF = KA$, $FJ = KB$, $JH = CB$, $HG = GC$;
   (*b*) B.

8. $x = 0.4$, $y = \frac{1}{4}$.   **9.** $a = 4$, $b = {}^-6$.

10. See Figure I. Required region is shaded.

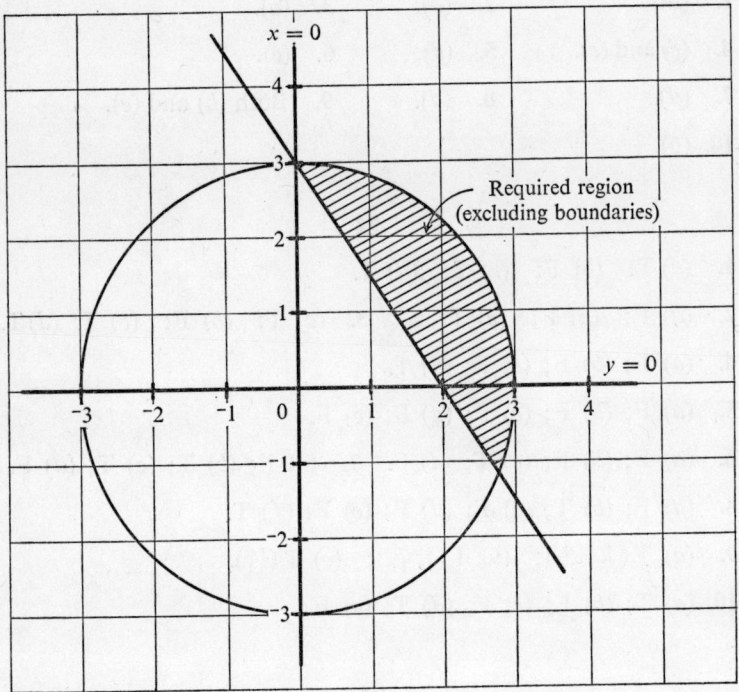

Required region
(excluding boundaries)

Fig. I

25

1. (a) 7·07 cm²; (b) 1·93 cm²; (c) $\dfrac{1\cdot93}{9} \approx 0\cdot21$.

2. (a) $x = 2$, $y = {}^-1$; (b) $(p \times 0) + (q \times 0)$ cannot equal 4.

3. (i) See Figure J.
(ii) A glide-reflection along line of symmetry parallel to AB and DC; the displacement $\mathbf{AD'}$.

4. (b) 1, 2, 4, 8, 16;
(c) (i) $2^6 = 64$, (ii) $2^9 = 512$, (iii) 2^{n-1}.

5. (a) $0\cdot\dot{1}$; (b) $0\cdot2\dot{3}$; (c) $\frac{1}{3} - \frac{1}{10} = \frac{7}{30}$; (d) $\frac{5}{9} - \frac{1}{10} = \frac{41}{90}$; (e) $\frac{34}{333}$.

6. $\{3, 0, ^-\frac{5}{3}, -3, ^-2\frac{1}{5}\}.$ **7.** $\begin{pmatrix} 1 & 0 \\ \frac{3}{2} & 1 \end{pmatrix}.$

8. 1·34 cm (3 S.F.).

9. $\angle ABC = 64°$, $\angle BCD = 154°$,

10. (a) 61·9°;   (b) 8 m.

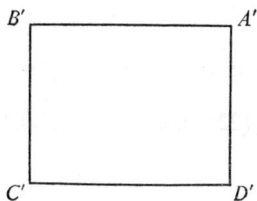   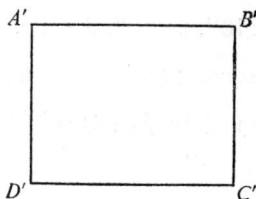

(a)   (b)

Fig. J

26

1. (a) 100_{12}, 121_{11}, 170_9, 196_{10}, 169_{10}, 121_{10}.
The exception is 170_9. $(18_{10})^2 = (13_9)^2 = (10_9 + 3_9)^2 = 169_9$ or 170_9.
(b) (3, 23), (2, 15), (1, 7); (26, 23), (17, 15), (8, 7); 208 planks.

2. (a) (1, 10), (2, 5), (3, $3\frac{1}{3}$), (4, $2\frac{1}{2}$), (5, 2), (6, $1\frac{2}{3}$), (7, $1\frac{3}{7}$), (8, $1\frac{1}{4}$).
(9, $1\frac{1}{9}$), (10, 1). Hence (b) and (c).
(e) £4·17;   (f) 3·16;   (g) 217 km/h.

3. (b) 115 cm.   **4.** (b) Possible examples shown in Figure K.

5. 1940 km; $n \geqslant 11$.

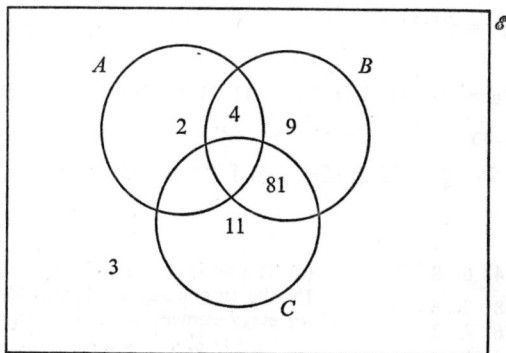

Fig. K

27

1. About £460 000.

2. $y = {}^{-}\frac{1}{2}x + 3$; $(\frac{-3}{2}, 0)$; from the origin, a rotation $^{-}90°$ and an enlargement, scale factor 2.

3. 2×10^{11}, 8×10^{33}, 8×10^{37}.

4. A square; (i) isosceles trapezium; (ii) rhombus; (iii) kite.

5. $x + y \leqslant 36$, $5x + 2y = 120$; (24, 0), (22, 5), etc. to (16, 20); $\frac{1}{3}$.

28

1. (a) 3·9 kg; (b) 2·2 kg.

2. (b) 5; (c) 3·99; (d) 36·9, 143·1; (e) $f(60) = 4·73$, $f(90) = 5$, $f(120) = 4·73$.

3. (a) $S_1 \cap S_2 = \{(x, y): x = 1, 5·2\}$; (b) $x = 2·4, 4·6$.

4. 1·5 m.

29

1. $7x + 5y \leqslant 140$; $y \geqslant 7$, $x + y \leqslant 24$; $x = 10$, $y = 14$.

2. (a) (4, 1), (1, 4), (2, 5), (3, 6); (b) (4, 3), (3, 4), (2, 5), (1, 6); $\frac{1}{24}$.

3. (a) 7·15 cm; (b) 8·72 cm; (c) 67·2°.

4. (a) $\frac{506}{24} = 21·1$;
(b)

No. of appearances	1–10	11–20	21–30	31–40	41–50
Frequency	11	2	2	2	7

(c) $25·5 - \frac{80}{24} = 22·2$. (Groups 1–9, 10–18 etc. give mean $20\frac{3}{8}$.)

5.

	2	4	6	8
2	4	8	2	6
4	8	6	4	2
6	2	4	6	8
8	6	2	8	4

(a) The set is closed under the operation,
(b) the set contains an identity (6),
(c) every element has an inverse,
$2^{-1} = 8$, $4^{-1} = 4$, $8^{-1} = 2$.
(d) Yes.

30

1. (a) 137 m, 187 m; (b) 232 m; (c) 324°.
2. Max $4\frac{3}{5}$ at $(-\frac{1}{5}, 4\frac{4}{5})$; min. 1 at $(1, 0)$.
3. (a) 4, 2, 3, 3; (b), e.g. 4, 6, 8.   4. Mean age, 16.
5. (b) (i) Yes; (ii) isosceles; (iii) each equals TA;
   (iv) $\angle A = \angle P + \angle Q = 90°$.

31

1. (a) $\frac{6}{35}$; (b) $\frac{2}{7}$; (c) $\frac{8}{35}$.
2. $a = 4, b = -0.375, c = 0$;
   (a) about 6.3; (b) $0.4 \leqslant x \leqslant 2$.
3. (b) 2 km, 4 km; $A(-2, -4)$, $B(4, -2)$, $C(2, 4)$, $D(-2, 1)$.
5. (a) $m = 3, c = \frac{4}{3}$; (b) $\frac{8}{27}$.

32

1. (a) (i) $\frac{1}{2}$; (ii) $\frac{1}{8}$.   (b) (i) 0.14; (ii) 0.53.
2. (a) 50; (b) 31, 67; (c) 56 %.
3. (a) $\sqrt{40} \approx 6.3$ units, $\sqrt{134} \approx 11.6$ units; (b) 15°; 3 planes of symmetry; $\angle SPB$.
4. $x \approx 68.5$.
5. $x \geqslant 4, y > 2x, 2x + y \leqslant 22$.
   (4, 9), (4, 10), (4, 11), (4, 12), (4, 13) (4, 14), (5, 11), (5, 12).

33

1. (a) 4.25×10^7 km²; (b) 25° E.
2. (a) (i) (4, 8); (ii) (8, -2).
   (b) $\mathbf{AB} = \mathbf{b} - \mathbf{a}; \mathbf{XY} = \frac{1}{2}\mathbf{b} - \frac{1}{2}\mathbf{a} = \frac{1}{2}(\mathbf{b} - \mathbf{a}) = \frac{1}{2}\mathbf{AB}$.
3. (a) 1000 cm³ (1 s.f.) or 970 cm³ (2 s.f.). [The volume is about 968 cm³.] (b) 500 cm³ (2 s.f.).
4. Take $n(F \cap G \cap R) = x$; then $x = 2$.

5. (a) $\begin{pmatrix} x \\ -y \end{pmatrix}$, P is reflection in $y = 0$; Q is $+\frac{1}{4}$-turn about $(0, 0)$.

(b) QP is reflection in $y = x$; its matrix is $\begin{pmatrix} 0 & 1 \\ 1 & 0 \end{pmatrix}$.

(c)

Transformation	P	Q	QP
Invariants	Points on $y = 0$	$(0, 0)$	Points on $y = x$

34

1. All by similar triangles. (a) $AB = 15$ cm; (b) $CM = 4\cdot8$ cm. $CN = 15\cdot4$ cm; (c) $AC = 17$ cm, hence required distance is $\frac{7}{17} \times 15\cdot4 = 6\cdot34$ cm (3 s.f.).

2. (a) (i) $\frac{1}{6}$; (ii) $\frac{1}{2}$; $\frac{3}{36} = \frac{1}{12}$.
(b) Mean 6, interquartile range $2\cdot41$.

3. (a) (i) $8 \leqslant x \leqslant 11$; (ii) $7 \leqslant x \leqslant 9$;
(b) (i) 21, $(1\frac{1}{2}, 5)$; (ii) 22, $(1, 6)$.

4. (a) (i) $\begin{pmatrix} 5 & 6 \\ 6 & 10 \end{pmatrix}$; (ii) $\begin{pmatrix} 10 & 4 \\ 9 & 5 \end{pmatrix}$;

(iii) $\begin{pmatrix} 2 & 0 \\ 0 & 2 \end{pmatrix}$; (iv) $\begin{pmatrix} 2 & 0 \\ 0 & 2 \end{pmatrix}$.

(b) $x = 2, y = -1$; (d) $\begin{pmatrix} 11 \\ 16 \end{pmatrix}$, $\begin{pmatrix} 14 \\ 14 \end{pmatrix}$.

5.

	I	X	Y	Z
I	I	X	Y	Z
X	X	I	Z	Y
Y	Y	Z	I	X
Z	Z	Y	X	I

(a) Each element is self-inverse.
(b) (i) $\quad XW = Z$ (ii) $\quad WY = Z$
$\qquad X(XW) = XZ \qquad\qquad (WY)Y = ZY$
$\qquad (XX)W = Y \qquad\qquad W(YY) = X$
$\qquad\quad IW = Y \qquad\qquad\quad WI = X$
$\qquad\quad W = Y \qquad\qquad\quad\; W = X.$

MISCELLANEOUS REVISION EXERCISES

35

1. (a) Mode 6, median 6; (b) mean 6·17; (c) bar chart; (d) 0·14.

2. 4·36 km.

3. $NA = 2\sqrt{3} = 3·46$ m (3 S.F.), so initially $PA = 3·04$ m (3 S.F.), (a) $\sqrt{30·3} = 5·5$ m; (b) $\sqrt{66·3} = 8·15$ m (3 S.F.).

4. (i) 4, (ii) 7; (i) 47, (ii) 109, 121.

5. (i) (a) (5, 2); (b) (3, ⁻2); (c) (5, ⁻2); (d) (2, 5); (e) (4, ⁻3); (f) (7, 2).
(ii) (1, 0); 90° anticlockwise.

36

1. (a) Other vertices are (⁻2, 4), (⁻4, 2), (⁻4, ⁻2), (⁻2, ⁻4), (2, ⁻4), (4, ⁻2), (4, 2).
(b) Other lines of symmetry are $x = 0$, $y = 0$, $x+y = 0$.

2. (a) 200 m; (b) 292 m; (c) 213 m; (d) 46·8°.

3. Other vertices are (⁻1, 1), (2, ⁻2), (3, ⁻4), (4, ⁻2), (7, 1), (9, 2), (7, 3), (4, 6). Mediator is $x+y = 5$. Centre of symmetry is (3, 2) order 4.

4. (a) 3; (b) 3, 2; (c) 4.

5. 6 cm × 18 cm × 24 cm; 27 packets; 50 p; 4 cm².

37

1. (a) 54; (b) 0·86; (c) 45.

2. (a) $v = 1+7t$; (c) 1:8; (d) 1:2.

3. (a) $c = 9/T^2$; (b) 14·9 cm².

4. (i) True for all value of x; (ii) one value, $x = \frac{7}{16}$; (iii) two values, $x = 2, 4$.

5. $2y = 3x+1$, $y = 38$.

38

1. (a) *B* (least interquartile range); (b) *C* (largest mean); (c) *B* (median 7·5 mm).

2. (1, 5), (2, 3), (3, 6), (4, 2), (5, 5), (6, 4), (7, 7), $(a, 8-b)$; reflection in $y = 4$.

3. $p = 380, q = 180, r = 170, s = 270$.

   When 240 tonnes are worked from Face 1, 100 tonnes from Face 2 and 500 tonnes from Face 3, then p is the total of Grade A coal produced; similarly q, r, s.

4. E' is at position D. $D'E' = 5$ cm, $FF' = 2·5$ cm, $AF' = \sqrt{4·33}$ cm, $\angle C'D'E' = 90°$, area $ABC'D'E'F' = 64·9$ cm².

5. (a) 28; (b) $y = \dfrac{x^3}{40}$, $y = 43·2$.

39

1. Reflection in $y = x$; shear with $y = 0$ invariant; one-way stretch ($\times 7$), parallel to $y = 0$, with $x = 0$ invariant;

$$\begin{pmatrix} 0 & -1 \\ 1 & 0 \end{pmatrix}; \quad \begin{pmatrix} 7 & 0 \\ 0 & 7 \end{pmatrix}.$$

2. Height of Spencer's is about 28·5 m, of Tracy's is about 29·1 m; so Tracy's is the higher by about 0·6 m.

3. 785 (3 s.f.); about 4·3 % $\left(\dfrac{0·21}{4·90} \times 100\,\%\right)$.

4. $V = \dfrac{2r^4}{25}$; $V = 20·48, r = 10$.

5. (a) All my pencils are chewed or blunt,
   (b) All my red pencils are blunt;
   (c) My red or blunt pencils are my chewed ones;
   (d) I have no unchewed red pencils;
   (e) My blunt red pencils are all chewed.
   $C = \varnothing$; $(A \cap C)' \cap B' = \varnothing$.

40

1. $\dfrac{41}{625} \approx 0.0656.$

2. (a) P' is $(-4, 13)$; gradient of PP' is -2.
(b) Points on $2y = x$ are invariant.
(c) -2.   (d) 6.
(e) Combination of shear (with $2y = x$ invariant) and one-way stretch ($\times 6$) perpendicular to $2y = x$.

3. If the segments are $P_1 P_2$ and $Q_1 Q_2$, then the axes of the glides are found by joining the mid-points of (a) $P_1 Q_1$ and $P_2 Q_2$, (b) $P_1 Q_2$ and $P_2 Q_1$.

4. (a) Less than;   (b) $k = 625$.

5. $(A-B)(A+B) = A^2 + AB - BA - B^2$
$$= A^2 - B^2 \text{ only if } AB = BA, \text{ so the result is only}$$
true if A and B are commutative under multiplication.
Any matrix commutative with $\begin{pmatrix} 3 & 1 \\ 2 & 4 \end{pmatrix}$ must be of the form $\begin{pmatrix} a & b \\ 2b & a+b \end{pmatrix}$.

197

INDEX

addition, of vectors, 11, 12, 13
addition machine, 100
addition tables, 104
affine transformations, 56, 59, 60
algebra, for transformation geometry, 160
algebraic statements, relations as, 110
allowances, against income tax, 53–4
angles: between lines, preserved in isometries, 57, 58; polygons, polyhedra, and, 141–3
antimeridian, 29, 33
Archimedes, 24
arcs, 174
area, preserved in isometries, 57, 58
area scale factor, 109
areas: comparison of, by weighing, 2; of irregular figures, 1–3; of surfaces, (cylinders), 26, (spheres), 24–6; of trapeziums, 3; under graphs, 4–7
arithmetic, finite, 104
arrow diagrams, 110
arrowhead, symmetry of, 142
associativity, 99, 102, 104, 161
averages, 131–2
axes, 133; of symmetry, 143

bar charts, 132, 135

calculus, 24, 110
Cayley–Hamilton theorem, 102
centre of rotation, 64
circles: projected into ellipses, 58; in three dimensions, 20–1
closure, 99, 102
collinearity, 67
column matrices, 157, 158
combination: of displacements, 12; of isometries, 154–7; of matrices, 160–2; of velocities, 13
commutativity, 103
compasses, gyro and magnetic, 34
computation, 128–30
computers, navigational, 12
cone, envelope for, 23
construction work, 71
coordinates: Cartesian, 141; and mappings, 110–17; polar 141; spherical polar, 31
cosine, 33
cost, lines of equal, 85–6
cumulative frequency curves, 132
cylinder: area of curved surface of, 26; envelope for, 22

direction, invariant in translation, 57
displacement vectors, 12–13, 157, 158
displacements, combination of, 12
distances: on a parallel of latitude, 30, 33–4; represented by areas, 4; shortest, between points on a sphere, 22–3

earth, the: as a sphere, 28–34
elements: inverse, solution of equations by, 104; operations, relations, and, 99–100
ellipses, as projected circles, 58
endowment assurance policies, 50, 53
enlargement, 67–8, 149–51, 152; invariants in, 56, 69
equal cost, lines of, 85–6
equal profit, lines of, 86
'equals', meaning of, 100–1
equations: in finite arithmetics, 104; linear, cubic, and quadratic, 35; quadratic, solution of, by inverse functions, 42–4; simple, 103–4; simultaneous, 162–9; with two operations, 104–9
equator, 29, 31
equilateral triangles, 57, 103
equivalence, topological, 153
experiments, design of, 134

factors, 44; solution of quadratic equations by, 45–7
family allowances, 54
finite groups, 101–3
flow diagrams, 10, 24, 41–4
force vector, 157
frequency diagrams, 132
frequency distributions, grouped, 132, 135

199

transformations (*cont.*)
  invariants in, 55; matrices for, 16–
  19, 169–77; topological, 55, 148
translation, 148; description of, 147;
  invariants in, 69
trapezium, area of, 3
trapezium rule, 7–9
tree diagrams, 133, 137
triangle rule, of addition of vectors, 11
triangles: equilateral, 57, 103; isosceles,
  142
trigonometry, 11; in three dimensions,
  33

unimodular group, 109

variability, of machine-made goods,
  134
variables, discrete and continuous, 132,
  133
vector quantity, 157
vector space, 157
vectors, 11–12, 157–9; displacement,
  12–13; under rotation, 16–19; velocity, 13–16
velocities, combination of, 13
velocity vectors, 13–16
volume of a sphere, 26–8

zero matrix, 45